GAY AND LESBIAN ELDERS

Gay and Lesbian Elders
History, Law, and Identity Politics in the United States

NANCY J. KNAUER
Beasley School of Law,
Temple University, USA

ASHGATE

Published by
Ashgate Publishing Limited
Wey Court East
Union Road
Farnham
Surrey, GU9 7PT
England

Ashgate Publishing Company
Suite 420
101 Cherry Street
Burlington
VT 05401-4405
USA

www.ashgate.com

British Library Cataloguing in Publication Data
Knauer, Nancy J., 1961-
  Gay and lesbian elders : history, law, and identity
  politics in the United States.
  1. Older gays--Legal status, laws, etc.--United States.
  2. Older gays--United States--Social conditions.
  I. Title
  342.7'308774-dc22

Library of Congress Control Number: 2010933966

ISBN 978 1 4094 0233 6 (hbk)
ISBN 978 1 4094 0234 3 (ebk)

Printed and bound in Great Britain by the
MPG Books Group, UK

Contents

Preface

Many of the ideas presented in this book were first explored in an earlier article, LGBT Elder Law: Toward Equity in Aging, which appeared in the *Harvard Journal of Gender and the Law* in 2009. The article received a 2010 Dukeminier Award for the best scholarship in the area of sexual orientation and gender identity and the 2010 Stu Walter Prize for outstanding scholarship from the Williams Institute, UCLA School of Law. Unlike the article, however, this book does not attempt to address the specific concerns of transgender elders. Despite the fact that gay men and lesbians and transgender individuals share common cultural space and are subject to similar and inter-related forms of bias and harassment, it proved ultimately unworkable to present a full treatment of sexual orientation *and* gender identity in a single book. I concluded that transgender elders warrant separate consideration due to their unique history, identity formation, and complex relationship with the medical profession.

For example, transgender elders face some very specific health concerns, and research has just begun to catalogue their needs in terms of health care. Currently, very little is known about the long-term effects of hormone therapy as individuals age (Cahill, South and Spade 2000: 17). Transgender elders who have transitioned without medical intervention may be unwilling to seek medical help or accept assistance from caregivers, thereby placing them at risk and further reducing their likelihood of successful aging. This sort of reluctance may have contributed to the death of Billy Tipton, the famous jazz musician and transman, who died at the age of 74 from a bleeding ulcer in 1989. Tipton was unwilling to seek medical assistance for his condition, presumably because an examination would have revealed that he was a transman. When Tipton died, it was reported that he had not seen a doctor in 50 years (Minter 2002).

Obviously, the challenges confronted by transgender elders are no less significant than those confronted by gay and lesbian elders, and the two groups are not mutually exclusive because some transgender elders may also identify as gay or lesbian. However, the history and identity formation of transgender elders presents a distinct and singular story about gender and embodiment in 20th century America. Although the story of today's transgender elders overlaps with the gay and lesbian experience and intersects at many points, it deserves its own telling and should be more than an aside in a larger discussion about gay and lesbian elders.

Limiting the book to gay and lesbian elders necessarily raises the important question of who counts as gay or lesbian. As used in this book, the term "gay and lesbian elder" refers to a broad range of individuals who are 65 years of age or older and may or may not identify as gay or lesbian. It includes individuals who self-identify as gay or lesbian or bisexual or homosexual or queer or who have had a same-sex partner, engaged in same-sex sexual activity, or experienced significant periods of same-sex attraction. Such a broad definition is necessary to encompass all of the elders who may face (or fear) harassment on account of their non-normative sexuality or sexual attraction, but who may not identify as gay or lesbian. To illustrate, an elder who lives with her same-sex partner may be subject to anti-gay bias regardless of whether the elder identifies as gay. In fact, studies suggest that identification with the term "gay" is a strongly correlated with age. As a result of this generational component, many of the individuals whose lives and experiences are discussed in this book might not recognize themselves in the title.

Of course, this book's focus on the experience of gay and lesbian elders is not intended in any way to diminish or detract from the daily struggles encountered by elders generally. Aging in the United States is not for the faint of heart. Although Americans are living longer, elders grapple with financial insecurity, declining health, increased disability, and inadequate senior-specific services. U.S. aging policy relies on informal caregiving, usually performed by younger family members, but elders who age in place may find themselves isolated and far removed from family given our increasingly mobile society. The goal of this book is to highlight the specific barriers to successful aging faced by gay and lesbian elders without minimizing the difficulties associated with aging generally.

In addition to LGBT Elder Law: Toward Equity in Aging, I have explored a number of the ideas expressed in this book in earlier articles, including: Same-Sex Marriage and Federalism (Knauer 2008); The Recognition of Same-Sex Relationships: Comparative Institutional Analysis, Contested Social Goals, and Strategic Institutional Choice (Knauer 2005a); The September 11 Relief Efforts and Surviving Same-Sex Partners: Reflections on Relationships in the Absence of Uniform Legal Recognition (Knauer 2005b); Defining Capacity: Balancing the Competing Interests of Autonomy and Need (Knauer 2003a); Science, Identity, and the Construction of the Gay Political Narrative (Knauer 2003b); The September 11 Attacks and Surviving Same-Sex Partners: Defining Family Through Tragedy (Knauer 2002); "Simply So Different": the Uniquely Expressive Character of the Openly Gay Individual after Boy Scouts of America v. Dale (Knauer 2001); and Homosexuality as Contagion: From *The Well of Loneliness* to the Boy Scouts (Knauer 2000).

The development of this book has benefited along the way from many excellent comments and suggestions from a variety of sources. I presented the initial outline for the book at the 16th annual Conference for Feminist Law Professors, organized by my colleague Marina Angel, and received helpful feedback from many of the participants. I also presented a portion of the book at the 2010 Annual Law & Society Conference. I twice presented the project to my colleagues at Temple University, Beasley School of Law, and again received great encouragement and guidance. In particular, Debra H. Kroll, who directs the Beasley School of Law

Elder Law Clinic, shared many of her experiences representing gay and lesbian elders and confirmed that I was on the right track. I would also like to thank Karen Taylor, the former director of Community Advocacy & Capacity Building at SAGE, for her encouragement and early interest in the project. In addition, Mark Allen Taylor, the former director of the Temple University Health Sciences Library and one of my former students, provided invaluable research assistance and helped guide me through the confusing and frustratingly incomplete empirical data on gay and lesbian elders. My research assistant, Theresa D. Giamanco, was an incredible asset and an ace proofreader. Deep thanks goes to Eric J. Levy of Ashgate Publishing, who first suggested that LGBT Elder Law should be expanded into a book. Many others have been exceedingly giving of their time as they have answered my queries and read chunks of the book along the way, offering their wisdom and critiques. I would like to thank Jane A. Bassett, Frances Frick Burden, Amanda Baulme, Robert Espinoza, Alicia Kelly, Marylouise Esten, Kathy Mandelbaum, James McGrath, Clifford Rosky, Rebecca Schatschneider, William F. Signer, and especially Robin S. Maril, who has read the entire manuscript more than once. Finally, I would like to acknowledge my grandmother, the Hon. Virginia H. Knauer, who just celebrated her 95th birthday – may we all age as gracefully.

Introduction

On June 16, 2008, Del Martin and Phyllis Lyon, longtime lesbian activists who were both well into their 80s, became the first same-sex couple to marry legally in California (McKinley 2008). Widely covered in the press, their wedding ceremony was presided over by San Francisco Mayor Gavin Newsom, as a jubilant crowd of supporters and a scattering of protestors waited outside City Hall (McKinley 2008). The elderly couple had been together for 55 years (McKinley 2008). They started the first lesbian organization in the United States and jointly authored the groundbreaking book *Lesbian/Woman* in 1972 – when homosexuality was still classified as a mental illness by the American Psychiatric Association. The couple's long-standing commitment to the movement for gay and lesbian equality, and to each other, made them the obvious choice for this historic first.

Phyllis later commented that when she met Del in the 1950s, she "never imagined there would be a day that we would actually be able to get married" (Gordon 2008). The *New York Times* described Del and Phyllis' wedding ceremony as a "landmark," but the couple's married life together was fleeting, as was legally recognized same-sex marriage in the state of California (McKinley 2008). Del, who had been in declining health, passed away a little more than two months after the wedding at the age of 87 (Gordon 2008). When Del died, Phyllis noted that she "took some solace in knowing we were able to enjoy the ultimate rite of love and commitment before [Del] passed" (Gordon 2008).

Del and Phyllis' marriage had been made possible by a 2008 California Supreme Court decision, *In re Marriage Cases*, which invalidated California's prohibition against same-sex marriage on the grounds that it violated a fundamental right guaranteed by the state constitution. The decision proved highly controversial, and, by the time Del and Phyllis exchanged their wedding vows, efforts were already underway to amend the state constitution through a ballot initiative, known as Proposition 8, and restrict marriage to one man and one woman. Consistent with their life of public activism, Del and Phyllis allowed their wedding video to be used by organizations working to secure marriage equality and defeat Proposition 8 (Martin and Lyon Wedding Video 2008). Less than four months after their wedding, the voters narrowly approved Proposition 8 and brought an end to legally sanctioned same-sex marriages in California. A subsequent court case preserved the validity of the approximately 18,000 same-sex marriages that occurred prior to the enactment of Proposition 8 (*Strauss v. Horton 2009*), and the Proposition remains the focus of a high-profile federal lawsuit, *Perry v. Schwarzenegger.*

As the events in California were unfolding, I was working on an article about same-sex marriage and federalism, and I thought that the media attention surrounding Del and Phyllis' wedding provided an excellent illustration of how easily the personal can become politicized when dealing with matters of sexual orientation. I had earlier noted this phenomenon in the context of surviving same-sex partners who are forced to go to court to preserve their rights. These reluctant litigants often find themselves thrust into the spotlight and labeled "gay activists" when they are simply trying to do any number of things that grieving spouses are permitted to do as a matter of course, such as retrieving a partner's body from the morgue (Edgar 2009). There is no question that heterosexual marriage carries significant social meaning, but, when Del and Phyllis exchanged vows, their ceremony also conveyed a distinctly political message. Del's many obituaries and memorials characterized her marriage to Phyllis as a political milestone, referring to the wedding as Del's "last public political act" or "last act of activism" (Rothaus 2008, Gordon 2008).

My intention was to include the story of Del and Phyllis' wedding as an epilogue to the marriage and federalism piece. I thought it offered an inspiring narrative of resilience and progressive social change. The media accounts of the wedding firmly established Del and Phyllis as the public face of the gay and lesbian members of the Greatest Generation – the generation who served the United States during World War II, weathered the storms of the McCarthy Era, witnessed the birth of Gay Liberation, and lived long enough to see the fall of repressive sodomy laws and the legalization of same-sex marriage. To me, the image of a frail white-haired Del Martin, resplendent in a lavender suit, rising slowly from her wheelchair to exchange marriage vows with her long-time partner symbolized the ultimate triumph of her generation (Martin and Lyon Wedding Video 2008).

The notoriety accompanying Del and Phyllis' wedding seemed to signal a happy ending for the generation of gay men and lesbians who came of age long before the 1969 Stonewall riots that marked the start of Gay Liberation. I wanted to believe that this pre-Stonewall generation would now be able to enjoy their twilight years in relative peace, secure in their identities and their equal standing in society. Although Proposition 8 and the continuing cultural skirmishes remind us that legal inequities and anti-gay bias remain, I thought that the years of overt homophobia and violence were, thankfully, in the past. In my mind, Del and Phyllis' joyful nuptials validated the decades of struggle and, in a symbolic way, rectified some of the innumerable past wrongs. The wedding also reaffirmed my core liberal belief that progressive social change is inevitable in a free society, and I found it intensely gratifying to imagine a bunch of elderly newlywed same-sex couples playing canasta at the Rainbow Retirement Village while swapping stories about being "in the life" back in the day.

As I started to gather more information on the pre-Stonewall generation of gay and lesbian elders, however, it became clear that the triumphant narrative arc that I had constructed bore little resemblance to the day-to-day lives of many of the estimated 1.6 to 2.4 million gay and lesbian seniors. Unlike Del and Phyllis, who were celebrated by the gay community and remained close to biological family members, many gay and lesbian elders face the daily challenges of aging isolated from family, detached from the larger gay and lesbian community, and ignored by mainstream aging initiatives. They lead lives that are solitary and closeted, plagued by fear of disclosure and financial insecurity. I was shocked to learn that the brave souls who came out in the 1950s and 1960s, when homosexuality was still a crime *and* a mental disorder, were spending their final years locked in an anxious silence, denied the basic dignity of sharing the memories of a life well lived.

The disconnect between the advances made in gay and lesbian civil rights and the conditions endured by many gay and lesbian seniors was jarring. Because I was raised by my grandmother, seniors have always been a big part of my life. It was simply untenable to me that our gay and lesbian elders were so vulnerable and friendless. As a legal scholar, my immediate impulse was normative – I would describe the problem and propose a series of broad-based reforms designed to insure equity (and dignity) in aging regardless of sexual orientation. Not surprisingly, my initial prescription centered on expanded legislative and market-based anti-discrimination measures. For example, gay and lesbian elders report that they face hostility and prejudice from health-care providers and feel silenced and unwelcome in institutional settings, such as assisted living facilities, nursing homes, and senior centers. They find the nursing home environment especially difficult to navigate, and some nursing homes will banish gay residents to Alzheimer or "memory" wards in order to mollify the prejudice of other residents (Gross 2007). In this context, it is easy to see how an already vulnerable nursing home resident could be harassed, abused, and neglected on account of his or her sexual orientation. And, I have to say, it was equally easy to propose a series of top-down anti-discrimination protections and "anti-bullying" measures to address this problem.

The seemingly quick fix of anti-discrimination protections, however, belied the complexity of the problem, not to mention the numerous obstacles to successful implementation. Beyond the pressing question of "what can be done to alleviate the suffering of gay and lesbian elders," there was a host of difficult and thorny follow-up questions. Why have gay and lesbian elders remained largely silent? Why has the gay and lesbian community failed to prioritize aging issues in its advocacy agenda? Why has the senior community ignored the needs of its gay and lesbian peers? And, the most puzzling of all – how can this happen at a time when gay men and lesbians enjoy an unprecedented level of legal and societal acceptance? Our gay and lesbian elders had been the vanguard of the contemporary gay and lesbian civil rights movement, but somehow they had been left behind.

Considering these questions, I quickly realized that the challenges facing gay and lesbian elders could not be attributed solely to the usual culprits of anti-gay bias and homophobia, although they both had important roles to play. The current crisis experienced by gay and lesbian elders involves a complicated interplay of historical forces, identity politics, and the failure of our heteronormative aging initiatives. In my attempt to address the concerns of gay and lesbian elders, I found myself confronting the corrosive legacy of the pre-Stonewall views of homosexuality, as well as the pervasive pattern of ageism within both the larger community and the gay and lesbian community. Positioning myself as an advocate for gay and lesbian elders, it became clear to me that the prevailing identity or ethnic model of sexual orientation is not equipped to champion their concerns because it has failed to incorporate a much-needed theory of difference. I also recognized that there is an inherent generational component to gay and lesbian identity because identity formation for the homosexual subject is uniquely the product of his or her historical context.

These were big thoughts to add to what had started as a modest set of policy proposals. Each observation seemed to have the potential to advance our understanding of the contemporary construction of sexuality and identity in exciting new ways, and each one seemed to deserve its own book-length exposition. Take, for example, my last assertion that gay men and lesbians are historically contingent subjects. With this observation, I am not referring to the type of cultural "generation gap" that captivated the United States during the Vietnam years, even though the gay and lesbian community has more than its fair share of inter-generational miscommunication. According to sociologists, the gay and lesbian community actually suffers from a multiplicity of generation gaps because it is comprised of highly compressed age cohorts delimited by relatively narrow social and political periods (Russell and Bohan 2005). Instead, I am suggesting a type of historical contingency that is deeply ontological and goes to the core of an individual's understanding of self and his or her right to exist in the world.

Since the late 19th century, an individual who experiences same-sex desire has been viewed as a distinct and identifiable type of person. Over the course of the next 100 years, the medical profession classified such individuals as inverts, homosexuals, and, finally, gay. Each theory of same-sex desire presented a different view of causation, the efficacy of therapeutic intervention, and the prospect or desirability of a "cure." The beliefs and behaviors of gay and lesbian elders show that the pre-Stonewall generation differs from its post-Stonewall progeny in fundamental ways that, I would argue, rival those more typically associated with the great epochal shifts in intellectual thought, such as transition from the enlightenment to post-modernity.

Despite the appeal of this rather grand observation, it is important for us to remember that its foundation rests on the daily struggles of gay and lesbian elders. Throughout this book, I have endeavored to foreground these real-life challenges while, at the same time, engaging related issues of sexuality and identity. My goal in this regard is not simply to strike a "balance" between questions of practical application and theory, but to show the inescapable connectedness of practice and theory. In the legal academy, there is an ongoing debate concerning the appropriate emphasis to be given to practical training versus theoretical inquiry, but I have always believed that the practice/theory debate presents a false dichotomy. Practice necessarily informs theory, and theory necessarily elucidates practice. For example, I discovered that any discussion of gay and lesbian elders must incorporate an appreciation for the pre-Stonewall views of homosexuality because these views are at the root of certain fears and anxieties expressed by gay and lesbian seniors that otherwise would be quite inexplicable. Thus, theoretical considerations of the social (and historical) construction of identity can help policy-makers decipher the behavior of gay and lesbian elders. Likewise, the manner in which gay and lesbian elders construct and live their lives directly informs theories of identity formation. Their modes of dealing with the medical profession, internalized homophobia, and the closet all illustrate the historically contingent nature of gay and lesbian identity. More importantly, though, it is their daily struggles that give the notion of historical contingency a sense of meaning and urgency. From this perspective, I think it is evident that practice and theory are not in tension with one another, but rather they are two sides of the same coin.

I hope that others who are grappling with social issues regarding sexual orientation (and gender identity) will also try to reject the trap of the practice/theory either/or. An overly practical approach to the problems of gay and lesbian elders could misapprehend the underlying cause of the problem and thereby produce ineffective or incomplete policy proposals. It would also miss an opportunity to engage a number of important concepts dealing with sexuality and identity formation. Similarly, a book ostensibly about gay and lesbian elders that primarily focused on issues of social theory would run the risk of losing sight of the original reason for the inquiry and relegating the needs of lesbian and gay elders to a footnote. For this reason, although I believe that theory can help direct our practice, I feel strongly that practice should *always* drive our theory.

Following this advice, I have divided the book into three parts, broadly designated as history, identity, and advocacy. The organizational structure reflects my conviction that our past informs the present and, in so doing, it can help us plan for the future. The first section of the book provides an introduction to the current generation of gay and lesbian elders by summarizing existing demographic data and providing a historical overview of pre-Stonewall views regarding homosexuality. As noted, I believe that an understanding of the pre-Stonewall views of homosexuality is essential to diagnosing many of the problems facing gay and lesbian elders today. The history of homosexuality as a mental disorder that demands therapeutic intervention greatly complicates the relationships gay and lesbian seniors have with medical professionals. It also makes them wary when pursuing relationships with younger people for fear of invoking the sexual predator stereotype popularized by the American Freudians in the 1940s and 1950s (Terry 1999). Above all, it normalizes the closet as a coping mechanism.

Sadly, the closet is a defining feature in the lives of many gay and lesbian elders. Some elders have never ventured very far out of the closet, but even those who have lived openly in the past retreat to the closet as they age in order to avoid dangerous and debilitating anti-gay bias. Whenever I am asked to give a presentation on gay and lesbian elders, I always travel with a Powerpoint slideshow of vintage photos of same-sex couples that I run toward the end of my talk. I like to think that they represent all the pictures of happier times that are not displayed on the nightstands and bureaus of gay and lesbian elders who live in nursing homes and assisted living facilities or the pictures that are turned over in advance of a visit from a home health aide. In addition to the human costs involved, the closet is one of the greatest stumbling blocks encountered in the development and implementation of effective policy reforms for gay and lesbian elders (Kanapaux 2003). When they remain silent, gay and lesbian elders are attempting to avoid anti-gay bias and prejudice, but their silence also insures that their concerns remain unnoticed and unaddressed. Thus, the closet's promise of safety will always fall short, because, to paraphrase Audre Lorde, your silence will never protect you (Lorde 1984: 41).

I suspect that many people, particularly those who are not gay or lesbian, underestimate the human toll exacted by the closet – what it means for seniors to disavow or permanently silence their memories. Thinking about my own family for a moment, I can't imagine what it would be like if my grandmother could not tell her stories. To me, the act of telling and retelling her stories is one of the things that constitutes us as a family. It simultaneously establishes her past and secures her rightful place in the present. At family gatherings, we request the stories by name. One of my cousins will inevitably say, "Tell the story about the first time you danced with grandfather." As if on cue, my grandmother will chuckle and lean a little closer as she explains the obvious physics of an Italian strapless dress and how she once warned a dashing stranger, who later became her husband, to step lightly or risk certain embarrassment. Through this familiar process of repetition and appreciation, we invite our grandmother to touch the past, and she reminds us, with a mischievous wink, that in 1939 she was young and desirable and in charge.

I am certain that our gay and lesbian elders have similar tales of derring-do, as well as riveting tales of romance and heart-wrenching tales of great loss. It is unlikely, however, that we will find gay and lesbian elders sitting at the kitchen table holding court before a multi-generational audience. In the first instance, gay and lesbian elders are less likely to be partnered and considerably less likely to have children. They rely, instead, on single-generational "chosen families." Secondly, when interacting with people outside their chosen family, gay and lesbian elders will routinely edit their past to avoid anticipated rejection and reprisals. Sometimes the demands of the closet may require only a slight modification to a story, and a same-sex partner can easily become a best friend or a sibling. Other times, a more drastic rewrite might be required in order for the story to make sense. Eventually, the story may cease to exist entirely because there is simply no one left to tell.

In the second part of the book, I address the invisibility of gay and lesbian seniors and examine the multiple double binds central to their identity formation. Gay and lesbian elders currently exist at an unenviable intersection of identity bounded by ageism and homophobia. In the popular imagination, a powerful combination of ageism and homophobia has rendered the lives of gay and lesbian elders all but unthinkable. It is easy to do the math. If seniors are perceived to be asexual (or at least no longer sexual), and gay men and lesbians are primarily defined by their sexuality, then seniors, by definition, cannot be gay or lesbian. Additionally, pervasive ageism within the gay and lesbian community and homophobia within the mainstream senior community work in tandem to alienate gay and lesbian elders from their two natural constituencies. The result is that closeted gay and lesbian elders are afraid to speak for themselves and their most likely allies are unwilling to speak on their behalf.

In other venues, I have argued that the contemporary ethnic model of gay and lesbian identity is inadequate to theorize the multivalent nature of identity and, to the contrary, it exhibits a strong essentializing tendency that elides intersecting identities. Queer theory, critical race theory, and feminist theory have all produced sustained critiques of this essentializing quality, and its resulting construction of a minority group comprised of stable gay subjects who, by default, are coded white, heteronormative, middle class, and largely male. When I initially approached the topic of gay and lesbian elders, I assumed that age presented another example of an intersecting identity to be added to a growing list that already included race, gender, ethnicity, and disability. However, in light of my observations regarding the importance of historical context to gay and lesbian identity formation, I now see that the study of gay and lesbian elders adds another *dimension* to the critique – not merely another category of intersection. The existing ethnic model of gay and lesbian identity obscures a crucial longitudinal component. The pre-Stonewall generation is not the same as its "out and proud" post-Stonewall progeny. The identities of the former generation's members were formed at different times and under dramatically different circumstances. Thus, gay and lesbian identity, as it is lived and experienced, is not only multivalent, as I have previously asserted, but it is also historically contingent.

In the third part of the book, I look forward and outline a number of advocacy points and practical reforms that further my original goal, namely to insure equity (and dignity) in aging for gay and lesbian elders. Here, I examine the shortcomings of the ethnic model of identity from a slightly different vantage point. In addition to influencing identity formation on the individual level, the ethnic model has been instrumental in legal and political advocacy efforts to normalize homosexuality and advance the rights of gay men and lesbians. These advocacy efforts generally employ a two-part argument of shared identity and equivalence. Using the ethnic model of identity, the first part of the argument asserts that gay men and lesbians represent an identifiable and cohesive minority group. The second part then maintains that, as a deserving minority, gay men and lesbians are entitled to equal treatment. Not surprisingly, this argument tends to highlight the heteronormative aspects of gay and lesbian lives because it is based on the conviction that gay men and lesbians are *the same as* non-gay and lesbian individuals. Although this strategy has met with considerable success, I have argued elsewhere that it does a disservice to the larger gay and lesbian community by imposing a heteronormative ideal that does not necessarily reflect the diversity of gay and lesbian lives. This has the effect of excluding non-heteronormative gay men and lesbians, and it also directly ignores the more problematic aspects of some gay and lesbian lives, such as relationship dissolution and same-sex domestic violence.

This overwhelmingly positive and traditional emphasis is reflected in the three signature issues of the contemporary movement for gay and lesbian equality: marriage equality, anti-discrimination protection in employment, and repeal of the military's "don't ask, don't tell" (DADT) policy. Viewed together, they send the clear message that gay and lesbian people are just like everyone else. They want to marry, have children, go to work, and serve their country. The problem with this formulation is not that it is necessarily untrue, but that it is necessarily underinclusive. The current needs of gay and lesbian elders are not reflected in this heteronormative, white, middle class, 30-something version of the American Dream because it is based on an identity model that does not include them.

To illustrate this point, I address the three signature issues from the perspective of gay and lesbian elders and consider the ways in which each issue fails to encompass their unique needs. For example, gay and lesbians elders frequently rely on single-generational "chosen families" for care and support, in lieu of more conventional multi-generational families of origin (Weston 1997). The concept of chosen family has obvious legal implications in terms of relationship recognition and aging policies, but gay and lesbian advocacy efforts to secure relationship recognition have focused exclusively on partners and children. Although same-sex marriage would doubtless help many partnered gay and lesbian elders, it does not address the legal fragility of their chosen families.

In a brief conclusion, I call for a more holistic and nuanced model of gay and lesbian identity – one that extends over an individual's lifespan, incorporates pre-Stonewall gay and lesbian history, and confronts difficult issues, such as ageism and internalized homophobia. Central to this model would be a robust theory of difference designed to resist the pull of heteronormativity. Advocacy claims based on this model would emphasize equity, rather than equivalence. They would acknowledge that gay and lesbian elders are indeed different from their non-gay peers and assert that it is precisely because of this difference that they are vulnerable and underserved. Accordingly, gay and lesbian elders would be constituted as a deserving minority not because of their sameness or their approximation to a heteronormative ideal, but because of their difference.

PART I
History

The identities of the current cohort of gay and lesbian elders were forged within a historical period that seems far removed from today's reality of legalized same-sex marriage and openly gay celebrities. The pre-Stonewall generation came of age in a time when being "out and proud" was a surefire way to get a Section VIII discharge from the military or an appointment for electroshock therapy (Berube 2000, Eskridge 1999). Homosexuality was classified as a severe sociopathic mental illness and sodomy was uniformly criminalized. The closet was not only a survival mechanism – it was, quite simply, a way of life.

Today, gay men and lesbians who are age 65 and older ("gay and lesbian elders") are a largely invisible and silent minority. Existing demographic and gerontological research is frustratingly incomplete and partial. Growing anecdotal evidence, supported by data collected by advocacy groups, suggests that gay and lesbian elders struggle with financial insecurity and social isolation. They overwhelmingly rely on single-generational chosen families for support, underutilize aging resources, and face significant barriers to health care and related elder-care services. Fearful of discrimination, gay and lesbian elders are prone to retreat to the closet when dealing with health-care and elder-care professionals or living in institutional settings. The willingness and ability of gay and lesbian elders to conceal their identities contributes to their invisibility and, in so doing, allows heteronomative and homophobic practices to go unchallenged. As one study concluded, "The difficulty in undertaking change in an environment in which older gays and lesbians are profoundly silent cannot be underestimated" (Kanapaux 2003).

Pre-Stonewall history provides an important context for many of the struggles encountered by gay and lesbian elders. The painful legacy of the pre-Stonewall theories of sexuality continues to inform their behavior and beliefs, as well as that of their non-gay peers. The stereotypes promulgated by the American Freudians stubbornly linger in our popular imagination, and find voice in partisan politics and policies long after the medical profession has repudiated their homophobic assumptions.

This section first provides a brief overview of pre-Stonewall history and then discusses the congenital and psychoanalytic models of homosexuality that were advanced, respectively, by the early sexologists and the American Freudians. With this important background, it then summarizes the existing research on gay and lesbian elders. The picture that emerges is quite sobering, but it also remains provisional. As will become evident, writing about gay and lesbian elders necessarily involves dealing with absences, omissions, and silence. A combination of increased interest in the challenges faced by gay and lesbian elders and improved data collection would go a long way toward filling in some of the missing pieces and, hopefully, it could begin to bridge the isolation that currently places an entire generation at risk.

Chapter 1

The Making of the Pre-Stonewall Generation

For many gay and lesbian elders, the invisibility and isolation that they face in their later years are, unfortunately, familiar territory. As members of the pre-Stonewall generation, gay and lesbian elders are well acquainted with the themes of estrangement, alienation, and secrecy. Coming-out stories from this generation are marked by narratives of loneliness and struggle (Martin and Lyon 1972: 177–204). The topic of homosexuality was, in many ways, unspeakable; censored from movies and literature. Young people, confused by their feelings of same-sex attraction, sometimes did not even know there was a word to describe what they were experiencing and were left to conclude that they must indeed be "the only one." In the days before the Internet, young people who consulted the library might not have found a reference to homosexuality in the card catalogue, but instead would be able to learn something about themselves under the entry of "sexuality, deviant" (McGreevey 2007). That reference would then lead the curious to titles such as *Neurotic Counterfeit-Sex; Impotence, Frigidity, "Mechanical" and Pseudosexuality, Homosexuality* (Bergler 1951) or the later *Homosexuality: Its Causes and Cures* (Ellis 1965). Some of the available "cures" could be found detailed in *Shock Treatments, Psychosurgery, and Other Somatic Treatments in Psychiatry* (Kalinowsky 1952). Understandably, many were repelled by what they learned about themselves from the abnormal psychology texts that they read surreptitiously in the stacks – their confusing feelings of same-sex attraction were a symptom of a severe form of mental illness and acting on those feelings was a crime.

Some homosexuals rejected and repressed their feelings of same-sex attraction and attempted to have a "normal" life complete with marriage and children. Others accepted the prevailing medical diagnosis that homosexuality was a mental disorder and labored for years in psychoanalysis to try to effect a cure (Berzon 2002, Duberman 1991). Still others moved on and tried to build a life despite the dire prognosis. Many members of the pre-Stonewall generation struggled through a variety of iterations of self before finally making peace with their sexuality.

The Pre- and Post-Stonewall Divide

At the outset, it is important to establish the parameters of the current cohort of gay and lesbian elders in order to situate pre-Stonewall events and trends within the course of their life experiences and make some general observations about the historical and cultural forces that helped shape their worldview. As of 2010, the youngest of today's gay and lesbian elders would have been born in 1945. That being said, however, it is not immediately apparent where to set the upper age limit for the age cohort. As explained in Chapter 3, the U.S. Census Bureau dose not collect data on sexual orientation, so it is not possible to pinpoint with any certainty the oldest gay or lesbian elder, although anecdotal accounts attest to their longevity. For example, Ruth Ellis, an African-American lesbian who lived in Detroit, was widely described as the oldest out lesbian when she died in 2000 at the age of 101 (Capeloto 2000). Rather than skew the discussion by focusing on outlying centenarians, it is reasonable to assume for illustrative purposes that the vast majority of gay and lesbian elders are between the ages of 65 and 95 (Hobbs, U.S. Census Bureau 2008).

Assuming that the current cohort of gay and lesbian elders were between the ages of 65 and 95 in 2010, the oldest members of the pre-Stonewall generation would have been born in 1915, before the United States entered World War I. The youngest would have been born in 1945, at the close of World War II. Naturally, the life experiences of those at either end of the age cohort would have been very different. The oldest members lived through the Depression and World War II. The youngest members were born during World War II and grew up in a period of post-war affluence. According to conventional attempts by sociologists to categorize individuals born between 1915 and 1945, gay and lesbian elders actually span three different American generations: the G.I. Generation (1901–1925), the Silent Generation (1926–1942), and the Baby Boom Generation (1943–1960) (Strauss and Howe 1991).

Notwithstanding the diversity of their life experiences, gay and lesbian elders are united in a single generation because they all share a common historical and cultural understanding of homosexuality. They came of age when the notion that one should be open and proud about his or her sexual orientation was unthinkable to all but a handful of free spirits and early homophile activists. It was not until the early 1970s that Gay Liberation popularized the belief that coming out publicly was essential to self-actualization and individual well-being. By that time, the youngest of today's gay and lesbian elders were well into adulthood and the oldest were approaching retirement age. Following a liberationist ideology, Gay Liberationists theorized that the act of coming out would have the dual benefit of liberating the individual and transforming society (Jagose 1996: 38). The public narrative of pride and openness introduced by Gay Liberation set the stage for the contemporary movement for gay and lesbian equality and signaled the beginning of a new type of discourse concerning sexuality and gender (Jagose 1996).

Conventional generational divides are marked by wars or periods of great economic or technological upheaval, but the divide between the pre- and post-Stonewall generations reflects this seismic shift in the views regarding homosexuality that took place in the years following the 1969 Stonewall riots. The Stonewall riots began on June 27, 1969, when the New York City police raided a gay bar on Christopher Street in Greenwich Village named the Stonewall Inn, and the gay and transgender clientele resisted (Duberman 1993: 194–212).

The disturbances and clashes with police spread to the streets and continued sporadically for several days (Duberman 1993: 200–205). The Stonewall riots hold a cherished place in LGBT history and are widely accepted as marking the beginning of the contemporary Gay Pride Movement (Bravmann 1997: 68–96). The first Gay Pride march was held in New York City on the one-year anniversary of the Stonewall riots (Bravmann 1997: 71), and Gay Pride Day is still celebrated on the last weekend in June to commemorate the riots (Jagose 1996: 30).

When the raid on the Stonewall Inn took place, the youngest members of today's gay and lesbian elders were 24 years old, whereas the older members of this generation were a mature 54 years of age. No doubt, individuals at opposite ends of the age range could have interpreted the significance of the events that transpired on Christopher Street quite differently, but the riots themselves were not widely reported by the media and arguably did not resonate in the everyday lives of homosexuals, even those living in New York City. *The New York Times* introduced a brief story on what is now referred to as "riots" with the following headline: "4 Policemen Hurt in 'Village' Raid: Melee Near Sheridan Square Follows Action at Bar" (Rupp 1999: 176–177). *The New York Daily News* was, not surprisingly, a bit more sensational. Its headline read: "Homo Nest Raided: Queen Bees are Stinging Mad" (Lisker 1969). There was no mention of the incident in the *Washington Post* or other urban newspapers with large gay populations, such as the *San Francisco Examiner/Chronicle* (Rupp 1999: 176–177).

Despite this lack of notoriety, the Stonewall riots provide an important historical line of demarcation because the public face of homosexuality was forever changed in the years immediately following the riots with the emergence of the vocal and confrontational Gay Liberation Movement that introduced the nation to the concept of "gay pride" (Jagose 1996: 30). In the early 1970s, Gay Liberation organizations, such as the Gay Liberation Front and the Gay Activist Alliance, quickly eclipsed the fledging Homophile Movement that had started in the mid-1950s and had pursued a more cautious and assimilationist path. The short-lived Gay Liberation Movement lasted only from 1969 until the mid-1970s, but its effective use of the media and political theater to deploy gay-positive images sparked a much larger cultural conversation about homosexuality and sexuality more generally.[1] Taking their cues from the anti-war and feminist movements, gay liberationists constructed a public counter-narrative that "Gay Is Good" and urged gay and lesbian individuals to declare themselves and leave the false security of

---

1   For example, Mark Segal, a member of the Philadelphia-based activist group the Gay Raiders, managed to bring Gay Pride into the living rooms of millions of Americans when he "zapped" the *CBS Evening News* with Walter Cronkite in 1973 (M. Stein 2004: 381). Similar protests that year disrupted *The Today Show*, *The Tonight Show*, and the popular daytime talk show, *The Mike Douglas Show* (M. Stein 2004: 381). The activism paid off. Two years later, *Time* magazine put an openly gay man on its cover when it ran a fair and balanced story about Sergeant Leonard Matlovich, a decorated veteran of the Vietnam War who challenged the military's ban on homosexuals (The Sexes 1975).

the closet with slogans such as: "Closets are for Clothes" and "Out of the Closet and Into the Streets" (D'Erasmo 1999: BR8, Noble 1981).

Prior to the Stonewall riots, there were estimated to be only 50 gay or lesbian organizations in the United States, including the two major homophile organizations: the Daughters of Bilitis founded by Del Martin and Phyllis Lyon in 1955 and the Mattachine Society founded by Harry Hay in 1950 (Hunter 2005: 16). After Stonewall, gay and lesbian organizations proliferated on college campuses and in major metropolitan areas and, their number grew to over 700 by 1973 (Hunter 2005:16). During the same period, some cities and municipalities began to extend anti-discrimination protections to include sexual orientation or, as it was referred to at the time, "sexual or affectional preference" (Eskridge 1999: 354–371). In December 1973, a true watershed event occurred that touched the lives of homosexuals everywhere. The American Psychiatric Association (APA) declassified homosexuality as a mental disorder, largely in response to aggressive lobbying by gay activists (Bayer 1987). As one Philadelphia newspaper explained, "20 Million Gain Instant Cure" (LeVay 1996: 224). By the time the official "cure" was announced at the close of 1973, the youngest of today's elders were 28 years of age and the oldest were 58. That same year, the District of Columbia became the first jurisdiction to pass comprehensive anti-discrimination protections in employment, housing, public accommodations, lending, and education (Eskridge 1999: 357).

Of course, the early successes of the Gay Liberation Movement have to be viewed in context. The social and political disabilities imposed on gay men and lesbians did not disappear overnight, and the radical calls for gay liberation were eventually replaced by a movement for civil and political equality that took a longer and more pragmatic view of social change. Post-declassification, the United States remained a deeply homophobic nation where sodomy was criminalized in the majority of states, and no state-wide antidiscrimination protections were enacted until 1982 (Eskridge 1999: 361). The Gay Liberation Movement, however, had started a public counter-narrative that advocated pride and openness. As this message of gay pride began to resonate on the cultural and political level throughout the 1970s, the days when a young gay person could grow up thinking that he or she was "the only one" were quickly drawing to a close.

A Generation in Hiding

Individuals who came of age before the advent of the Gay Liberation Movement did not have the benefit of this public pro-gay counter-narrative. Members of the pre-Stonewall generation formed their ideas regarding homosexuality, and necessarily themselves, by reference to the established views expressed by religion, science, and the law. These three forces presented an unappealing and frightening portrait of the homosexual who was simultaneously characterized as a sinner, a mentally ill pervert, and a criminal. Unlike other minority groups, gay men and lesbians do not typically grow up in households where their family members also share their minority status. For the pre-Stonewall generation, this meant that parents and other relatives often subscribed to the prevailing negative views of homosexuality and homosexuals. News that a child was "that way" could be greeted with hostility and disgust, resulting in estrangement or worse – the family could attempt to secure a "cure" for the afflicted family member. The ever-present threat of estrangement prompted homosexuals to remain secretive and distance themselves from their families. Without support from their family, homosexuals relied heavily on what anthropologists refer to as "chosen family," as they tried to plot a course through the all-encompassing social, political, and legal disabilities that were imposed on homosexuals.

During the period when today's gay and lesbian elders were entering their adult years, an individual who openly admitted to being a homosexual was not simply risking social disapproval and religious condemnation. As a severe mental disorder, homosexuality was grounds for civil commitment, and the malady was "treated" with a wide range of therapies, including electro-shock therapy, aversion therapy, drugs, and the occasional prefrontal lobotomy (Eskridge 1999: 62). Tennessee Williams used the growing connection between psychosurgery and homosexuality to dramatic effect in his 1958 play, *Suddenly Last Summer*, which was later made into a popular movie staring Elizabeth Taylor, Katherine Hepburn, and Montgomery Cliff (*Suddenly Last Summer* (dir. Joseph Mankiewicz, 1959)). Williams' plot illustrates the extreme lengths a family would employ to silence homosexuality within its ranks. The family matriarch, Violet Venable, arranges for her niece to be committed to a psychiatric hospital and evaluated for a lobotomy because the young woman refuses to remain silent about the circumstances surrounding the death of her cousin, the matriarch's beloved son, Sebastian. Although deeply coded, it gradually becomes clear that a retelling of the unseemly circumstances of Sebastian's death would threaten to out him posthumously. Rather than risk this unwanted disclosure, the matriarch appeals to a man of science to excise the disturbing memory. Referring to her niece, Violet urges the doctor to "cut this hideous story out of her brain" (*Suddenly Last Summer* (dir. Joseph Mankiewicz, 1959)).

In addition to the possibility of "therapeutic" intervention, the classification of homosexuality as a mental disorder was also used to justify a wide range of social and political disabilities. Homosexuals were considered to be unfit for the vast majority of jobs, as well as parenthood. They were officially labeled perverts and deviants, and they lived with the constant fear of exposure. They had to choose their confidants wisely and carefully monitor their actions and associates. For the pre-Stonewall generation, the closet was a way of life, and it makes sense that they would once again embrace its promise of relative safety as they begin to encounter the vulnerabilities associated with aging. As Ski Hunter explains, today's gay and lesbian elders are the "last generation to have lived their adolescence and young adulthood in hiding" (Hunter 2005: 13).

Beyond the diagnosis of homosexuality as a mental disorder, the lives of the pre-Stonewall generation were also constrained by multiple and overlapping prohibitions imposed by the criminal law. Sodomy was criminalized in all states until 1961, when Illinois adopted of the Uniform Penal Code that favored sexual privacy (Eskridge 1999: 104).[2] Illinois remained an outlier until 10 years later, when Connecticut repealed its sodomy law in 1971.[3] At the time, the repeal of sodomy laws was consistent with a trend to decriminalize the so-called "victimless crimes." In 1957, *The Report of the Departmental Committee on Homosexual Offences and Prostitution Committee* (known as the *Wolfenden Report*) was published in Great Britain and concluded that homosexual behavior between "consenting adults in private" should no longer be criminalized (Committee on Homosexual Offences and Prostitution 1964: 46). Although it was another 10 years before Great Britain repealed its laws criminalizing homosexual conduct,[4] the recommendation of the *Wolfenden Report* sparked a celebrated debate between H.L.A. Hart, a leading legal scholar, who agreed with the *Report*, and Lord Devlin, a well-respected British jurist, who did not. Following John Stuart Mill, Hart argued that criminal sanctions were inappropriate when only a moral law had been transgressed and there was no victim (Hart 1963). Lord Devlin, on the other hand, maintained that homosexual acts should be criminalized in order to preserve the moral fabric of society and prevent its disintegration – an argument that is very similar to the one currently waged against marriage equality (Devlin 1965).

---

2   Historically, sodomy was but one variation in a broad range of sexual practices that were subject to religious and criminal proscriptions. In England, sodomy was first criminalized during the reign of Henry VIII (Eskridge 1999: 157). Until 1861, the penalty for "the detestable and abominable vice of buggery committed with mankind or beast" was death (Eskridge 1999: 157). Both Sir Edward Coke and Sir William Blackstone believed that the very nature of the act was unmentionable and described sodomy as "the infamous crime against nature" (Eskridge 1999: 158). In his Commentaries, Blackstone promised his readers that he would not "dwell any longer upon a subject, the very mention of which is a disgrace to human nature" (Blackstone 1769: 215). Instead, he elected "to imitate ... the delicacy of our English law, which treats it, in it's [sic] very indictments, as a crime not fit to be named; peccatum illud horribile, inter christianos non nominandum" (Blackstone 1769: 215). William Eskridge (1999) reports that the "English crime of buggery was generally applicable in the American colonies, either as a matter of common law or statutory decree" (Eskridge 1999: 157).

3   After Illinois, other states were slow to repeal their sodomy laws. By the time the APA declassified homosexuality as a mental illness in 1973, only five additional states had repealed their sodomy laws: Connecticut (1971), Colorado (1972), Oregon (1972), Delaware (1973), and North Dakota (1973). In 1986, the U.S. Supreme Court ruled in *Bowers v. Hardwick* that the criminalization of adult consensual sodomy did not violate the U.S. Constitution. Bowers was not overruled until *Lawrence v. Texas* in 2003.

4   Unlike the United States, Great Britain had never criminalized consensual sexual conduct between women.

During the pre-Stonewall era, sodomy laws in the United States were selectively enforced, but the fact that homosexual conduct was criminalized made all homosexuals presumptive felons – a status that did not cease until 2003 when the U.S. Supreme Court ruled in *Lawrence v. Texas* that the U.S. Constitution prohibited the criminalization of consensual same-sex sexuality. Beginning in the 1930s, the criminal sodomy laws were augmented by the sexual psychopath laws that had been created specifically to address the perceived threat that homosexuals posed to children and other innocents. These laws authorized the psychiatric commitment of an individual charged with a sex crime for an indeterminate period of treatment either before or after standing trial for the underlying offense (Eskridge 1999: 42). Criminal laws governing loitering, indecency, and disorderly conduct were also used to regulate homosexuals who ventured into public spaces, whether bars and coffeehouses or "cruising" areas frequented by male homosexuals. Criminal obscenity laws banned even restrained depictions of same-sex attraction, as well as political newsletters and magazines published by the early homophile organizations and activists. The chilling effect of the obscenity laws kept frank discussions of homosexuality confined to medical texts that were largely outside the reach of average people.

As presumptive felons, homosexuals had difficulty socializing and organizing. From a legal standpoint, the power of the state to disrupt peaceful and private gatherings raised obvious issues with respect to associational freedoms, but, from an individual perspective, it also greatly increased the importance of the closet. In 1959, simply attending a homophile conference would have been a dangerous proposition. That year, the Mattachine Society held a national conference in Denver, and the organizers were arrested and one was jailed for 60 days (D'Emilio 1983: 120–121). The police searched the home of the organizer who was jailed, and he lost his job due to the publicity surrounding his arrest (Hunter 2005: 65). The following year, 84 gay men and lesbians who were attending an organizational meeting of the Mattachine Society were arrested in suburban Philadelphia (M. Stein 2004: 180–184).

Going to meet other homosexuals in a public place, such as a gay bar, was fraught with anxiety because of the potential for anti-gay violence outside the bar, and police activity inside the bar. As an alternative to bars, many homosexuals relied on private friendship circles and socialized in their homes. Bars frequented by homosexuals existed in many cities and towns, but they were often controlled by organized crime and were under constant police surveillance. Gay bars could be raided by the police for no cause and, in some cities, the patrons' names would be published in the newspaper. With no anti-discrimination protections and rampant anti-gay sentiment, exposure as a homosexual, or even as a fellow traveler, could easily ruin a career. It could also ruin a heterosexual marriage. If children were involved, the homosexual parent would be considered *per se* unfit. The constant fear of exposure made homosexuals vulnerable to extortion and, in some cases, led to suicide.

During this period, politicians and prosecutors frequently targeted homosexuals to signal that they were tough on crime, and rounding up the perverts and sex deviants sent a definite message to the voters. The large metropolitan areas most closely associated with homosexuality, such as San Francisco and New York City, would periodically crack down on gay bars and cruising areas. The famous 1969 raid on the Stonewall Inn was part of a larger "police cleanup" in New York City that was initiated by the incumbent mayor John Lindsay, who was facing a difficult re-election challenge (D'Emilio 1983: 269). Throughout the 1950s and 1960s, Philadelphia was notorious for the Saturday night raids on gay bars led by police captain Frank Rizzo, who was later promoted to police commissioner and then served as mayor for two terms on a law-and-order platform (M. Stein 2004: 157).

Smaller towns were also susceptible to homosexual panic. From 1954 to 1956, the town of Boise, Idaho, was consumed by allegations of a "homosexual underground" of men who had sex with minors (Gerassi 2001). Lasting for two years, the ensuing police investigation involved the questioning of close to 1,500 men and resulted in 15 convictions with sentences that ranged from probation to life in prison (Gerassi 2001). One of the men implicated in the scandal later committed suicide (Gerassi 2001: xxi). At the same time, Sioux City, Iowa, was struggling with its own homosexual panic that was triggered by two cases of child molestation and murder (Miller 2002). Conflating homosexuality with pedophilia and homicidal tendencies, the authorities in Sioux City rounded up men who were suspected homosexuals and questioned them regarding the murders (Miller 2002). Although none of the men was implicated in the murder, and one of the victims was a little girl, 20 of the men were adjudged to be criminal sexual psychopaths and committed to a state facility for the criminally insane for an indeterminate period of time (Miller 2002: 122).

The abuses that occurred in Boise and Sioux City had been preceded by the military witch hunts that took place toward the end of World War II and the purges of homosexuals from the executive branch of the federal government during the early 1950s (Berube 2000). At the close of World War II, the military began to investigate and discharge homosexual service members in great numbers (Berube 2000). Sodomy was proscribed by the military code of conduct, but service members who were accused of homosexuality were discharged from the military on the basis that they were mentally unfit for service on account of their "psychopathic personality" (Berube 2000: 12). Service members discharged on these grounds forfeited all veterans benefits and received what was referred to as an undesirable or "blue" discharge. This type of discharge made future employment extremely difficult. (Berube 2000: 133). The near-universal conscription that occurred during World War II, and the continued draft after the war, made it highly likely that male job applicants would have a service record, which meant that prospective employers would routinely ask to see an applicant's discharge papers (Berube 2000: 229). Given that an undesirable discharge was associated with homosexuality or sexual perversion, a job applicant with a blue discharge would quickly be out of the running. Landlords, schools, and insurance companies also discriminated against individuals who received blue discharges (Berube 2000: 229).

The Cold War purges of homosexuals from the executive branch were conducted in the name of national security and had the effect of branding homosexuals as Communists (Johnson 2006). In 1953, President Eisenhower issued Executive Order 10,450, expressly stating that "sexual perversion" was grounds for expulsion from government service (Johnson 2006: 123). With that executive order, homosexuals were no longer simply sinners, mentally ill, and criminal, they were also un-American, subversive, and capable of treason. Under this reasoning, homosexuals posed a threat to the entire nation and warranted swift action at the highest level. Consistent with this belief, the Daughters of Bilitis and the Mattachine Society were under constant surveillance by the FBI from the date of their founding, and the Daughters of Bilitis even garnered the attention of the CIA (Gallo 2007).

Throughout the Cold War, homosexuality was linked with Communism and considered subversive and un-American. Senator Joseph McCarthy (R-WI) began his anti-communist crusade in 1950 by denouncing unnamed State Department employees as members of the Communist party in his well-known speech at a Republican Women's Club in Wheeling, West Virginia (Johnson 2006: 15). The speech drew immediate attention to his cause and led to the eventual creation of the Senate counterpart of the House Committee on Un-American Activities, known as the Senate Permanent Committee on Investigations. As it turned out, a number of the alleged Communists had already lost their jobs by the time the Senator delivered his speech. The twist was that they had not been dismissed from their posts for their alleged Communist sympathies. Instead, they had been accused of sexual perversion (Johnson 2006: 19).

In terms of the threat homosexuality posed to national security, it was never clear which came first – the Communist or the sexual deviant. Senator Wherry (R-NE) tried to explain the connection between the two in a *New York Post* interview in December 1950. The senator reasoned: "You can't hardly separate homosexuals from subversives. Mind you, I don't say that every homosexual is a subversive, and I don't say every subversive is a homosexual. But [people] of low morality are a menace in the government, whatever [they are], and they are all tied up together" (Faderman 1991: 143). Officially, the reason Congress demanded the dismissal of thousands of alleged homosexuals from federal service was twofold. First, homosexuals were considered prime targets for blackmail by foreign powers (Lewis 2001). This belief continued to be used as a justification to deny gay men and lesbians security clearances until the 1990s (*High Tech Gays v. Def. Indus. Sec. Clearance Office* 1990). Second, homosexuals were considered to be bad for morale. As a 1950 U.S. Senate report warned, "[o]ne homosexual can pollute an entire office" (Eskridge 1999: 69). A similar argument is still used today in the military context with respect to the DADT policy where one openly gay soldier can single-handedly destroy "unit cohesion."

The counter-intuitive pairing of homosexuality and Communism shows how easy it was for Cold War America to project its fears and anxieties onto a friendless minority group that had no public champion and enjoyed virtually no public sympathy. In 1959, Florida replicated the federal purges on the state level and turned the attention of its State Legislative Committee (known as the Johns Committee) to homosexuals (Graves 2009). Specifically, the Johns Committee believed that homosexuals, who by this time were understood also to be Communists, had infiltrated all levels of the state educational system (Graves 2009). The Johns Committee spent six years investigating college professors, students, and school teachers, but the danger posed by their alleged Communist sympathies was secondary to the conviction that homosexuals or perverts, as they were officially called, recruited children. The Johns Committee purportedly uncovered an elaborate multi-tiered homosexual cabal. It reported that "instructional personnel at the higher educational level are recruiting young people into homosexual practices and these young people are becoming school teachers in the public school system of Florida, and some of them are recruiting teen-aged students into homosexual practices" (Eskridge 1999: 73). As explained in the next chapter, the depiction of the homosexual as a sexual predator was an integral feature of the American Freudians' construction of homosexuality. The stereotype of the homosexual *qua* pedophile was used to justify a variety of social and political disabilities, and it continues to be used today to make the case against marriage equality.

Throughout these difficult times, both male and female homosexuals persevered. They managed to form lasting and rich relationships and constructed warm and vibrant communities. Oral histories of the period, such as Ester Newton's *Cherry Grove Fire Island: Sixty Years in America's First Gay and Lesbian Town* (1995) and Elizabeth Davis and Madeline Davis' *Boots of Leather and Slippers of Gold: History of a Lesbian Community* (1994), attest to the fact that homosexuals made a place for themselves despite being branded as mentally ill, criminal, and un-American. Estranged from their families of origins, they created chosen families and weathered the storms as best they could.

Chapter 2
Pre-Stonewall Views on Homosexuality

The declassification of homosexuality as a mental disorder by the APA in 1973 was a milestone in the lives of the pre-Stonewall generation, and, unlike the Stonewall riots, this event was widely publicized. The "instant cure" it promised did not put an immediate end to homophobia and discrimination, but it did remove a powerful justification for the many civil disabilities and criminal penalties that were imposed on homosexuals. At the time of declassification, today's gay and lesbian elders ranged in age from 28 to 58. They had come of age and spent much of their adulthood laboring under the stigma of mental illness. The construction of homosexuality as a mental disorder had informed their self-image and fostered a complex relationship between the medical profession and gay and lesbian individuals that arguably continues to the present day.

When today's elders were entering adulthood, the predominate view of homosexuality was the psychoanalytic model popularized by the American Freudians (Terry 1999). The oldest of today's gay and lesbian elders turned 21 in 1936 and the youngest turned 21 in 1966. During this 30-year period between 1936 and 1966, the psychoanalytic model held that homosexuality was a grave psychiatric disorder that stemmed from early childhood trauma and required therapeutic intervention to redirect the sex drive. The psychoanalytic understanding of homosexuality represented a significant change from the congenital model of homosexuality advanced by the early sexologists, most notably Richard von Krafft-Ebing and Havelock Ellis, toward the close of the 19th century. The congenital model considered homosexuality, or "inversion" as it was called, to be a naturally appearing variation that was not easily subject to change. Because the psychoanalytic model did not completely displace the older congenital model, it is likely that some members of the pre-Stonewall generation understood their sexuality in terms of inversion or an idiosyncratic amalgam of the two models.

These pre-Stonewall constructions of homosexuality have demonstrated considerable staying power despite the fact that both models have long been repudiated by the medical profession. The congenital model was based on an elaborate matrix of gender inversion that to some extent continues to inform contemporary stereotypes about gay men and lesbians, specifically the conflation of cross-gender performance with homosexuality (Foucault 1978: 43). Likewise, the psychoanalytic model spawned the sexual predator stereotype that continues to animate many of the contemporary anti-gay policy arguments.

The Early Sexologists and the Birth of the Modern Homosexual

In 1936, the year the oldest of today's gay and lesbian elders turned 21, the very concept that a homosexual was a distinct and identifiable type of individual was relatively new, which could help explain why some members of the pre-Stonewall generation report that when they first experienced same-sex attraction they did not know there was a word to describe their feelings (Cohler 2003). To 21st-century readers, however, it might come as a surprise to learn that the homosexual is a peculiarly modern creation. After all, it is now accepted as common knowledge that a number of prominent historical figures were gay or lesbian, leading one to conclude that homosexuality must be a transhistorical phenomenon.

The key to the quandary over whether homosexuality is transhistorical lies in the distinction between homosexuality and homosexuals. Although same-sex sexuality has existed across historical periods, the notion that same-sex attraction constitutes a master status that defines a specific type of person is, relatively speaking, a new idea. Scientists did not turn their attention to sexuality until the late 19th century, when they sought to catalogue the endless varieties of human sexual behavior, just as they had relentlessly organized the flora and fauna. The early sexologists, such as Krafft-Ebing and Ellis, produced an elaborate taxonomic scheme of inversion or "contrary sexual feeling" (Kraft-Ebing 1920: 187). They created the medico-scientific category of the invert as a distinct type of person with an identifiable constitution (Krafft-Ebing 1920: 230). It was this feat of historical naming that led Michel Foucault to declare that the sexologists had created a new "species" (Foucault 1978: 43). He famously asserted that whereas "the sodomite had been a temporary aberration; the homosexual was now a species" (Foucault 1978: 43).

Eve Sedgwick later characterized Foucault's bold assertion as "polemic bravado," and his claim should not be read as a strict statement of causality (Sedgwick 2008: 44). The invert did not spring full-born from the heads of the sexologists. Historians have established that some individuals who experienced same-sex attraction shared well-developed subcultural practices and allegiances prior to the elite naming by the sexologists[1] (Chauncey 1995: 27). Given that

---

1   The term "homosexuality" is credited to a journalist Karoly Maria Benkert, who used the term in an 1868 letter to the German sexologist and homosexual activist Karl Heinrich Ulrichs (Terry 1999: 44). Berkert, who later went by the name Kertbeny, introduced the term to public discourse in an 1869 open letter to the Prussian Minister of Justice urging the repeal of criminal sanctions for sodomy on the grounds that homosexuality was both innate and a matter of personal privacy (Benkert 1870). A German physician, Karl Westphal, is generally identified as the author of the first medical article on homosexuality published in 1869, although he referred to it as "contrary sexual feeling" (Terry 1999: 36, 45). Ronald Bayer establishes a much earlier date for the first article, noting that a description of homosexuality, although not the term, appeared in the medical literature in 1825 (Bayer 1987: 16). Foucault used the date of Westphal's article to establish the creation of the

the sexologists were empiricists, it makes sense that they presumably derived their theories from the study of an extant species. However, their production of a detailed matrix of "contrary sexual feeling" and inversion offered a systematic way for individuals to explain themselves and assert the naturalness of their feelings, in lieu of the otherwise idiosyncratic way that an individual would have to make sense of his non-normative sexuality. Many individuals who experienced "contrary sexual feelings" welcomed the sexologists' explanation of their condition, just as homosexuals later embraced psychoanalytic theory and contemporary gay men and lesbians follow the search for the "gay gene" (Minton 2001: 16). As one of Krafft-Ebing's readers wrote in a thankful letter to the sexologist, the scientific model of inversion provided "the comfort of belonging together and not being alone anymore" (Minton 2001:16).

The theory of inversion also facilitated the production of "reverse discourse" as the inverts appropriated the weight of this new objective scientific authority and used it instrumentally to argue for social and legal change (Foucault 1978: 101). In the 1920s, the German Homosexual Emancipation Movement[2] advanced the theories of the sexologists in order to educate inverts regarding their own nature and encourage them to forge a group identity (Steakly 1975). In 1928, the British author Radclyffe Hall published her novel *The Well of Loneliness* with the express purpose of exposing other inverts like herself to the theories of the sexologists. The book illustrates the potential explanatory and ordering force of the scientific model when the protagonist finds a book by Krafft-Ebing in her father's study and first learns the true (and scientific) nature of her feelings for other women (Hall 1990: 204). The novel had a devoted following in the United States, but was banned in Britain as obscene libel until 1949. For the current generation of gay and lesbian elders, *The Well of Loneliness* was a cultural touchstone, and countless

---

modern homosexual, but he was one year off (Foucault 1978: 43). Foucault's influential and much contested pronouncement reads:

> [T]he psychological, psychiatric, medical category of homosexuality was constituted from the moment it was characterized (Westphal's famous article of 1870 "contrary sexual sensations" can stand as its date of birth) less by a type of sexual relations than by a certain quality of sexual sensibility, a certain way of inverting the masculine and the feminine in oneself ... The sodomite had been a temporary aberration; the homosexual was now a species (Foucault 1978: 43).

2   There were a number of politically active homosexual organizations established in Germany beginning in the late 19th century, such as Magnus Hirschfield's Scientific-Humanitarian Committee (Steakley 1993). Although homosexual organizations proliferated during the Weimar Republic, many were primarily social in nature. The elections of 1933 marked the end of the German Homosexual Emancipation Movement. In May 1933, the Nazis targeted the Institute of Sexual Science in Berlin that had been founded by Hirschfeld (Steakley 1975: 104–105). In order to rid Berlin of "un-German spirit," the Nazis looted the building and later burned over 12,000 books taken from its libraries in a public ceremony (Steakley 1975: 104).

personal stories from the period credit reading the novel with a profound sense of personal self-discovery (O'Rourke 1989: 114–142).

The Psychoanalytic Model of Homosexuality

As Freudian views of psychosexual development became generally accepted in the medical and scientific communities throughout the 1930s and 1940s, experiential explanations for homosexuality replaced the congenital model of inversion. The early sexologists were empiricists who measured and mapped the bodies of inverts in an attempt to make sense of difference through the process of endless categorization. The human variations they observed were attributed to the existence of a biological predisposition. Psychoanalytic theory, to the contrary, offered an experiential explanation for homosexuality. Informed by an elaborate interior view of psychological development, it discarded the congenital determinants of the early sexologists and instead located the cause of homosexuality in an individual's experience or environment (Bayer 1987: 21). According to this new theory, homosexuals were made – not born.

Freudian psychoanalytic theory posited an original state of bisexuality and a natural progression out of that state toward heterosexuality (Terry 1999: 56). Homosexuality, thus, represented a perversion of the normal sex drive that occurred at some point during an individual's natural psychosexual development (Terry 1999: 56). The psychoanalytic model of homosexuality did not originally endorse therapeutic intervention because it characterized homosexuality as a perversion and not a neurosis, and a perversion of the sex drive was not easily re-directed (Bayer 1987: 26). On the topic of curing homosexuality, Sigmund Freud considered the question of intervention in connection with his case study of a 19-year-old woman in *Psychogenesis of a Case of Homosexuality in a Woman* (1920). Writing in 1920, he concluded:

> One must remember that normal sexuality also depends upon a restriction in the choice of object; in general to undertake to convert a fully developed homosexual into a heterosexual is not much more promising than to do the reverse, only that for good practical reasons the latter is never attempted (Freud 1920: 157).

By the 1940s, however, this relatively benign view of homosexuality had been rejected by the American Freudians, who ascribed strongly to the belief in universal heterosexuality and characterized homosexuality as a phobic response to the opposite sex (Bayer 1987: 28–29). Under this view, the homosexual lifecycle began with the seduction of an innocent by an older homosexual. The early seduction would trigger a phobic response to the opposite sex, causing the young victim to become a homosexual. The victim would then mature into an unhappy and disaffected homosexual who would in turn prey on young children and the cycle of perversion and seduction would continue.

According to this revised psychoanalytic narrative, the cause of homosexuality was neurotic and, therefore, a condition that could be cured (Bayer 1987: 33). This therapeutic optimism, coupled with an unwavering commitment that heterosexuality was optimal, led psychiatrists to develop an arsenal of procedures and protocols designed to cure homosexuality. Psychiatrists experimented with various methods designed to redirect sexual orientation to conform to the heterosexual norm, including, as mentioned earlier, psychotropic drugs, aversion therapy, electro-shock, and prefrontal lobotomies (Eskridge 1999: 62). As discussed in the prior chapter, the promise of a cure also influenced the laws regulating homosexuality with the enactment of the sexual psychopath laws that blurred the lines between criminal law and civil commitment (Terry 1999: 272–273, Eskridge 1999: 42–43, 61–62).

When the first *Diagnostic and Statistical Manual of Mental Disorders (DSM-I)* was published in 1952, it listed homosexuality as among the most severe sociopathic personality disorders (Bayer 1999: 39). Without intervention, the prognosis was grim. As homosexuals aged, they would become exaggerated caricatures of their former selves – solitary and bitter, obsessed with youth. As late as 1971, Dr. Clarence A. Tripp, a former Kinsey Institute researcher who later wrote the influential 1975 book *The Homosexual Matrix*, argued that therapists were intentionally "frightening [their] patient[s] with the image of the aging, lonely homosexual" (Kelly 1977: 331).

Throughout this time period, many homosexuals were motivated to enter therapy voluntarily in order to seek a cure. Martin Duberman, a distinguished professor of history and a noted scholar, has written eloquently about his own experience with psychoanalysis and his struggles with homosexuality in his memoir simply entitled *Cures* (1991). In addition, the psychotherapist Betty Berzon, who founded the first gay group within the APA, wrote an award-winning memoir, *Surviving Madness: A Therapist's Own Story* (2002), which movingly tells of her suicide attempt, institutionalization, and her decades-long battle to accept her sexuality.

These individual stories are consistent with the position of the early U.S. Homophile Movement that endorsed medical and psychiatric research into, not only the cause, but also the cure, of homosexuality (Bayer 1987: 78–88, Minton 2001: 238–241). The Daughters of Bilitis and the Mattachine Society both adopted a neutral stance regarding scientific research into homosexuality and included commitments to such research in their official statements of purpose. The first paragraph of the DOB's Statement of Purpose provides that the goal of the organization is:

> Education of the variant, with particular emphasis on the psychological, physiological and sociological aspects, to enable her to understand herself and make her adjustment to society in all its social, civic and economic implications this to be accomplished by establishing and maintaining as complete a library as possible of both fiction and non-fiction literature on the sex deviant theme; by sponsoring public discussions on pertinent subjects to be conducted by leading

members of the legal, psychiatric, religious and other professions; by advocating a mode of behavior and dress acceptable to society (DOB Statement of Purpose 1955).

Both organizations cooperated with the Kinsey Institute and made it a practice to invite researchers whose views, by today's standards, would be considered anti-gay, to speak at their conventions and contribute articles to their publications (Bayer 1987: 42, Minton 2001: 174–175). Richard Bayer, who has written a comprehensive history of psychiatry and homosexuality, explains the willingness of homosexuals to embrace the diagnosis with the simple statement "Better sick than criminal" (Bayer 1987: 9). For example, Edward Sagarin, who under the pseudonym Daniel Webster Cory authored the 1951 book, *The Homosexual in America: A Subjective Approach*, was a strong proponent of the psychoanalytic model. In 1956, Sagarin warned homosexuals against engaging in "a head-on clash with men of science" and argued "that there is nothing inconsistent between acceptance of the work of psychotherapists who report success, nay cure, and the struggle for the right to participate in the joys of life for those who cannot, will not or do not undergo change" (Bayer 1987: 84). As late as 1964, Sagarin admonished the Homophile Movement for "alienating itself from the scientific thinking ... by the constant, defensive, neurotic, disturbed denial that homosexuality was a sickness" (Minton 2001: 251).

By 1965, homophile activists and organizations increasingly began to identify the continued classification of homosexuality as a mental disorder as a major roadblock to achieving their goals. That year, Dr. Franklin (Frank) Kameny, an early homophile activist who had lost his job as a federal astronomer on account of his homosexuality, argued: "We cannot declare our equality and ask for acceptance and for judgment as whole persons, from a position of sickness" (Bayer 1987: 106). The same year, the Mattachine Society of Washington also voted to disaffirm the psychoanalytic model of homosexuality and adopted the following resolution:

> The Mattachine Society of Washington takes the position that in the absence of valid evidence to the contrary homosexuality is not a sickness, disturbance or other pathology in any sense but is merely a preference, orientation or propensity, on a par with, and not different in kind from heterosexuality (Bayer 1987: 88).

The cooperative relationship between the Homophile Movement and psychiatry was severed officially in 1968 when the North American Conference of Homophile Organizations adopted a platform that declared "Gay is Good" – in advance of the Gay Liberationists, who later appropriated it as their own (Bayer 1987: 91, LeVay 1996: 222). It then took five more years of lobbying and protests to secure the deletion of homosexuality from the *DSM*.

The first organized protest took place in 1968, when polite homophile activists picketed an American Medical Association convention to demand the inclusion of pro-homosexual views and speakers (Bayer 1987: 92). Homophile activists wearing suits and dresses were soon replaced by the much more confrontational gay activists. Working within a larger critique of psychiatry's enforcement of social convention, gay activists lobbied ferociously for the deletion of homosexuality from the *DSM-II*. Armed with empirical studies, such as Alfred Kinsey's massive collection of data on human sexual behavior and Evelyn Hooker's revolutionary 1957 study, *The Adjustment of the Male Overt Homosexual*, the activists argued that there was no evidence that homosexuals were actually maladjusted.

Kinsey's work helped normalize homosexuality by asserting that it was more prevalent than previously thought. Based on what is now referred to as the "Kinsey scale" of sexual orientation, Kinsey's research indicated that the incidence of homosexuality was as high as 10 percent among American men. Hooker's study cast considerable doubt on the notion that homosexuality was a severe mental disorder. Her study presented the results of psychological tests administered to self-identified male homosexuals and a control group of male heterosexuals. Hooker then submitted the test results to psychiatric experts, who proved unable to determine which of the test subjects were homosexual. The inability to identify the homosexual test results was considered shocking at the time, given the widely accepted pathology of homosexuality as a severe mental disorder. Based on her findings, Hooker openly challenged established medical opinion and concluded that "homosexuality is not necessarily a symptom of pathology" (Hooker 1957: 30). Instead, she reasoned that some of the personality disorders commonly observed in homosexuals could be due to external pressures or what is now referred to as minority stress. Hooker wrote:

> It would be strange indeed if all the traits due to victimization in minority groups were in the homosexual produced by inner dynamics of the personality, since he is also a member of an outgroup which is subject to extreme penalties involving, according to Kinsey, cruelties which have not been matched except in religious and social persecutions (Bayer 1987: 53).

Hooker also addressed the existence of homophobia within the ranks of physicians. She specifically warned that the personal views of a medical professional could interfere with treatment and compromise the objectivity of psychiatric evaluations. As evidence of institutional bias against homosexuals, Hooker quoted a scientific report on homosexuality that had been published shortly before her 1957 article. The report had asserted: "It is well known that many people, including physicians, react in an exaggerated way to sexual deviations and particularly to homosexuality with disgust, anger, and hostility" (Hooker 1957: 18). As discussed in Chapter 6, the Gay and Lesbian Medical Association (GLMA) reports that anti-gay bias on the part of health-care professionals remains a problem today.

Dr. Charles Socarides provides a case in point of a psychiatrist with a marked antipathy toward homosexuals. In the 1950s and 1960s, Dr. Socarides wrote extensively about homosexuality and later refused to accept its declassification as a mental illness by the APA. Socarides theorized that homosexuality was the result of a pre-oedipal phobic response to the opposite sex and considered homosexuals to be profoundly troubled (Bayer 1987: 35). Specifically, Socarides claimed that nearly one half of homosexuals were either "in the throes of a manic-depressive reaction" or suffered from "schizophrenia, paranoia, or latent pseudoneurotic schizophrenia" (Bayer 1987: 35). Until his death in 2005, Socarides remained committed to this view of homosexuality and belonged to a small group of psychiatrists who rejected the declassification of homosexuality as a mental illness. In 2001, Socarides wrote that "obligatory homosexuals are caught up in unconscious adaptations to early childhood abuse and neglect" and explained that what he referred to as "unconscious adaptations" was simply "a polite term for men going through the motions of mating not with the opposite sex but with one another."

In addition to dissenting psychiatrists such as Socarides who never accepted the declassification, the formal relationship between psychiatry and homosexuality did not end in 1973. At the same time the APA voted to declassify homosexuality, it also created the new category of mental disorder called "sexual orientation disturbance" to describe "individuals whose sexual interests are directed primarily towards people of the same sex and who are either disturbed by, in conflict with, or wish to change their sexual orientation" (Bayer 1987: 137). The name was later changed to "ego-dystonic homosexuality" and remained in the *DSM-III* until it was finally deleted in 1987. The concept of ego-dystonic homosexuality remains an integral part of the lexicon of reparative therapists who comprise the medical wing of the contemporary ex-gay movement, which argues that gays not only can change, but they should change.

Despite the initial optimism of gay activists, the numerous social and legal disabilities imposed on gay men and lesbians did not disappear with the deletion of homosexuality as an official diagnostic category. The positive trajectory that immediately followed declassification was interrupted in 1977 with the emergence of the first organized anti-gay political coalition, Save Our Children. Orchestrated by former recording star, beauty queen, and orange juice spokesperson Anita Bryant, Save Our Children relied on the repudiated sexual predator stereotype that had been popularized by the American Freudians to argue against anti-discrimination protections for gay men and lesbians. Bryant explained, "As a mother, I know that homosexuals cannot biologically reproduce children; therefore, they must recruit our children" (Ghaziani 2008: 33). Save Our Children was successful in repealing a number of anti-discrimination laws that included sexual orientation as a protected category, including a contentious ordinance adopted in Dade County, Florida in 1977 (Eskridge 1999: 131). Bryant argued that "If gays are granted rights, next we'll have to give rights to prostitutes and to people who sleep with St. Bernards" (Jones 2009). This type of slippery-slope argument would go on to feature prominently in later anti-gay speaking points, albeit the concern over bestiality is rarely breed-specific.

Bryant's rhetoric set the stage for the highly politicized anti-gay narrative that was popularized by Reverend Jerry Falwell's Moral Majority during the 1980s and later refined by the politically sophisticated organizations that waged the culture wars of the 1990s and beyond, such as the Family Research Council (FRC) and Lou Sheldon's Traditional Values Coalition. As discussed in Chapter 5, opponents of marriage equality have used both the slippery-slope argument and the stereotype of the predatory homosexual to great advantage.

Chapter 3
Gay and Lesbian Elders in the New Millennium

Today there are an estimated 1.6 million to 2.4 million gay men and lesbians in the United States who are 65 years of age or older. Despite their number, gay and lesbian elders remain largely invisible and, until recently, they were rarely studied. As a result, the information regarding how the pre-Stonewall generation has fared as its members have aged is limited, comprised mainly of census data on partnered same-sex households and a handful of small, non-random academic studies. When read in conjunction with increasing anecdotal evidence and research conducted by advocacy groups, this existing data strongly suggests that gay and lesbian elders grapple with isolation, financial insecurity, health concerns, and the persistent fear that they will experience discriminatory treatment at the hands of service providers.

The lack of information is a major obstacle to understanding the existing disparities between gay and lesbian elders and their non-gay peers, as well as the effect of intersecting identities. The failure of elder-care service providers and aging researchers to collect data on gay and lesbian seniors is not surprising, given the popular misconception that individuals who are 65 or older are asexual. Through the deep fog of heteronormativity, it may simply not occur to researchers or elder-care providers that their presumably asexual senior subjects or clients could be anything other than retired heterosexuals. As explained in the next section, the forces of ageism and homophobia can combine to render the notion of a gay or lesbian elder all but unthinkable because elders are not considered to be sexual and gay men and lesbians are, too often, viewed as only sexual.

The scope of the missing data on lesbian and gay elders also reflects tensions inherent in the construction of gay men and lesbians as a distinct minority. On the most basic level, there is no consensus regarding the percentage of the population that is gay or lesbian. This is partly due to underreporting on account of the continuing stigma associated with homosexuality. In addition to under-counting, there is a deeper definitional concern – it is not entirely clear who should "count" as gay or lesbian. Both of these problems are exacerbated in the case of gay and lesbian elders because elders are more likely to fear disclosure and less likely to self-identify as gay or lesbian. From a societal standpoint, the construction of gay men and lesbians as a valid minority remains highly politicized, and anti-gay organizations will openly challenge estimates of the number of gay men and lesbians in an effort to minimize the size of the group and de-legitimize claims for gay and lesbian equality.

The Missing Data

Comprehensive census data, large nationwide surveys, such as National Survey of Older Americans Act (Title III) Recipients, and countless academic studies have produced a wealth of information about seniors with respect to their gender, race, ethnicity, financial status, life expectancy, living situation, and health concerns. Very little of this information, however, takes into account sexual orientation and almost none of it considers sexual orientation in the context of intersecting identities, such as race or ethnicity. As a result, it is possible to calculate with some level of precision the percentage of seniors between the ages of 65 and 69 who are still in the workforce, but not how many of these working seniors are gay or lesbian. There are no reliable figures on the percentage of gay and lesbian elders who are subject to abuse or discrimination on account of their sexual orientation. Nor is it possible to answers any number of questions that would help assess the disparities that gay and lesbian elders may encounter with respect to aging and access to essential services and resources.

At the most basic level, the failure to collect information on sexual orientation means that there is no definitive estimate of the number of gay and lesbian elders in the United States. To estimate the number of gay and lesbian elders, researchers and advocates multiply the number of U.S. seniors by the percentage of the general population who are thought to be gay or lesbian. For example, in 2010, there were 40 million seniors in the United States, comprising approximately 13 percent of the general population. Estimates of the percentage of the general population that is gay or lesbian range from between 4 percent to 6 percent.[1] Assuming that gay men and lesbians are uniformly distributed throughout all age cohorts, it would then follow that, as of 2010, there were between 1.6 million and 2.4 million gay and lesbian elders in the United States.[2] Although this approach seems straightforward,

---

1   For purposes of estimating the number of gay and lesbian elders, SAGE uses the estimate produced by the Williams Institute that 4.1 percent of the population identifies as gay, lesbian, or bisexual (Improving the Lives of LGBT Older Adults 2010: 2). The higher 6 percent ceiling represents figures from state and federal health surveys reporting same-sex behavior (Grant 2010: 134). In any event, the estimate of between 4 and 6 percent may seem quite modest in comparison to the oft-repeated commonplace that 10 percent of the population is gay. The 10 percent figure was popularized by the first Kinsey Report, *Sexual Behavior in the Human Male* (1948), and continues to enjoy wide acceptance despite the fact that Kinsey's methodology has been roundly criticized and his findings have never been duplicated. Some of the early articles on gay and lesbian elders used Kinsey's 10 percent figure and accordingly reported much larger numbers of gay and lesbian elders (Jacobson and Grossman 1996). For example, applying the Kinsey estimate to the senior population, in 2010 there would have been approximately 4 million gay and lesbian elders.

2   The figures provided by the U.S. Administration on Aging (AoA) are slightly different because the AoA defines elder status to begin at age 60. The AoA estimates also include transgender elders. As of 2010, the AoA estimates that there are between 1.75 million and 4 million LGBT elders in the United States who are 60 years of age or

the large range in the second part of the equation belies the fact that there is no definitive count of gay and lesbian Americans nor agreement regarding who should be included in such a tally.

Even without an exact count of the number of gay and lesbian elders, it is clear that their absolute number will increase dramatically over the next several decades as the members of the Baby Boom Generation age. By the year 2030, there will be an estimated 72 million seniors, representing close to 20 percent of the general population (AoA 2009e). This projected growth in the senior population will translate to a corresponding increase in the number of gay and lesbian elders, raising their number by 2030 to between 2.88 million and 4.32 million. By 2050, the number of seniors is projected to increase to 88 million, which means there would be between 3.52 million and 5.28 million gay and lesbian elders.

To contemporary eyes, it may be difficult to comprehend that such a large number of gay and lesbian elders are potentially aging in the closet, beset by financial difficulties, and fearful of discrimination. It is important to remember, however, that, until relatively recently, the majority of gay men and lesbians labored their entire lives in the closet. As explained in Part II, gay and lesbian elders "choose" the closet in response to a powerful combination of ageism and homophobia, but it is a choice infused with duress. According to researchers and anecdotal reports, even those gay and lesbian elders who were once open about their sexual orientation sometimes feel compelled to retreat to the closet as they approach their senior years (Mock, Taylor and Savin-Williams 2006: 156). Although some could argue that the political invisibility of gay and lesbian elders is the natural consequence of their personal choice to hide their sexual orientation, this observation misunderstands the nature of the closet. The closet did not precede the political disempowerment of gay and lesbian elders, although it does help to perpetuate it. It is an adaptive strategy that is never solely self-imposed.

Enhanced information regarding gay and lesbian elders would help counter the longstanding social and political invisibility of gay and lesbian elders that is reinforced by the closet. More comprehensive data collection regarding sexual orientation would establish that not only do gay and lesbian elders exist, but they do so in great numbers. As recently as 2009, the Family Research Council, a conservative political organization with an aggressively anti-gay platform, capitalized on the invisibility of gay and lesbian elders when it denounced proposed federal funding for a program designed to assist LGBT elders. The FRC blasted a decision by the U.S. Department of Health and Human Services to fund the creation of a national clearinghouse on LGBT elder issue by arguing that there were not enough gay and lesbian elders to justify the proposed $250,000 expenditure (FRC 2009). The FRC's objections demonstrate the identity Catch-22 experienced by

---

older. Consistent with traditional gerontology and social science conventions, this book uses the age of 65 to distinguish when an individual is considered "old" or "elder"(Barker 2004: 31). The choice of 65 as the dividing line also comports with the popular understanding of when an individual becomes a senior citizen.

gay and lesbian elders, namely that seniors aren't gay and gays aren't seniors. First, the FRC asserted that seniors were less likely to be gay because "people who are 80 – or 90 years old didn't grow up in a culture where it was acceptable to identify with this lifestyle" (FRC 2009). Second, the FRC stated that gays and lesbians were not seniors because "these people are less likely to live long enough to become senior citizens" (FRC 2009). This last claim is related to a longstanding effort by anti-gay conservative groups to characterize homosexuality as inherently dangerous and unhealthy (Herman 1997). Anti-gay political tracts often distort HIV/AIDS public health information and speak authoritatively about reduced life expectancy and other health risks encountered primarily by gay men, but also by lesbians (Herman 1997: 78, 94).

The most straightforward way to solve the problem of the missing data on gay and lesbian elders would be to collect information on sexual orientation through the U.S. Census Bureau, but this solution raises political as well as conceptual and practical concerns that are discussed in greater detail below. Short of adding sexual orientation to the list of census categories, there are many opportunities to increase the visibility of gay and lesbian elders. For example, researchers and elder-care professionals could include questions about sexual orientation on general senior surveys and intake forms. One study reported that fewer than 35 percent of social service agencies include questions regarding sexual orientation as part of their intake procedures, and less than 25 percent of social service agencies provide LGBT-specific programming (Anetzberger et al. 2004: 32). When intake forms at a senior center only allow a respondent to choose among a range of ostensibly heterosexual options, such as "married," "widowed," "divorced," or "unmarried," it follows that the staff at the center would believe that all of their clients are heterosexual and see no reason for the center's policies and programs to address gay- or lesbian-specific concerns. Simply posing a question regarding sexual orientation on an intake form would provide a twofold benefit. First, it would collect important information that would then be available for larger studies. More immediately, however, it would also have a salutary effect on the individual level. The inclusion of a question on sexual orientation normalizes homosexuality and provides a more welcoming environment – even for those gay and lesbian elders who may not feel that they can answer honestly. Asking the question disrupts the silence surrounding seniors and sexual orientation and signals to gay and lesbian elders that they are not alone.

The problem of undercounting is endemic to all surveys compiling data on sexual orientation due to the continuing stigma attached to homosexuality (Grant 2010: 136). In light of their pre-Stonewall experiences, gay and lesbian elders may be especially reluctant to disclose information regarding sexual orientation to a stranger or on a government form. As explained in Chapters 1 and 2, gay men and lesbians are a unique minority who in living memory were both pathologized and criminalized. If the U.S. Census Bureau were to start to collect data on sexual orientation, it could very well trigger a skeptical and perhaps fearful response from some quarters of the gay and lesbian community. Indeed, for those suspicious of government intrusion, such a proposal could bring to mind the misuse of census data by the United States in connection with the internment of Japanese-Americans during World War II or even the role census data played in the Final Solution. In the absence of formal equality, gay men and lesbians may understandably be wary about putting their names on a government list.

Fundamental questions of identity and self-definition also complicate any effort to measure the size of the gay and lesbian population. Simply put, in order to count gay men and lesbians, there needs to be consensus regarding who qualifies as gay or lesbian. As the Preface explains, this book uses the term "gay and lesbian" very broadly to recognize individuals who self-identify as gay or lesbian or bisexual or homosexual or queer or who have had a same-sex partner, engaged in same-sex sexual activity, or experienced significant periods of same-sex attraction. A broad definition is important because much of the fear that elders report centers on the reactions of third parties to perceived non-normative sexuality or sexual attraction, thereby mooting questions of self-identification. An elder who lives with her same-sex partner can be subject to anti-gay harassment despite the fact that she does not personally identify as gay or lesbian. Thus, it is not necessary for someone to identify as gay or lesbian in order to fear disapproval or discrimination on account of a past relationship or a same-sex partner.

In terms of self-identification, even members of the pre-Stonewall generation who self-identify as something other than heterosexual may not embrace the more contemporary labels of gay or lesbian. In one study, there was a strong correlation between age and those who identified with the label "gay" (Rawls 2004: 129). More than 50 percent of the gay male respondents who were age 70 or older identified as homosexual rather than gay (Rawls 2004: 129). If this study is representative, then a sizable portion of the group described as gay and lesbian elders for the purposes of this book would not identify as such. Despite their failure to self-identify, these elders share a unifying characteristic of non-heterosexuality, and it is this characteristic that subjects them to homophobia and anti-gay bias.

This definitional issue underlies any attempt to count gay men and lesbians – not just gay and lesbian elders. The few large random surveys that address sexual orientation use different measures of sexual orientation and have not produced consistent results (Grant 2010: 132–138). Some surveys ask the respondents to self-identify, whereas others focus on behavior. Those focusing on behavior often restrict the question to specific time periods, such as whether the respondent has had sex with a person of the same sex within the last year. Before national aging surveys begin to collect information regarding sexual orientation, it will be necessary to determine how the question should be phrased. Should the question ask the participant to self-identify? If so, which categories should be included and what should they be called (e.g., gay, bisexual, lesbian, homosexual, queer)? To the extent that self-identification is not always congruent with behavior, should research instruments also inquire as to sexual behavior?[3] But, if so, what behavior and over what time frame?[4]

A 2010 controversial proposal in Great Britain to include a question on sexual orientation on the U.K. census raised many of these issues (Woolf 2009). The argument to include the question was a good one: Reliable estimates of the size of the gay and lesbian population are necessary to judge the success of anti-discrimination policies. The proposal sparked a discussion regarding how questions regarding sexual orientation should be phrased (i.e., should they focus on behavior or identification or both) and whether individuals are still too frightened by homophobia and possible reprisals to disclose such information on an official form. Gay and lesbian advocates in the United Kingdom expressed concern that the fear of disclosure might result in a significant undercount that in turn would jeopardize the larger cause of gay and lesbian equality because an accurate count is essential to establish the size of the minority group and the scope of the services required. The proposal was also met by fierce opposition by some citing privacy concerns.

In the United States, however, a similar proposal would likely meet fierce opposition from anti-gay organizations that would not be motivated by privacy concerns. As illustrated by the FRC attack on gay and lesbian elders, anti-gay organizations challenge the estimates regarding the percentage of the population that is gay or lesbian in an attempt to destabilize gay men and lesbians as a valid minority (Herman 1997: 74–75). They claim that the actual number of gay men and lesbians is much smaller than commonly believed in order to assert that gay men and lesbians are a tiny minority who wield vastly disproportionate political power. Under this reasoning, anti-discrimination protections are transformed into "special rights" for a wealthy minority (Herman 1997: 120).

A recent controversy involving the 2010 census provides a case in point. In preparing the 2010 census form, the question arose as to whether, in addition to same-sex partnered households, the Census Bureau should record same-sex *married* couples given that same-sex marriage is now legally recognized in a number of states and the District of Columbia (Morello 2009). Under the Bush Administration, the Census Bureau took the position that it would not include same-sex couples who listed their status as "married" instead of "partnered." The Census Bureau initially reasoned that counting same-sex couples as married for purposes of the census would constitute federal recognition and violate the federal Defense of Marriage Act (DOMA), which establishes that for all federal purposes, marriage is only between one man and one woman. The failure to count same-

---

3   The experience within the early years of the HIV/AIDS epidemic introduced researchers to the distinction between self-identification and behavior and led to the creation of the category of "MMS," or men who have sex with men.

4   Demographers at the Williams Institute at UCLA have developed a recommended set of Best Practices to be used when collecting data on sexual orientation that are designed to minimize these definitional issues (Sexual Minority Assessment Research Team 2009).

sex partnered households that checked the box "married" would have produced a governmental undercount of self-identifying same-sex couples. The Census Bureau later reversed its decision under the Obama administration (Morello 2009).

Census Data on Partnered Households and Other Studies

The existing empirical data on gay and lesbian elders consists of census figures for self-identifying elder same-sex partnered households gathered for the decennial census, as well as the annual American Community Survey, small largely non-random academic studies, and surveys conducted by advocacy and industry groups. The census information provides a large, but incomplete, national data set of gay and lesbian elders that allows comparisons between partnered elder same-sex households and their peers who are in different-sex partnered or married households. The academic studies encompass both partnered and unpartnered elders and provide more in depth information regarding the concerns and life experiences of gay and lesbian elders. However, these results are compromised by small sample sizes and the lack of diversity among the study participants. The industry and advocacy group surveys are generally larger, but they also have methodological shortcomings and lack the comparative feature inherent in the census data.

The census figures represent the largest data set on gay and lesbian individuals, encompassing nearly 1.2 million self-identified individuals who are in same-sex partnered relationships. According to the 2000 census, same-sex partnered households can be found across the United States, giving new meaning to the Gay Liberationist slogan "We are Everywhere." Same-sex partnered households exist in 99.3 percent of all counties in the United States, and elder same-sex partnered households can be found in 97 percent of counties in the United States (Gates 2003a). As promising as this sounds, the census data has three serious limitations. First, it fails to capture the large percentage of gay and lesbian elders who are not partnered and, therefore, it does not reflect the segment of the gay and lesbian elder population at the greatest risk of social isolation – unpartnered elders who live alone. Second, the census data does not account for underreporting by elders who are not willing to self-identify on a government form. Finally, same-sex couples with intersecting identities may not be adequately captured by the census as marginalized groups are historically underrepresented in census data. When added together, it appears that some of the most vulnerable gay and lesbian elders may *not* be reflected in the census data. These elders would include unpartnered elders, partnered same-sex couples so fearful of disclosure that they would not self-identify on a government form, and elders who are otherwise marginalized (Badgett and Rogers 2003: 1). With this rather large caveat, the census data remains an important, if hopelessly partial, source of information on today's gay and lesbian elders, and it is frequently cited and used to provide a baseline assessment on same-sex couples, as well as the gay and lesbian community more generally (Gates 2007).

The U.S. Census Bureau unintentionally began collecting information on same-sex partnered households in 1990 when it first included the status of "unmarried partner" on the census form in an effort to track the number of cohabiting different-sex couples. To the surprise of the Census Bureau, some same-sex couples also self-identified as "unmarried partners," and since then the census has provided an intriguing glimpse into a limited segment of the gay and lesbian community. The response of same-sex couples in 1990 was fairly lukewarm, and only 145,130 same-sex partnered households outed themselves on the census form (Gates 2007). Ten years later, the same question on the 2000 census garnered a much more robust response. The preliminary analysis of the data indicated a total of 594,391 same-sex households, although it has since undergone a number of refinements (Gates 2009). Demographers attribute the increase in the number of same-sex partnered households from 1990 to 2000 to the growing social acceptance of gay men and lesbians, as well as a public education campaign by gay and lesbian advocacy groups that urged same-sex partners to declare themselves on the census form, saying: "The more we are counted, the more we count."

Although researchers are still analyzing the census data regarding elder same-sex partnered households, it is possible to make some preliminary observations with respect to the demographic and financial characteristics of the group. Researchers estimate that 11.8 percent of all same-sex partnered households include one partner age 65 or older (Bennett and Gates 2004: 13). This figure increases dramatically when expanded to include the Baby Boom generation. An estimated 23.4 percent of all same-sex partnered households include a partner 55 years of age or older (Bennett and Gates 2004: 13). Elder same-sex partnered households are located in states and metropolitan areas with high concentrations of seniors generally. However, same-sex partnered African-American and Latino households tend to be located in areas with high concentrations of members of their respective racial and ethnic minorities (Gates and Ost 2004). The top three states with the highest number of elder same-sex partnered households are also the states with the largest numbers of elder different-sex couples: California, Florida, and New York (Census 2003, Grant 2010: 23). Although there is little research on rural gay and lesbian elders, 15 percent of all same-sex partnered households reside in rural areas (Grant 2010: 33–34).

In terms of financial security, elder same-sex partnered households lag behind elder different-sex married households with respect to income, assets, and home ownership. Most striking, however, is the number of elder same-sex partnered households that live at or near the poverty level (Albelda et al. 2009). Elder same-sex partnered households are more likely to live below the poverty line than elder different-sex married couples (Albelda et al. 2009). In the case of elder different-sex married couples, 4.6 percent live below the poverty line, whereas 4.9 percent of male same-sex couples live below the poverty line (Albelda et al. 2009). The figure for elder female same-sex partnered households living below the poverty line is a startling 9.6 percent – almost twice that of different-sex married couples (Albelda et al. 2009). Elder same-sex couples are 72 percent more likely than different-sex married couples to be receiving supplemental Social Security income and 84 percent more likely to be receiving public assistance (Goldberg 2009: 8).

Elder different-sex married couples earn more income than elder same-sex partnered households (Bennett and Gates 2004: 4). Specifically, elder same-sex partnered households also have 34.7 percent less income from retirement savings than elder different-sex married couples (Bennett and Gates 2004: 5). They are less likely to own their own home than different-sex married couples. When they do own a home, its median value is less and they are more likely to still be paying a mortgage on it (Bennett and Gates 2004: 6). This fact can make continued home ownership for gay and lesbian elders a precarious proposition when combined with certain tax and Medicaid rules discussed in Chapter 9. It also gives weight to a study conducted in San Francisco that identified homelessness as a growing problem among gay and lesbian elders (San Francisco Human Rights Commission 2003, Grant 2010: 26).

Until recently, academic interest in gay and lesbian aging was sporadic and dispersed across a number of disciplines, including gerontology, psychology, and anthropology. Judith C. Barker reports that prior to 1990, there was no mention of gay men or lesbians in standard gerontology texts and studies on sexuality rarely included people beyond the age of 60 (Barker 2004: 30). The existing academic studies on gay and lesbian elders consist of a confusing array of small non-random surveys that tend to use homogeneous convenience samples of middle-class urban white men. A 2006 article on LGBT elders concludes: "An inclusive review of all the published literature in LGBT gerontology is of only historical curiosity because most of the samples are small and idiosyncratic" (Kimmel et al. 2006b: 6). The studies also seem to report contradictory findings, with some studies predicting that gay and lesbian elders will demonstrate superior aging skills and others reporting that gay and lesbian elders face formidable challenges to successful aging.

The reason the studies have produced disparate findings is that the academic research into gay and lesbian aging has proceeded in two distinct tracts. The early "gay positive" research was designed primarily to counter the depressing stereotype of the aging homosexual that had been popularized by the psychoanalytic view of homosexuality – what Frank Kameny described as the "universal stereotype of older homosexuals as lonely frustrated miserable people" (in Lee 1991: 1). The "gay positive" studies focused on the mental well-being of older homosexuals and, in the case of gay men, issues of sexuality. Lesbians were not well represented in these early studies and when they were included, the impact of aging on lesbian sexuality was largely ignored (Garnets and Peplau 2006: 82). More recent gerontological research and advocacy work has been less focused on debunking old stereotypes and more concerned with addressing questions related to successful aging and identifying barriers to effective care. As a result, this line of aging research accentuates the challenges and disparities encountered by gay and lesbian elders, rather than their triumphs. It focuses on the more negative aspects of gay and lesbian aging, such as the prevalence of closet, fear of discrimination, and financial insecurity, and how these factors can impede successful aging.

Raymond Berger's 1982 *Gay and Gray* was the first book-length discussion of gay aging and provides an excellent example of "gay positive" research. The book takes direct aim at the negative portrayal of the aging homosexual by the American Freudians and argues that the mental health and well-being of gay men will actually increase with age. This focus on the psychoanalytic model of homosexuality makes sense given that Berger conducted his study in 1978, only five years after declassification, when the pernicious stereotypes produced by the American Freudians were still fresh in the popular imagination. Berger described the stereotype of the aging homosexual as follows:

> The older homosexual ... becomes increasingly effeminate with age, he is alienated from friends and family alike, and he lives alone, not by choice but by necessity. At thirty he is old. Since he is no longer sexually attractive to other homosexuals, he is forced to prey on children and to pursue anonymous sexual contacts in public places such as restrooms and parks. He is desperately unhappy (Berger 1996: 25).

The findings in Berger's book are based on in-depth interviews with ten white gay men aged 44 to 72 and the questionnaire responses of 212 men in the same age range who were largely non-diverse. At the time, the stereotype of the aging homosexual was so pervasive that the ability to document *any* well-adjusted older homosexuals was arguably cause for celebration. Several years earlier, Jim Kelly had published *The Aging Male Homosexual: Myth and Reality*, in which he summarized his 1973–1974 non-random survey of 241 gay men from the Los Angeles metropolitan area concerning their views on aging (Kelly 1977). Kelly identified the participants through contacts made at a gay beach, the Metropolitan Community Church, advertisements in gay publications, and friendship groups (Kelly 1977: 328). He concluded that, based on his findings, "there seems to be *no further rationale* for the application of certain 'blanket' stereotypes about aging gay men" [emphasis in original] (Kelly 1977: 331). Kelly asserted that the participants in his study were "living proof that such assertions are not always accurate" (Kelly 1977: 331).

Consistent with the exuberance that characterized the years immediately following Stonewall, some of the early "gay positive" researchers were not content simply to dispel the damaging stereotype and, instead, claimed that gay and lesbian elders would actually age *more* successfully than their non-gay peers. This claim was based on the theories of "crisis competence" and "mastery of stigma" (Berger 1996). The notion was that gay and lesbian elders would more easily adjust to the demands of aging because, over the course of their lives, they had weathered the crisis of coming out in a homophobic society and endured the continuing stigma associated with homosexuality. Berger explained the phenomenon by use of a garden metaphor. He wrote: "Every gardener knows that placing his seedlings in the harsh outdoors early in the season creates plants that are better able than the greenhouse variety to withstand the stressors of the growing season. So it is with people ... Early weathering promotes survival" (Berger 1996: 4).

Later studies have not borne out the theory of superior aging ability (Kertzner, Meyer and Dolezal 2004:109). The gerontologist John Allen Lee has dismissed the gay positive school of thought as the "new mythology" of gay and lesbian aging (Lee 1991: xiv). Even though gay and lesbian elders may not have turned out to be super seniors who excelled in areas of crisis competence and mastery of stigma, a relatively large study of 416 gay men and lesbians who were 60 years of age and older that was conducted in 2001 (the "D'Aguelli and Grossman study") found that the majority of the respondents were well adjusted and had good self-esteem (D'Augelli and Grossman 2001). A later 2006 survey of LGBT Baby Boomers conducted by Metlife found that 38 percent of the respondents reported that they have developed positive character traits, greater resilience, or better support networks as a consequence of being lesbian, gay, bisexual or transgender (Metlife 2006: 14). In the Metlife study, African-American respondents, in particular, thought their sexual orientation gave them coping skills that would help them as they entered the aging process (Metlife 2006: 14). In addition, research shows that older same-sex couples have a more equalitarian division of labor, which is thought to assist in the aging process because when a partner dies the surviving partner is better equipped to handle a broader range of life activities (De Vries and Blando 2004: 7).

Despite the promise of the "gay positive" theories of aging, a careful reading of some of the studies suggests that decades of minority stress may have taken their toll on many of today's gay and lesbian elders. Although the D'Augelli and Grossman study of 416 older gay men and lesbians concluded that the majority of the participants were well adjusted, it also found a pronounced undercurrent of distress (Grossman 2006: 64). Twenty-seven percent of the participants reported that they felt lonely, 13 percent said they felt isolated, 10 percent reported that they "sometimes or often" considered suicide, and 17 percent affirmatively wished they were heterosexual (Grossman 2006: 64). One explanation is that the participants are experiencing the cumulative effect of repeated victimization experienced over the course of a lifetime (D'Augelli and Grossman 2001: 1023).

As Todd W. Rawls notes, "it appears that a larger minority of older gay males than previously assumed may be suffering from depression, perhaps as a result of enduring the trials and tribulations of being gay in a homophobic society" (Rawls 2004: 126). This finding would be consistent with other studies that point to a higher incidence of mental health problems among individuals who identify as gay or lesbian (Grant 2010: 80–84). For example, in an advocacy report prepared by the National Gay and Lesbian Task Force, Jaime M. Grant notes that based on "a review of five large studies, gay and bisexual men were twice as likely as individuals in the general population to have had a mental disorder, and lesbian women were more than three times as likely" (Grant 2010: 81).

Both older gay men and lesbians report significant anxiety and fear that they will be discriminated against on account of their sexual orientation (Metlife 2006:

14). This fear is understandable, given the high level of victimization that has been reported among older gay men and lesbians. In the D'Augelli and Grossman study, two-thirds of the participants experienced verbal abuse, 29 percent had been threatened with violence, 16 percent had been assaulted, and 29 percent had been threatened with the unwanted disclosure of their sexual orientation (D'Augelli and Grossman 2001: 1016–1017). Moreover, when gay and lesbian elders encounter discrimination or anti-gay bias, they often have no legal recourse because, as explained in Chapter 10, anti-gay discrimination is not prohibited under federal law or under the laws of a majority of the states.

Chapter 6 discusses the problem of anti-gay bias on the part of various service providers, but gay and lesbian elders also worry about the attitudes and reactions of their non-gay peers whom they might encounter at senior centers or retirement facilities. In this regard, gay and lesbian elders are right to be concerned because non-gay seniors are also members of the pre-Stonewall generation and their views of homosexuality were also formed during the heyday of the American Freudians. Public opinion polls consistently show that individuals age 65 and older are the age cohort least likely to have accepting attitudes toward gay men and lesbians (Herdt and De Vries 2004: xiii, Kaiser Family Foundation 2001).

For at least a decade, advocates have warned about the high risk of social isolation among gay and lesbian elders (Cahill, South and Spade 2000: 10). Social isolation is not simply living alone, but refers to a state that can be devastating for seniors in terms of emotional and physical well-being. An individual who is socially isolated is cut off from the larger society and unable to access needed social and medical services (Grant 2010: 86). Gay and lesbian elders are at a greater risk for social isolation than their non-gay peers because they are significantly more likely to live alone and less likely to be partnered or to have children (De Vries and Blando 2004: 7). The potential for social isolation is aggravated by the fear of encountering anti-gay bias that can cause gay and lesbian elders to withdraw from social interaction and underutilize senior services. Additionally, ageism within the gay and lesbian community can further marginalize gay and lesbian elders and make them less likely to be involved in community activities.

Short of social isolation, living alone and being single are both considered factors that reduce the likelihood for successful aging. Douglas C. Kimmel explains that "[a] partner may also serve as a *buffer* against losses and someone who can aid with challenges of aging. A partner may also be a caregiver, a reason for living, or a spiritual soul mate who promotes successful aging just by being around" (Kimmel 2004: 275). For example, the D'Augelli and Grossman study found that the majority of respondents lived alone. Sixty-three percent of the respondents lived alone, 29 percent lived with a partner, 4 percent lived with friends or relatives, and 4 percent were homeless (D'Augelli and Grossman 2001: 1011). If the D'Augelli and Grossman study is representative of gay and lesbian elders generally, then the percentage of gay and lesbian elders who live alone is much greater than that of their non-gay peers. According to the 2000 census, only

28 percent of people 65 years of age or older lived alone, whereas 66 percent lived with someone else, and 6 percent resided in group quarters (Gist and Hetzel 2004). Another study found that fewer than one-fifth of LGBT elders lived with a partner as compared to one-half of non-LGBT seniors (Cahill, South and Spade 2000: 10). In addition to impeding successful aging, elders who live alone in urban centers are at a higher risk of poverty (Grant 2010: 30). A recent study of housing data from New York City found that gay men over 50 were twice as likely as heterosexual men over 50 to live alone and lesbians over 50 were one-third more likely to live alone than heterosexual women over 50 (Grant 2010: 30).

In some studies on gay and lesbian elders, up to 90 percent of the respondents did not have children, compared with only 20 percent of non-gay elders generally (Cahill, South and Spade 2000: 10). The census results regarding same-sex partnered households, however, suggest that the figures from some of the small academic studies may overstate the number of gay and lesbian elders who do not have children. According to the census data, a relatively large percentage of same-sex partnered households include minor children (Gates and Ost 2004: 44–47). It is unclear whether the prevalence of same-sex partnered households with minor children translates cross-generationally or whether it represents the current shift toward intentional childrearing on the part of same-sex couples. For the pre-Stonewall generation, children are most likely the product of prior heterosexual relationships, rather than intentionally conceived within same-sex relationships. Even gay and lesbian elders who do have children from prior heterosexual relationships may be estranged from them and, therefore, not able to call on them for support as they age. As discussed in greater detail below, gay men and women of all age cohorts rely on support groups comprised of what anthropologists have termed "chosen families" in lieu of their traditional or biological family members (Weston 1997).

The isolation experienced by gay and lesbian elders can be further complicated by health concerns. According to the census data on same-sex partnered households, a greater proportion of elder individuals in same-sex partnered households report having a disability than do those in elder different-sex married households (Baumle and Romero 2009). The census measures a number of different types of disability, including hearing, vision, mobility, and memory (Baumle and Romero 2009). Elders in same-sex partnered households lead in all categories (Baumle and Romero 2009). These statistics are consistent with the findings of one small study of gay and lesbian elders where 27 percent of all elders reported that they were in poor health (Cahill, South and Spade 2000: 6).

For all gay and lesbian elders, not just those in poor health, the fear of disclosure is a significant barrier to health care because gay and lesbian elders report they are reluctant to disclose their sexual orientation to health-care and elder-care providers (Grant 2010: 69). This reluctance is especially pronounced in the case of further marginalized subsets of the gay and lesbian community and those who do not identify as gay or lesbian (Grant 2010: 138). Older gay men in particular have been disproportionately affected by the HIV epidemic, in terms of both infection and loss, and the prevalence of HIV infection weighs heavily on the population of older gay men and communities of color. Gorman and Nelson attempt to illustrate the scale of loss experienced by older gay men with the following comparisons:

> By the year 2002, there had been approximately 460,000 U.S. adult deaths from AIDS or AIDS-related causes, with the number of adult male deaths being on the order of 400,000. Of these deaths, some 267,000 of these were MSMs, a very large number when one considers the relatively small likely size of the gay/ bisexual male population (some estimates range from [2 to 4 percent] of the adult male population). By comparison, the United States experienced 57,000 combat deaths in Vietnam, 37,000 in the Korean conflict, and 404,000 combat-related deaths in World War II, but these combat deaths were spread over an entire generation and more, as well as across all geographical areas of the country, not primarily in a concentrated subgroup (Gorman and Nelson 2003: 76).

Little research has been devoted to aging with HIV since long-term HIV management only became possible after the advent of protease inhibitors in the mid-1990s (Cahill, South and Spade 2000: 61). In addition to the gay elders who are long-time survivors, 15 percent of all new cases of HIV infection occur in men 50 years of age and older (Evans 2007). Despite this alarming rate of new infection, relatively few prevention efforts are targeted at older gay men (Cahill, South and Spade 2000: 15, Waysdorf 2002).

The population of HIV-positive elders is especially prone to isolation because many long-time survivors lost partners and friends to the disease and now face aging without a peer support group – without a chosen family. A 2006 study of individuals living with HIV/AIDS reported that close to 70 percent of the participants lived alone (Grant 2010: 30). As explained below in greater detail, gay and lesbian elders depend on friendship groups to take the place of family and rely on these chosen families to provide all manner of support. Thus, gay men who have lost partners and friends may find themselves not only widowed, but also orphaned – left to cope with what is now referred to in the literature as multiple loss syndrome (Gorman and Nelson 2004: 82–83). Not surprisingly, HIV-positive elders are at an increased risk of suicide (Gorman and Nelson 2004: 83). Steven Schwartzberg situates older gay men in what he refers to the "unavoidable climate of loss." He writes:

> [T]he enormity of loss in the gay community has a secondary, cumulative effect that is greater than the sum total of the various deaths. It creates an unavoidable climate of loss in the community as a whole ... survivors grieve not only for their most personal losses, but also for all the victims, for strangers and for the loss of community and culture" (Schwartzberg 2004: 13).

The Importance of Chosen Family

Gay men and lesbians of all ages rely on fictive kinship networks referred to as "chosen families" for a wide range of support. These chosen families are based on affinity rather than consanguinity and help compensate for the fact that, even today, many gay men and lesbians are estranged or distanced from their families of origin (Weston 1997). Chosen families also provide a uniquely affirming gay or lesbian alternative to an individual's presumably heterosexual natal family (Weston 1997). In a study of social support networks of gay men and lesbians 60 years of age and older, the vast majority of the respondents reported receiving support from chosen family or friendship networks (Grossman et al. 2000: 174). Seventy-two percent reported receiving general social support from their network, 62 percent receive emotional support, 54 percent receive practical support, 41 percent receive advice and guidance, and 13 percent receive financial support (Grossman et al. 2000: 175). To further underscore the importance of this support, the D'Augelli and Grossman study involving the same age cohort found that 63 percent of the respondents lived alone (D'Augelli and Grossman 2001: 1011).

In her 1991 book, *Families We Choose: Lesbians, Gays, Kinship*, anthropologist Kath Weston presented the field work she conducted from 1985 to 1987 in the San Francisco Bay area on gay kinship patterns. She explained that, traditionally, gay or lesbian individuals existed outside the family because their homosexuality would cause them to be alienated from their parents and their family of origin, and they would be unlikely to have children and form a family of their own (Weston 1997). In a chapter titled "Exiles from Kinship," Weston explained:

> Looking backward and forward across the life cycle, people who equated their adoption of a lesbian or gay identity with a renunciation of family did so in the double-sided sense of fearing rejection by the families in which they had grown up, and not expecting to marry or have children as adults. Although few in numbers, there were still those who had considered "going straight" or getting married [to a different-sex partner] specifically in order to "have a family" (Weston 1997: 24).

As noted in the previous section, this notion of lingering heterosexual regret was also present in the D'Augelli and Grossman study where 17 percent of the respondents actively wished that they were heterosexual (Grossman 2006: 64). Weston specifically ties this regret to the desire to have a family (Weston 1997: 24).

As explained in Chapter 1, the contemporary concept of gay pride was popularized by the gay liberationists who advocated self-disclosure as a pathway to personal fulfillment, as well as to political equality. Prior to the Gay Liberation Movement, very few individuals would have considered affirmatively disclosing their homosexuality to family members because homosexuality would have been cause for great shame and concern (Barker 2004: 61). Thus, unlike today's gay men and lesbians, the pre-Stonewall generation did not typically grapple with the weighty question of whether or on what terms they should come out to their family (Weston 1997: 44). For the pre-Stonewall generation, a family's knowledge of homosexuality would likely proceed from inference and, indeed, could turn out to be dangerous if the family decided to attempt a "cure" (Weston 1997: 45). Even if the family did not have actual knowledge of a loved one's homosexuality, the simple fact that the loved one failed to conform to the prevailing heterosexual norms would have been sufficient cause for alarm. As one of Weston's interviewees explained, the danger of institutionalization was quite real:

> [Y]ou just didn't talk about anything about [being] gay. . . if you did ... you ended up in an insane asylum. Your family would sign you in for your own good. They could get you into there ... You couldn't do anything about it ... your best friend might decide for your own good that you needed some help ... What you'd be doing if you came out, you'd be declaring yourself fit for the insane asylum (Weston 1997: 45).

Weston reported that gay teenagers continued to fear institutionalization well into the 1980s (Weston 1997: 46), and even today there are quasi-psychiatric religious-based facilities where parents can send their minor children to effect a "cure" for homosexuality (Bannerman 2008).

For the pre-Stonewall generation, a chosen family consisted of kindred spirits who shared a common culture and values. They celebrated holidays together, vacationed together, and took care of each other when they were sick. As the members of these chosen families age together, they serve as mutual caregivers for one another. It is quite possible that future generations of gay and lesbian elders will no longer rely on chosen families as homosexuality is normalized and families of origin learn to embrace and celebrate their openly gay family members. Moreover, same-sex couples are increasingly choosing to become parents, which means that gay men and lesbians may now be able to stay connected to their inter-generational families of origin *and* start their own inter-generational families through assisted-reproductive technologies or adoption. The current trend of intentional parenting, sometimes referred to as the "gayby boom," began among lesbians in the mid- to late 1980s and has continued to gain momentum, as well as social and legal acceptance. For the pre-Stonewall generation, however, parenting was fraught with numerous social and legal disabilities.

Aside from the emotional and interpersonal benefits of parenthood, children (and grandchildren) are an important resource for aging parents (and grandparents). Aging policy in the United States relies heavily on children and the existence of an inter-generational support network. In this regard, gay and lesbian elders are at a considerable disadvantage because they are much less likely than their non-gay peers to have children and, given the possibility of estrangement from their family of origin, they are less likely to be able to call on younger family members, such as nieces or nephews, for assistance. Those gay and lesbian elders who have children may be at a high risk of estrangement because the children were most likely the result of a heterosexual marriage.

Members of the pre-Stonewall generation entered into heterosexual marriages due to a combination of social pressure, a later average age of coming out, and an earlier age of first marriage. For example, in 1950 the median age of first marriage was 20.3 years of age for women and 22.8 years of age for men, as compared with a median age of first marriage in 2003 of 25.3 for women and 27.1 for men (U.S. Census Bureau). However, the 2001 study of older gay men and lesbians indicates that, for gay men and lesbians 60 and older, the average age of coming out was 23 years of age (D'Augelli and Grossman 2001: 1015). As a result, many gay and lesbian elders came to terms with their homosexuality while in a heterosexual marriage. According to a 2009 study, today the average age of coming out is 13.4 years of age, making it less likely that an individual would come out after already in a different-sex marriage (Ryan 2009: 2).[5]

The fact that the children of today's gay and lesbian elders were largely the product of failed heterosexual marriages would have added an additional layer of stress on the parent-child relationship because at the time divorce itself was not without controversy – let alone a divorce that might have involved claims of sexual perversion. It would have been highly unlikely that the homosexual parent would have been granted custody or even visitation rights given that the medical establishment held that homosexuality was a severe mental illness. Even in the absence of negative legal intervention, the pressures of pre-Stonewall homophobia could have made effective parenting difficult, and gay and lesbian elders who have children may face retirement estranged from them.

Gay and lesbian elders who rely on chosen family for support in lieu of their family of origin are also disadvantaged because chosen families tend to be comprised of members of the same age cohort (Weston 1997: 111). The single-generational nature of chosen families can be explained in part by ageism within the gay and lesbian community and internalized homophobia that can keep elders from attempting to form cross-generational relationships, both of which are discussed in greater detail in Part II. As the members of a chosen family all age in unison, the resources of the group will become increasingly strained. The level of care the chosen family members can provide for one another naturally declines as they become progressively older and more infirm.

Both the likelihood that gay and lesbian elders may be estranged from their family of origin and the single-generational structure of chosen families can decrease their chances for successful aging because, as noted above, existing aging policies in the United States rely heavily on family members to arrange and coordinate services and support. As spouses or partners age together, they can

---

5   The same study found that between 17 percent and 24 percent of gay adolescents experienced family rejection on account of their sexual orientation and, most importantly, that this rejection was a predictor for a number of negative health outcomes, such as HIV infection, substance abuse, and suicide (Ryan et al. 2009).

help each other plot a course through the complicated eldercare systems. When an individual is widowed or single, however, the responsibilities for care and support most often fall on children and other family members. Judith C. Barker notes: "The moral obligation of lineal kin to provide care for one another is a taken-for-granted cultural value underpinning much interaction within natal families and is reflected in both social theory distinguishing family from other social groups and throughout social policy" (Barker 2004: 59).

In the United States, approximately 80 percent of long-term care is provided by informal unpaid caregivers (Coleman and Pandya 2002: 1), and that care is overwhelmingly provided by younger relatives. According to a 2009 national study on the prevalence of unpaid caregiving conducted by the National Alliance for Caregiving (NAC) in collaboration with the American Association for Retired Persons (AARP), 89 percent of all unpaid caregivers for individuals over 50 years of age are relatives (NAC 2009: 21), and the average age of caregivers for individuals who are age 75 and older is 51 years of age (NAC 2009: 19). For the majority of individuals who are "aging in place" (i.e., aging within the community), this unpaid caregiving is their only source of assistance (NAC 2009: 38). Gay and lesbian elders, like the majority of Americans, also desire to "age in place," but this preference is reinforced by intense fear that they will experience discrimination and anti-gay bias in mainstream senior housing options (Orel 2006: 233). The absence of inter-generational support or caregiving works against their desire to age in place because almost a quarter of those individuals receiving care in the national NAC study lived with their caregivers (NAC 2009: 43).

It is also clear from the NAC study that caregiving can exact both an emotional and a financial toll on gay and lesbian elders. Although it is expected that partners will care for one another as they age, gay and lesbian elders who are members of a chosen family will have multiple, and at times reciprocal, caregiving responsibilities. According to the NAC study, 19 percent of the population (43.5 million people) had served as unpaid caregivers to someone 50 years of age or older in the prior year (NAC 2009: 15). Thirty-two percent of the caregivers reported that they were in a "high burden" situation with respect to the level of care they provided and performed an average of 19 hours of care a week (NAC 2009: 26, 34). Fifty-three percent reported either moderate or high emotional stress, with 31 percent reporting high emotional stress (NAC 2009: 53). Twenty-three percent of the caregivers reported that they experienced moderate or high financial stress because of the caregiving (NAC 2009: 55).

As explained more fully in Chapter 8, the second major drawback of chosen families is that chosen family structures are not recognized by the law, and this produces a multitude of difficulties and uncertainties when trying to organize and coordinate elder care. The legal fragility of chosen families first became apparent on a wide scale during the initial years of the HIV/AIDS epidemic that decimated the gay male community from the beginning of the 1980s through the mid-1990s. At the time, persons living with HIV were often estranged from their families of origin due to the dual stigmas of homosexuality and HIV/AIDS (Weston 1997:

185–187). Writing in 1991, Weston noted, "The number of PWAs [person with AIDS] without homes, family, or resources has grown year by year" (Weston 1997: 186). When people living with HIV/AIDS became too ill to direct their own care, they would rely on partners and friends. All too frequently, however, medical professionals or family members would ignore or simply countermand the patient's stated wishes. Andrew Holleran wrote movingly of this dilemma in *Chronicle of a Plague*, originally published in 1988, when he observed that "friendships that would have evolved over time were tested by AIDS long before old age could. AIDS made people ask: What are you to one another? Even in New York, walking into a hospital and identifying oneself to the person at the desk, the word 'friend' sounded flimsy" (Holleran 2008: 10).

Gay and Lesbian Elders with Intersecting Identities

The dearth of information on gay and lesbians elders is most pronounced in the case of elders of color and elders with other intersecting identities. In terms of demographic information, the census and general aging research routinely collects information on age, race, and ethnicity. As a result, it is possible to break down the senior population in terms of sex, race, and ethnicity and produce a detailed profile of today's seniors. For example, the life expectancy of African-American men who reached the age of 65 in 2007 was 80.3 years of age (AoA 2009a). Seventy percent of the senior Hispanic population lives in only four states: California, Texas, Florida, and New York (AoA 2009c). Twenty percent of Asian-American women age 65 and above live alone, and 12 percent of senior Asian-Americans live below the poverty level (AoA 2009b). With the exception of the limited data that is available on same-sex partnered households, it is not possible to cross-reference any of this information by sexual orientation because, as explained earlier, the census and general aging research does not inquire as to sexual orientation.

Of course, statistics alone cannot begin to express the unique experience of being a gay or lesbian elder of color, but they can help measure health disparities and assess related barriers to access. The same calculus used to estimate the number of gay and lesbian elders can be employed to estimate the number of gay and lesbian elders of color. Using the general guidepost that between 4 and 6 percent of the population is gay or lesbian, it is then possible to approximate the number of gay and lesbian elders of color, assuming that the incidence of homosexuality is constant across racial and ethnic lines. For example, as of 2008 there were 3.2 million African-American seniors in the United States, which amounts to between 128,000 and 192,000 African-American gay and lesbian elders.

As discussed in Chapter 2, the pre-Stonewall generation came of age at a time when homophobia masqueraded as scientific knowledge, as did racism and sexism. The process of identity formation experienced by gay and lesbian elders was radically different from that of the post-Stonewall and MTV generations. However, gay and lesbian elders of color had to deal with multiple vectors of oppression and discrimination. Their identity was formed not only during a time of officially mandated homophobia; it was also a period of government-imposed segregation and widespread racism. Gay and lesbian elders of color spent their formative years in a climate that sanctioned extra-legal violence against persons of color, and they experienced their homosexuality within this larger context of race and ethnicity. The result was a multivalent identity where intersecting identifications coalesce to form a distinct identity, such that an individual is not merely gay *and* African-American, but rather is uniquely constituted as a gay African-American. Today, gay and lesbian elders of color have to add their senior status to their already complex identities, and experience their senior status differently to the extent they age within their respective racial and ethnic communities.

Similar observations can be made regarding gender. Lesbian elders came of age before the advent of Title VII and Second Wave feminism. Coming out during a period when sex roles were much more rigid and help-wanted ads were sex segregated, pre-Stonewall lesbians had to face not only homophobia, but also misogyny. Like elders of color, they had access to fewer opportunities in terms of education and jobs. Lesbian stereotypes emphasized cross-gender performance such that the so-called "mannish" lesbian challenged the mid-century dictates of gender, as well as those of sexuality. Lesbians of color, of course, faced multiple overlapping disabilities. Given these considerable challenges, it is not surprising that female same-sex partnered households of color lag significantly behind other same-sex partnered households in terms of financial security (Dang and Frazer 2005).

Until more complete data is available, it is reasonable to assume that gay and lesbian elders of color share the burdens of their racial or ethnic identification in terms of life expectancy, income, and education. The 2000 census data on African-American same-sex partnered households confirms this and suggests that gay and lesbians of color struggle financially (Dang and Frazer 2005). Households where at least one same-sex partner identified as African-American represent 14 percent of the overall number of same-sex partnered households and 10 percent of these African American households had at least one partner who is 65 years of age or older (Dang and Frazer 2005: 15). The median income of African-American same-sex partnered households is lower than that of white same-sex partnered households (Dang and Frazer 2005: 16). African-American same-sex partnered households are also less likely to own a home (Dang and Frazer 2005: 18). These observations suggest that race may play a factor in terms of financial security, but that race cannot be the only factor because African-American same-sex partnered households also lag behind African-American different-sex married couples in terms of economic well-being (Dang and Frazer 2005). African-American same-sex female partnered households labor under the three-fold burden of race, gender, and sexuality, and, not surprisingly, they have the lowest median income of any of the couples and are least likely to own their home (Dang and Frazer 2005: 16, 19).

Despite their lower median income, African-American same-sex partnered households are twice as likely as white same-sex partnered households to be raising biological children and more likely to be parenting non-biological children, including adopted children, foster children, and minor relatives (Dang and Frazer 2005: 22–25). In fact, African-American female same-sex partnered households are just as likely to be living with a minor child as African-American different-sex married couples (Dang and Frazer 2005: 22). The added financial burden of children increases the likelihood that African-American partnered households live below the poverty line.

Beyond this limited snapshot of self-identifying same-sex partnered households provided by the census, there is very little demographic data on gay men and lesbians of color, and virtually no information on gay and lesbian elders of color, who are almost completely absent from the academic studies discussed earlier in this chapter (Kimmel et al. 2006b: 9). Despite the growing interest in the topic of gay and lesbian elders, it is common for a review of the literature to start with a disclaimer explaining that the extant studies are primarily based on small convenience samples of urban, white, middle-class gay men, with only secondary attention paid to urban, white, middle-class lesbians (Barker 2004: 39).

In addition to learning more about gay and lesbian elders with intersecting identities, future research specifically targeting gays and lesbians of color could help discredit the attempts of anti-gay organizations to pit the African-American community against the movement for gay and lesbian equality. This divisive strategy is based on the false premise that an individual is either gay or African-American, but certainly not both. It began in earnest during the Amendment 2 controversy in Colorado in the mid-1990s that ensued when the voters amended the state constitution to prohibit the enactment of laws extending anti-discrimination protection on account of sexual orientation. The resulting court challenge led to the groundbreaking U.S. Supreme Court decision *Romer v. Evans* that invalidated Amendment 2 to the Colorado state constitution on the basis that its passage was motivated by animus toward gay men and lesbians and animus is not a legitimate state interest (*Romer v. Evans* 1996).

In support of Amendment 2, the anti-gay organization Colorado for Family Values (CFV) argued that anti-discrimination protections on account of sexual orientation amounted to "special rights," as opposed to basic civil rights that are afforded to African-Americans (Badgett and Rogers 2003). The CFV produced informational pamphlets in support of Amendment 2 that purported to compare the income and general financial well-being of gay men and lesbians with that of "disadvantaged African Americans" (Knauer 2003b: 71). The materials were designed to illustrate the stereotype that gay men and lesbians are a wealthy minority who wield disproportionate political power and are not disadvantaged by their minority status (Herman 1997: 119).

The absence of diversity within the academic studies is due, at least in part, to the non-random nature of the samples that are based instead on "convenience samples" and "snowball referrals." It is to be expected that non-random convenience samples will reflect the demographic characteristics of the researcher and the dominant gay and lesbian community. Researchers recruit participants by posting flyers at gay and lesbian community centers and using so-called "snowball referrals," where an individual who responds to a flyer or advertisement then suggests his or her friends. For example, the participants in a study of 125 self-identified gay men 55 years of age in Texas were recruited through "social organizations for aging gay men" and "gay/lesbian churches and several friendship networks" using "snowball and convenience methodology" (Cruz 2003: 82). Only two of the participants in that study identified as African-American, four identified as Latino, and one identified as Native American (Cruz 2003).

One of the largest studies of older gay men and lesbians was conducted by D'Augelli and Grossman and involved 416 gay, lesbian, and bisexual elders who were aged 60 to 91 (D'Augelli and Grossman 2001). The study identified participants through "groups providing social, recreation, and support services to older LGB adults" (Grossman et al. 2000: 172). Only 3 percent of the respondents identified as African-American and 2 percent identified as Latino (Grossman et al. 2000: 172). To further skew the sample, 71 percent of the participants in the survey were male (Grossman et al. 2000: 172). The lack of attention paid to women is even more shocking, given that women are disproportionately represented among those who are age 65 and older (Barker 2004: 34). In 2008, there were 22.4 million women aged 65 and older compared to 16.5 million men (AoA 2009d). Overall, this distribution translates to a sex ratio of 136 women for every 100 men (AoA 2009d). The proportion of women increases markedly as the population ages. In the age group of seniors who are 85 and older, there are 207 women for every 100 men (AoA 2009d).

The racial, ethnic, and gender makeup of the academic samples also reflect the segregated nature of the gay community. If a white researcher conducts outreach in predominantly white gay venues, the sample is going to be white. The racial divisions that exist within the gay community compound the challenges faced by gay and lesbian elders of color – not only do elders face ageism within the gay and lesbian communities, but also racism. The weight of this additional burden tightens the circle around them and could further increase the risk of social isolation. The census data for partnered same-sex households suggests residential segregation patterns for both African-American and Hispanic same-sex couples. Areas with higher African-American populations have higher concentrations of African-American same-sex couples (Gates and Ost 2004: 50). The same is true of Hispanic same-sex couples (Gates and Ost 2004: 51). Of particular note is the fact that African-American same-sex partnered households tend to be concentrated in smaller metropolitan and rural areas, which is not the case for same-sex partnered households generally. The three states with the highest concentration of African-American same-sex partnered households are Mississippi, Louisiana, and South Carolina (Gates and Ost 2004: 50). The metropolitan areas with the largest concentration of African-American same-sex partnered households are:

Sumter, South Carolina; Albany, Georgia; and Pine Bluff, Arkansas (Gates and Ost 2004: 50). These locales are a far cry from the cities boasting the highest overall concentration of same-sex partnered households: San Francisco, Oakland, and Seattle (Gates and Ost 2004: 26).

In terms of class, the samples used in the academic studies represent, by and large, well-educated middle-class respondents who are actively engaged in the gay community. Accordingly, there is a lack of information on working-class gay and lesbian elders, except what can be gleaned from the census data. Based on that information, it is safe to say that financial insecurity is a problem as discussed in detail in Chapter 9. This observation leads to the conclusion that poverty reforms may be more closely linked to the cause of gay and lesbian equality than previously thought. Further research with respect to gay and lesbian economic security generally could also help put to bed the myth of gay affluence that anti-gay organizations have championed since the mid-1990s.

Finally, almost all of the studies were conducted in major metropolitan areas, and, as a result, there is no information regarding the elders who are scattered across the United States in rural settings. According to the census data, 15 percent of all partnered same-sex households are in areas classified as rural. Despite the limited applicability of the studies, and the shortcomings of the census data, they do show recurring themes, at least for urban, middle class, white, gay men. These general themes of isolation, financial insecurity, and barriers to access to health care and senior services are addressed in the following chapters.

PART II
Identity

The historical forces discussed in the preceding chapters offer important insights with respect to many of the behaviors and beliefs that are common among gay and lesbian elders, such as their attachment to the closet, their apprehension when dealing with health-care and elder-care professionals, and their reliance on chosen family. Although their self-imposed silence may be rooted in painful lessons from pre-Stonewall America, it is reinforced daily by the continuing legal and social disabilities imposed on gay men and lesbians. Gay and lesbian elders remain silent because they fear anti-gay bias and violence, and studies show that, unfortunately, this fear is not misplaced. Older gay and lesbian elders report high levels of victimization and violence over the course of their lifetimes (D'Augelli and Grossman 2001).

Today, a complex interplay of ageism and homophobia further obscures the identities of gay and lesbian elders and keeps their concerns securely removed from public view. Stereotypical ageist and homophobic constructions work in tandem to make the very notion of a gay and lesbian elder impossible because seniors are not sexual and homosexuals are, by definition, only sexual. Under this reasoning, a senior cannot also be a homosexual nor can a homosexual also be a senior. As noted in Chapter 3, the FRC used this very argument when it objected to federal funding for a project benefitting gay and lesbian seniors.

Ageism and homophobia also operate to alienate gay and lesbian elders from the two communities with whom they share the greatest affinity: the gay and lesbian community and the larger senior community. Although gay and lesbian elders would seem to have a foot firmly planted in both of these well-organized and influential minority groups, existing prejudices within each community can alienate gay and lesbian elders from their natural constituent groups. Ageism within the gay and lesbian community compounds the isolation experienced by gay and lesbian elders and impairs their ability to form cross-generational support networks. Homophobia within the senior community presents a roadblock to full participation by gay and lesbian elders in senior-specific programs and aging services. The interplay of ageism and homophobia decreases the likelihood of successful aging and leaves the needs of gay and lesbian elders unrecognized and unaddressed.

These chapters explore the contemporary iteration of senior gay and lesbian identities within society at large and within both the gay and lesbian community and the senior community.

Chapter 4

The Invisibility of Gay and Lesbian Elders: The De-sexualized Senior and the Hyper-sexualized Homosexual

The notion of a gay or lesbian elder presents an oxymoron in the classic sense of the term in that the very existence of a gay or lesbian senior "is something that is surprisingly true, a paradox" (Willis 2009). The source of this paradox is the clash of two powerful stereotypes: the de-sexualized senior and the hyper-sexualized homosexual. The larger culture ignores or denies senior sexuality and perceives seniors to be asexual or, at least, no longer sexual[1] (Barker 2003: 53). Sex over 65 is considered not only unappealing but also unlikely. To the contrary, gay men and lesbians are often defined principally by reference to their sexuality — their *sexual* orientation. Anti-gay rhetoric, in particular, emphasizes the sexual aspects of the lives and relationships of gay men and lesbians. If gay men and lesbians are defined primarily by their sexuality, and seniors are not sexual, then it follows that seniors cannot be gay or lesbian. Obviously, this thinking misapprehends the nature of human sexuality. It also mischaracterizes gay and lesbian identity by privileging its sexual aspects over questions of relationships and commitment. Simply put, gay men and lesbians are more than the sum of their sex acts.

Pre-Stonewall Stereotypes of the Aging Homosexual

If one takes a long view, the fact that gay and lesbian elders are an invisible minority could be perceived as progress because it signals the demise of the pre-Stonewall stereotypes of the aging homosexual. As described in Chapter 2, the psychoanalytic theory of homosexuality produced two distinct, yet interrelated, stereotypes of homosexuals that have particular relevance to gay and lesbian elders: the sexual predator and the aging homosexual. In many ways, the aging homosexual is still

---

1   The exception to this would be the stereotype of the "dirty old man." This stereotype seems to have many characteristics in common with that of the aging homosexual in that they are both pathetic and childish creatures. The sexuality of a "dirty old man" is not taken seriously. To the contrary, there is a sense that he is well past his prime and there is something inappropriate about his continued interest in sex. In this way, the "dirty old man" actually reinforces the notion of the asexual senior.

a sexual predator – just more pathetic. For the pre-Stonewall generation, the stereotypical image of an aging homosexual served as a strong cautionary tale. Its message was clear: unless homosexuals embraced the therapeutic promise of a cure, they would end up as bitter, lonely malcontents, clinging pathetically to their lost youth and preying on children. This stereotype provided a secular version of the familiar religious admonition that homosexuals should "repent now or face eternal damnation" or, as the rabidly anti-gay Westboro Baptist Church in Topeka, Kansas, puts it, "turn or burn."

Writing in 1977, Jim Kelly offered the following summary of the stereotype of the aging homosexual as it appeared in the "scientific literature" prior to declassification (Kelly 1977: 329).

> He no longer goes to bars, having lost his physical attractiveness and his sexual appeal to the young men he craves. He is over-sexed, but his sex life is very unsatisfactory. He has been unable to form a lasting relationship with a sexual partner, and he is seldom active sexually anymore. When he does have sex it is usually in a "tearoom" (public toilet). He has disengaged from the gay world and his acquaintances in it. He is retreating further and further into the "closet" – fearful of disclosure of his "perversion." Most of his associations now are increasingly with heterosexuals. In a bizarre and deviant world centered around age he is labeled "an old queen," as he has become quite effeminate.

Kelly's summary of the scientific literature is strikingly similar to the one provided by Berger in his book *Gay and Gray*, discussed in Chapter 3.

The stereotype of the aging homosexual was not limited to medical texts, and it could be found in both popular and literary descriptions of homosexuals, such as they were. For example, in his 1961 sensational exposé, *The Sixth Man: The Startling Investigation of the Spread of Homosexuality in America,* Jess Stearn, a former *Newsweek* editor and the future chronicler of the American psychic Edgar Cayce, described the archetypical older homosexual in deplorable terms. According to Stearn, older homosexuals could be found living "in the Bowery, seeking oblivion in handouts and cheap wine" (Kelly 1977: 329) More ominously, Stearn warned that the older (male) homosexual would inevitably "regress to the point where he preys on small children" (Kelly 1977: 329).

In terms of literary depictions, the notion of the aging queen *qua* pedophile is at the heart of Thomas Mann's novella, *Death in Venice.* Mann's protagonist, Gustave (von) Aschenbach, is a 50-something author who becomes hopelessly besotted with a young boy and finds himself quite literally chasing youth through the streets of Venice (Mann 2009). Early in the story, Gustave encounters an elderly man in a wig and makeup surrounded by young men, and Gustave is filled with disgust at the "ancient" homosexual who is nothing more than a "cheap counterfeit" with a "shrill voice" (Mann 2009: 12). As the story unfolds, Gustave quickly disintegrates, and he too eventually resorts to hair dye and rouge in a futile attempt to reclaim his looks (Mann 2009: 50). In the end, Gustave succumbs to the pestilence (i.e., cholera) that has taken hold of the city (Mann 2009: 53). Predictably, he dies alone, a grotesque caricature of his former self and a fair approximation of the "cheap counterfeit" whom he earlier had found so repulsive (Mann 2009: 12).

A comparable portrait of an aging lesbian is offered in the play *The Killing of Sister George*, written by Frank Marcus in 1964. The play was staged on the West End and Broadway during the 1960s to critical acclaim, but the 1968 movie version earned an X rating due to the inclusion of a lesbian sex scene and some brief nudity. The protagonist, June Buckridge, is an aging actress who plays a beloved nurse, Sister George, on a popular soap opera. In real life, June, whom everyone calls George, is a sadistic and mannish lesbian who drinks too much and smokes cigars. In the movie, her much younger partner, whom George calls Childie, flits around their apartment in short chiffon negligees and plays with dolls (*Sister George* 1968). George verbally and physically abuses Childie, and, at one point, a drunken George memorably molests two novitiate nuns in a taxi cab. In the end, George loses her job and Childie (*Sister George* 1968). George is literally put out to pasture when the only role she is offered is that of the voice of a cow on a children's show. The movie ends with George pathetically "mooing" backstage lost among the props – alone in her desperation (*Sister George* 1968).

As explained in Chapter 3, the first "gay positive" studies by Kelly (1977), Berger (1982), and others were aimed directly at what they termed the "myth" of gay aging. The successful repudiation of this stereotype, however, created a vacuum in terms of the popular understanding of gay and lesbian elders. Although gay and lesbian elders no longer labor under an age-specific negative stereotype, they are now burdened by a near universal invisibility that presents its own set of disabilities with respect to policy development and needs assessments. As both the senior community and the gay and lesbian community grew substantially in terms of their political strength and influence during the 1980s and 1990s, neither community embraced the specific concerns of gay and lesbian elders. The result has been a resounding silence on the topic of gay and lesbian aging. Admittedly, this silence may be preferable to the widespread demonization that had been prevalent during the pre-Stonewall period, but social invisibility reinforces the sense of isolation reported by a significant number of gay and lesbian elders and further decreases their likelihood of successful aging.

De-sexualized Seniors and the Denial of Identity

The denial of senior sexuality can have negative consequences in terms of overall senior health and emotional well-being for seniors generally, but it can have far-reaching ramifications for gay and lesbian elders whose identities are easily conflated with sexuality. In such cases, the denial of senior sexuality can be paramount to denying gay and lesbian identity.

Despite the widespread refusal to acknowledge that seniors remain sexual, studies show that individuals enjoy healthy and active sex lives well past age

65 (Kamel 2003: 204–205). A 2007 random survey of more than 3,000 seniors between the ages of 57 and 85 published in *The New England Journal of Medicine* revealed levels of sexual activity that could make even the "Golden Girls" blush (Lindau, et al. 2007). Among adults ages 65 to 74, 53 percent reported that they were sexually active, whereas 26 percent of the respondents ages 75 to 85 responded that they were sexually active (Lindau, et al. 2007: 762). Sexual activity decreased with age and, among those who were sexually active, approximately one half disclosed some form of sexual difficulty, including erectile dysfunction in men and or low desire in women (Lindau, et al. 2007: 762). Among those who were sexually active, however, the frequency of sexual activity was comparable to the results of a 1992 national study of adults aged 16 to 54 (Lindau, et al. 2007: 768). Frequency was the lowest for the 75 to 85 age group, but even in this age group over one half of the sexually active seniors reported having sex two or three times a month, and almost a quarter (23 percent) reported having sex one or more times a week (Lindau, et al. 2007: 768).

Studies such as this one demonstrate that sexuality does not stop with retirement and continues across the lifespan. Both seniors and health-care providers would benefit from greater candor regarding sexuality because ignoring it can have medical consequences, in addition to a negative impact in terms of a senior's self-image and emotional well-being. For example, certain types of sexual dysfunction can indicate more serious health concerns, including diabetes and certain cancers. With respect to HIV prevention and education, ignoring senior sexuality can have tragic consequences. For example, the CDC only recommends routine HIV testing up to age 64, despite the continued risk of infection in older age groups (Branson et al. 2006). If health-care and elder-care professionals are reluctant to raise issues of sexuality, the onus is placed on seniors to raise the topic – something that could be very difficult for gay and lesbian elders given their reluctance to disclose and their general discomfort with the medical profession.

Where senior sexuality is not denied out of hand, it is often closely regulated. For example, it is common for senior living facilities to impose prohibitions on expressions of sexuality. To some degree, this regulation is other-regarding and reflects shared norms regarding the differences between permissible behavior in public versus private space (Casta-Kaufteil 2003/2004, Perlin 1993/1994). The regulation of senior sexuality is also justified as necessary to safeguard a potentially vulnerable population easily subject to exploitation and abuse (Toy 2002). It is tempting to dismiss this argument as a paternalistic attempt to regulate senior sexuality. Today, seniors may be staying in the workforce and remaining active long after the traditional age of retirement, but there are also many seniors who spend part of their twilight years in poor health, with diminishing levels of capacity, and susceptible to manipulation. Even though sexual abuse constitutes only a small fraction of the reported cases of elder abuse, the threat still remains (National Center on Elder Abuse 2005). Accordingly, it is important to differentiate the paternalistic impulse to deny senior sexuality from the effort to protect vulnerable seniors.

Studies suggest that a significant percentage of individuals who live into their senior years will experience some form of dementia or diminished capacity. In legal terms, there is no single monolithic standard to determine whether an individual has capacity. The law imposes differing standards on a number of important life activities, such as the ability to refuse medical treatment, enter into a contract, marry, execute a will, donate organs, stand trial, hire a lawyer, or consent to sex. It is possible that an individual may not have the legal capacity to enter into a contract, yet still have the requisite capacity to get married.

Generally, capacity doctrines disfavor non-normative choices and, therefore, could more easily invalidate certain choices involving senior sexuality and gay and lesbian identity in particular. Capacity doctrines typically take into account an individual's ability to engage in deliberative decision-making and, in some instances, the perceived reasonableness of the individual's actions. Thus, the relative value assigned to a particular decision or action may ultimately determine whether an individual has the requisite capacity to engage in the activity. If a health-care professional, nursing home administrator, or even a judge views senior sexuality as aberrational, rather than a healthy component of successful aging, then expressions of sexuality could be interpreted as evidence of lack of capacity. In other words, the myth of the asexual senior could become the standard against which choices and behavior are evaluated.

The danger of such imbedded bias is even greater in the case of gay and lesbian elders where a finding of a lack of capacity has the potential to silence not just sexual autonomy, but also identity. As noted earlier, the myth of the asexual senior is, perhaps paradoxically, coded with a heterosexual default setting. If senior sexuality is considered unusual when it is heterosexual, then imagine the potential concern when senior sexuality is homosexual. In the case of closeted gay and lesbian elders, the elder's family of origin might reasonably believe that homosexual behavior is aberrational. For gay and lesbian elders, the sex of a partner could be sufficient to invalidate the choice of that partner because the choice of a same-sex partner would serve as proof of incapacity.

One of the most well-known instances where the capacity doctrine was used to invalidate a non-normative life choice and deny gay or lesbian identity was the prolonged and heartbreaking case of Sharon Kowalski that began in the early 1980s and extended into the next decade (Lewin 1991). Although this case involved a young person rather than an elder, the protracted litigation raised issues that are highly relevant to gay and lesbian elders, namely the law's preference for family, the meaning of the closet, and the continuing specter of the sexual predator. The case took place during the initial years of the HIV/AIDS epidemic and together with the stories about the partners of persons living with AIDS who were denied visitation rights or decision-making authority, Sharon's case became a rallying call to educate the gay and lesbian community concerning the importance of durable powers of attorney and comprehensive estate planning.

In 1983, the car Sharon was driving was struck by a drunk driver, and she suffered brain stem damage leaving her paralyzed and with short-term memory loss (Brozan 1988). At the time of the accident, Sharon was 27 years old and had lived with her partner, Karen Thompson, for four years in a home they had bought together (Brozan 1988). Sharon and Karen had exchanged rings in a private commitment ceremony, but they had not told their parents about their relationship (Brozan 1988). After the accident, Karen told Sharon's parents that she and Sharon were partners, but the parents refused to believe Karen and accused her of lying (Brozan 1988). When Karen petitioned the local probate court to be appointed Sharon's guardian in 1984, Sharon's father cross-petitioned, and the court declared Sharon incapacitated and appointed Sharon's father as her guardian (*In re Guardianship of Kowalski* 1986). As soon as he was appointed guardian, Sharon's father terminated Karen's visitation rights (Brozan 1989).

Karen appealed to the Minnesota Court of Appeals, but the appellate court upheld the probate court's decision (*In re Guardianship of Kowalski* 1986). The court found it simply incredible that a daughter would not tell her parents that she was gay and, therefore, refused to believe that Sharon and Karen were partners. It concluded:

> The relationship between Sharon Kowalski and Karen Thompson is uncertain. They had been roommates for four years prior to the accident, had exchanged rings, and had named each other as beneficiary in their life insurance policies. Prior to the accident, Sharon had closed their joint bank account and had also told her sister she was considering moving to Colorado or moving home and that Karen Thompson was becoming very possessive. Karen Thompson claims a lesbian relationship with Sharon Kowalski. Sharon never told her family of such a relationship or admitted it prior to the accident (*In re Guardianship of Kowalski* 1986).

Rolling out the sexual predator stereotype, a doctor who testified for Sharon's parents warned the court that "visits by Karen Thompson ... would expose Sharon Kowalski to a high risk of sexual abuse" (Brozan 1988). It was unclear whether the court agreed with this assertion, but it disallowed visits from Karen on the grounds that they were contrary to the "quietude" that was an essential part of Sharon's treatment (*In re Guardianship of Kowalski* 1986). As a result of the court order, Karen was not permitted to visit or speak with Sharon for three and a half years (Brozan 1988). Karen's visitation privileges were eventually restored in 1989, but it took Karen two more years to be appointed as Sharon's guardian, notwithstanding the fact that Sharon could express her desire to live with Karen through the use of a "speak board" (Brozan 1989).

By the time of the final court proceedings in 1991, Sharon's case had become a national cause célèbre for the gay and lesbian civil rights movement and the disability movement. After seven years of litigation, a Minnesota appellate court finally found, consistent with Minnesota law, that Sharon had sufficient capacity to express her wish to name Karen as her guardian (*In re Guardianship of Kowalski* 1991). The court ruled that "all the medical testimony established that Sharon has the capacity reliably to express a preference in this case, and she has clearly chosen to return home with [Karen] if possible" (*In re Guardianship of Kowalski* 1991: 797). As Karen's lawyer explained, "Sharon doesn't have the short-term memory to remember what happened an hour ago, but she does remember Karen and the past, and that she is a lesbian" (Lewin 1991).

Hyper-Sexualized Homosexuals and the Identity Model

The Culture Wars of the 1990s produced a new stereotype of gay men as rapacious sexual animals who engage in kinky sex with countless anonymous partners (Herman: 1997: 80). Contemporary anti-gay rhetoric continues to cast gay men and lesbians primarily in sexual terms and conservative organizations with anti-gay platforms seem to take great relish in cataloguing the different types of sexual acts practiced by homosexuals, always against the backdrop of the health risks associated with sexually transmitted diseases. Their goal is to expose homosexuality as a disease-ridden and debauched lifestyle, thereby undermining arguments in favor of marriage equality and equal parenting rights. As Didi Herman explains, this hypersexual hypermasculine image has displaced the traditional cross-gendered stereotype of the effeminate male homosexual who is now represented as a form of "masculinity out of control ... aggressive, powerful, and unrestrained" (Herman 1997: 80). Much of this sort of anti-gay propaganda treats lesbians as an afterthought. Although lesbians are sometimes portrayed as exhibiting unbridled sexuality, the fit has not been perfect given the constraints of gender (Herman 1997: 100). More often, lesbian relationships are portrayed as violent and abusive, and lesbians are cast as both the victims and perpetrators of rape and domestic violence (Herman 1997: 100).

It is clearly difficult, if not impossible, to reconcile this view of homosexuality with the notion of the de-sexualized senior, but both stereotypes have something in common in that they both miscalculate the relative importance of sexuality. The de-sexualized senior greatly underestimates the role of sexuality across the lifespan, whereas the hyper-sexualized homosexual greatly overestimates the role of sexuality in the performance of gay and lesbian identity. In both instances, the weight assigned to sexuality obscures and inhibits the appreciation of the individual. Sexuality is an essential feature of gay and lesbian identity, and its denial can work to silence identity. However, sexuality alone is not sufficient to express the depth and complexity of gay and lesbian lives.

Merely revealing the fallacy of the de-sexualized senior and affirming the right of seniors to express their sexuality would not fully address the concerns of gay and lesbian elders because sexuality is only one aspect of gay and lesbian identity. Being gay or lesbian involves more than a non-normative libidinal object choice. When gay and lesbian elders retreat to the closet, they are not necessarily giving up sex. They are giving up the ability to be open and honest about a host of facets about their lives and relationships because the social meaning of homosexuality permeates even the most mundane aspects of an individual's life.

The contemporary pro-gay model of homosexuality reflects this understanding of sexual orientation as a master status – a fundamental and defining feature of an individual's identity. Following the lead of the sexologists and the psychoanalytic model of homosexuality, the contemporary identity model of homosexuality accepts the view that a homosexual is a distinct and identifiable type of individual. It then throws these two previous understandings of homosexuality on their heads by declaring that homosexuality is a positive attribute. It asserts that sexual orientation is an immutable, unchosen, benign characteristic that should be the source of pride and not shame.

This well-defined gay and lesbian identity emerged during the last quarter of the 20th century after the initial burst of liberationist fervor following Stonewall (Jagose 1996: 61). Similar to existing minority or ethnic identity models, the so-called identity model of homosexuality enjoys broad support among gay men and lesbians and has produced a vibrant gay and lesbian culture (E. Stein 2001). Studies suggest that gay and lesbian elders, however, may be less likely to embrace the identity model and identify as gay or lesbian than younger gay men and lesbians. That being said, the identity model remains a useful way to understand the contemporary burdens of the closet.

The closet does not demand celibacy – it demands silence. The silence surrounding the lives of gay and lesbian elders makes it exceedingly difficult to identify their needs and take steps to remedy their social isolation. The silence of the closet also exacts a heavy toll on elders as they face the vulnerabilities that come with aging. In a recent *New York Times* article, Dr. Melinda Lantz, chief of geriatric psychiatry at Beth Israel Medical Center in New York, explained that "there is something special about having to hide this part of your identity at a time when your entire identity is threatened" (Gross 2007). She notes that closeted seniors face "a faster pathway to depression, failure to thrive and even premature death" (Gross 2007). The pressure to remain closeted is particularly acute in institutional settings with congregate living facilities such as nursing homes. A 2000 advocacy study on gay and lesbian elders explains the demands of conformity that exist in these settings:

> As LGBT old people enter assisted living situations, nursing homes, independent elderly housing, or retirement communities, they are often presumed heterosexual and may feel the need to go back into the closet; often their long-term relationships are devalued and not recognized. Even if they have lived openly in the past, they may suddenly find themselves in situations where disclosing their sexual orientation makes them vulnerable to discrimination or even abuse. The lack of sensitivity to sexual orientation in housing and supportive care programs for elders often places LGBT elders in vulnerable and uncomfortable circumstances (Cahill, South and Spade 2000: 53).

In order to successfully manage the closet, gay and lesbian elders have to redact many important details of their lives and choose their memories carefully. Denied the opportunity to retell stories and revisit past events, the resulting isolation can literally leave gay and lesbian elders alone with their memories. Some gay and lesbian elders report that they create an alternate set of memories to share with others where a same-sex partner might become a brother or simply a "best friend" (Gross 2007). Certain stories regarding gay-specific rites of passage, such as the first time the elder "knew" or the first time the elder ventured into a gay bar, would not be suitable for retelling even with extensive editing. If the elder still lives with a romantic partner, then the partners must present as roommates or best friends or perhaps cousins. They have to monitor their comments to each other and guard against any inappropriate signs of affection or familiarity. If a closeted elder has to open up his or her home to health-care workers or lives in congregate housing, then all of the elder's pictures, books, music, and life's souvenirs have to be evaluated to determine whether they might raise suspicion. Closeted elders have to banish from their speech any campy humor, gay cultural references, and stereotypical gestures. Given the persistent conflation of homosexuality with cross-gender performance, closeted elders might even avoid certain gender "inappropriate" interests, such as musical theater for men or sports for women. In short, being in the closet requires intense information management and constant vigilance regarding the facts of one's life and one's place in the world because being a homosexual involves more than sex.

Chapter 5
Ageism Within the Gay and Lesbian Community

Ageism within the gay and lesbian community compounds the isolation experienced by gay and lesbian elders, who are already marginalized by homophobia, and further decreases their chances for successful aging. As explained in Chapter 3, one of the main challenges faced by gay and lesbian elders is the absence of an intergenerational support system because they are often estranged from their family of origin and chosen families are typically comprised of individuals who are in the same age cohort. The absence of cross-generational chosen families is partly the result of the strong strain of ageism that runs through the youth-conscious gay and lesbian community, but studies also indicate that, over the years, gay and lesbian elders may have been reluctant to pursue intergenerational relationships partly due to the internalized fear of being perceived as a sexual predator.

The focus on youth may explain why the contemporary movement for gay and lesbian equality has largely been silent regarding issues of particular concern to gay and lesbian elders, and instead has championed issues that posit a young, white, heteronormative, and predominantly male subject – marriage equality, employment non-discrimination protections, and the repeal of DADT. It may also provide an explanation as to why the gay and lesbian community has not responded to the current crisis in aging faced by gay and lesbian elders in the same way it did to the first wave of the HIV/AIDS epidemic in the 1980s. Despite the fact that there are between 1.6 and 2.4 million gay and lesbian elders, the mainstream gay and lesbian advocacy organizations have only recently added aging concerns to their agendas, and the gay and lesbian community has not responded with an outpouring of community time and resources to alleviate the isolation of today's gay and lesbian elders.

Age Cohorts and Cross-Generational Relations

Historically, intergenerational relationships have not been common in the gay and lesbian community. Andrew J. Hostetler notes that "[a]ge-related divisions are exacerbated by the nature of inter-generational contacts in the gay community, which do not typically follow the heterosexual, extended-family pattern but rather involve strangers and non-kin interacting in bars and similar venues" (Hostetler 2003: 159). Existing research on age cohorts within the gay community focuses almost exclusively on the divisions that exist between youth and those in middle age. This emphasis on youth and the disregard for older gay men and lesbians is symptomatic of the ageism that is prevalent in the gay and lesbian community. Quentin Crisp, the author of *A Naked Civil Servant* and renowned raconteur, explained: "For gay men, they are indeed not long – the days of wine and roses ... [a]s soon as one can no longer be described as a boy, one's social and sexual life is finished" (in Berger 1982: xi).

Researchers who study age cohorts within the gay and lesbian community suggest that during the post-Stonewall period the rapid change in the status of gay men and lesbians has resulted in a fractured gay and lesbian community that is divided by specific social and political experiences into highly compressed generations (Russell and Bohan 2005: 2–3). Members of these abbreviated generations have difficulty relating to individuals who do not share their common social and political experiences (Russell and Bohan 2005). Thus, for gay men and lesbians, a generation "may span only a few years" (Russell and Bohan 2005: 3). For example, the arrival of HIV/AIDS provides a stark dividing line between post-Stonewall generations. There is the natural division between those gay men who came of age before safer sex and those who have never known sexuality without the danger of a life-threatening disease. However, even among the post-HIV/AIDS age cohort, there is another very important distinction. The first post-HIV/AIDS age cohort who came of age between the early 1980s and the early 1990s did so during a fearful time before the advent of protease inhibitors when men older than 30 were considered synonymous with disease (Gorman and Nelson 2003: 77). Conversely, the turn-of-the-century generation came of age at a time of optimism with openly gay celebrities and same-sex marriage announcements in *The New York Times*. For many in this later generation, HIV/AIDS is now viewed as an undesirable but manageable chronic disease (Buchanan 2006).

Studies indicate that conditions for gay men and lesbians have changed so rapidly that the turn-of-the-century age cohort has difficulty relating to the more classic coming-out stories of gay and lesbian isolation and suffering (Russell and Bohan 2005: 5–6). Today, there are gay and lesbian-oriented cable networks, gay and lesbian characters on television, and even gay and lesbian cruises. When talk show host Ellen DeGeneres legally married her long-time girlfriend, the actress Portia DeRossi, their wedding was splashed on the front page of *People* magazine (Jordan 2008) and covered in the entertainment press as respectfully as any other celebrity marriage. With widespread media coverage of gay and lesbian issues, it is nearly inconceivable that a young person struggling with same-sex attraction in 2010 would for one moment worry that he or she is "the only one." They might have difficulty coming to terms with the remaining religious or moral objections to homosexuality, but they would know that they are not alone.

One study on the generation gap between young and middle-aged gay men and lesbians reports that the youth age cohort resents what they perceive to be a "privileging of suffering" on the part of older generations of gay men and lesbians

(Russell and Bohan 2005: 5–6). There is more than a hint of irony in this finding because the ease with which many in the turn-of-the-century generation have been able to come to terms with their sexuality is a direct result of the outreach efforts to improve conditions for gay and lesbian youth that were fueled by the very stories that the younger generation is unable to comprehend. Many older gay men and lesbians experienced horrific childhoods marked by bullying, physical violence, and isolation. These accounts, along with statistics indicating that gay and lesbian youth are at a higher risk of suicide and are more likely to drop out of school, led organizations such as the Gay Lesbian and Straight Education Network (GLSSEN) to advocate for anti-bullying laws, Gay/Straight Alliances (GSA), and youth-oriented activities such as alternative proms. High-profile court cases, such as *Nabozny v. Podlesny* (1996), have helped secure the right of public school students to be free from anti-gay harassment and bullying. Other federal court cases, such as *East High Gay/Straight Alliance v. Board of Education of Salt Lake City School Dist.* (1999), have recognized the right of public high school students under the federal Equal Access Act to organize GSAs in their schools. Consistent with the emphasis on youth within the gay and lesbian community, however, similar advocacy resources have not been directed toward improving the conditions of gay and lesbian elders.

Given that the post-Stonewall generations have difficulty relating to each other, it is not surprising that there has been so little outreach to the pre-Stonewall generation. For many years, Services & Advocacy for Gay, Lesbian, Bisexual, and Transgender Elders (SAGE) was one of the few gay and lesbian organizations that prioritized issues related to aging. SAGE was founded in 1978 as Senior Action in a Gay Environment, and it provides a wide range of services for LGBT elders. Its website states that "SAGE works with LGBT elders to address and overcome the challenges of discrimination in senior service settings, while also being an essential component in the creation of informal caregiving support, and development of new 'family' networks." The large LGBT advocacy organizations, such as the Human Rights Campaign, the National Gay and Lesbian Task Force, and the National Center for Lesbian Rights have added "aging" to their list of action issues, but only recently.

The few commentators who have addressed the failure of the gay and lesbian community to prioritize the needs of its elders have all pointed to persistent ageism within the community as the primary cause. The gay and lesbian community, especially the gay male community, is commonly described as a youth culture. Lesbians generally do not report the same degree of anxiety with respect to aging, and studies suggest that ageism is not as great a problem within the women's community (Cahill, South and Spade 2000: 16). Although researchers may have debunked the stereotype of the aging homosexual, it continues to resonate in some quarters of the gay (male) community. Hostetler notes, "For many gay men, the spectacle of an older gay man in a gay bar provides a cautionary tale about developmental failure" (Hostetler 2003: 160). Ageism also colors who qualifies as "old" in the gay community. For example, Berger's 1982 book, *Gay and Gray*, defined "older" gay men as those who were at least 40 years of age. Only 11 percent of the Berger's relatively small sample of 112 participants were age 70 or older (Berger 1982). In the forward of Berger's book (1982), Quentin Crisp explained:

> I have sat with groups of middle-aged gay men who are discussing a guest who had not yet arrived at some gathering. Such phrases as, "mind you, he used to be sensational" fell from their haggard lips. When the individual in question arrived, he turned out not to be some stooping, shuffling person. He was a young man of about twenty-eight years of age but he could no longer be described as 'a boy' (in Berger 1982: xi).

The phenomenon so colorfully described by Crisp is what some researchers have described as "accelerated aging" (De Vries and Blando 2004: 20). The term does not refer to actual aging but rather to an individual's self-assessment of his relative age (Bennett and Thompson 1991). In other words, there is some evidence to suggest that gay men (and lesbians to some extent) consider themselves "old" at an earlier age than their non-gay peers (De Vries and Blando 2004: 20).

As mentioned earlier, the current crisis in aging experienced by gay and lesbian elders has strong parallels to the first wave of the HIV/AIDS epidemic, when homophobia and ignorance concerning the disease needlessly compounded the anguish and suffering of those struggling with HIV/AIDS (National Gay and Lesbian Task Force 2006: 5). Gay and lesbian elders, however, have not benefited from the type of mass community outreach that began during the mid-1980s and brought a much-needed level of compassion and caring to a tragic time. The wide spectrum of services provided by the gay and lesbian community and its allies during the first wave of the HIV/AIDS epidemic corresponds to many of the needs presented by today's gay and lesbian elders. AIDS/HIV buddy programs provided companionship. Community volunteers delivered hot meals, walked dogs, catalogued art works, and wrote wills. The gay and lesbian community raised money for research, educated policy-makers and the public, challenged the government and pharmaceutical companies, and otherwise humanized the face of a deadly epidemic.

Unlike the HIV/AIDS epidemic, age segregation within the gay and lesbian community operates to keep the current crisis out of sight. The primacy of the gay bar as a historically important meeting place and epicenter of community reinforces the preference for youth. In a community where 20-something gay men consider 30-something gay men to be irrelevant, getting either group to take an interest in the lives and well-being of octogenarians presents an obvious challenge. The age-segregated nature of the gay and lesbian community and the absence of elder gay role models means that gay men and lesbians do not have the benefit of seeing examples of successful gay and lesbian aging.

The post-Stonewall generations have fought hard for greater openness and protections from harassment and violence, but many of the most vulnerable members of their community currently live in silence and increasing isolation.

One way to bridge this isolation is to facilitate inter-generational dialogue, which would also benefit members of the post-Stonewall generations. Kimmel notes that such contact "is important because most lesbians, gay men, and bisexuals do not have role models for aging within their family of origin, as most heterosexuals do" (Kimmel 2004: 265). Gay and lesbian elders can provide a different and valuable perspective based on experience – what gerontologists refer to as "wisdom" (Russell and Bohan 2005: 4). To this end, a number of LGBT organizations have established local visitor programs and chore assistance networks similar to the early HIV/AIDS support efforts. Philadelphia's "Connecting Generations" program, run out of the William Way Center, offers inter-generational visiting programs and chore assistance to homebound LGBT older adults (Grant 2010: 97). In Brooklyn, New York, the GRIOT Circle's "Buddy to Buddy" program matches homebound elders of color with older volunteers to make sure that the elder is able to maintain a connection to the broader gay and lesbian community (Grant 2010: 97).

Internalized Fear of the Predatory Homosexual

Ageism most commonly refers to a set of beliefs and attitudes that devalue older people and the aging process. A variation on this theme has been reported in the case of gay and lesbian elders who have internalized the stereotype of the predatory homosexual and report hesitation in pursuing inter-generational relationships for fear of being perceived as a sexual predator (Russell and Bohan 2005: 1). As explained in Chapter 2, the notion of the predatory homosexual figured prominently in the theory of homosexuality developed by the American Freudians and precipitated the enactment of the sexual psychopath laws, as well as other laws restricting the access of homosexuals to children (Terry 1999: 272). The predatory older homosexual was essential to the homosexual lifecycle that began when a young person was seduced and initiated into the fold by an older homosexual predator. The youth would then mature into a predator, who would go on to prey on youth and the cycle would continue.

The resilience of this discredited stereotype underscores the importance of understanding the historical background of the pre-Stonewall period. It directly impacted the lives of members of the pre-Stonewall generation and the way they structured their relationships. It also continues to animate many contemporary anti-gay attitudes and policies. Until relatively recently, the law aggressively policed the interactions between gay and lesbian individuals and young people and imposed severe legal disabilities on gay and lesbian individuals in areas such as education, custody, and adoption. Despite considerable legal progress in all three areas, the notion of the homosexual-as-pedophile remains a staple of anti-gay political rhetoric and continues to have currency in the popular understanding of homosexuality, as well as in certain areas of the law and public policy.

Some of the earliest clashes in the post-Stonewall culture wars involved the influence of homosexuals on children, such as the 1977 "Save Our Children" crusade discussed in Chapter 2 and the unsuccessful 1978 California ballot measure known as the Briggs initiative that would have banned homosexual public schoolteachers (Eskridge 1999: 131). Today, the notion that gay men and lesbians will push a "gay agenda" on schoolchildren continues to loom large in the public debate regarding marriage equality. In 2009, Maine voters approved a ballot initiative that repealed marriage equality passed by the legislature (Sacchetti 2009). The opponents of marriage equality argued that the law authorizing same-sex marriage would force the elementary public schools to teach "homosexual marriage" (Sacchetti 2009). In a television advertisement titled "Everything to Do with Schools," anxious parents and educators warned that second-graders would be taught that "boys could marry other boys" (Everything to Do with Schools 2009). The Maine state attorney general felt compelled to respond to the ad and issued an advisory opinion stating that the marriage legislation would not mandate changes in the public school curriculum, but this did not quell voters' fears (Vick 2009).

In 2008, opponents of Proposition 8 in California argued that marriage equality would harm children. Using the slippery-slope argument popularized by Anita Bryant in the 1970s, the Traditional Family Coalition warned in a fundraising letter that, after securing the right to marry, gay activists would fight to "legalize having sex with children" (Tam 2008). The letter warned that unless the voters passed Proposition 8: "Every child, when growing up, would fantasize marrying someone of the same sex. More children would become homosexuals. Even if our children is [sic] safe, our grandchildren may not. What about our children's grandchildren?" (Tam 2008). The plaintiffs in *Perry v. Schwarzenegger* submitted Tam's letter with their trial brief as evidence that the passage of Proposition 8 was motivated by animus and, therefore, violates both the due process and equal protection clauses of the U.S. Constitution (Plaintiff's Trial Brief 2009).

During the pre-Stonewall era, efforts to regulate the influence of homosexuality in education focused almost exclusively on removing teachers. Today, the state-sponsored witch hunts endorsed by the Johns Committee are over, but gay and lesbians teachers can still be fired from their jobs on account of their sexual orientation in a majority of jurisdictions. The flashpoint in public education, however, has moved to the student level. As the age of coming out has steadily decreased, the front line in the education culture wars is now manned by high school and middle school students fighting to establish GSAs or to bring a same-sex partner to the prom.

The continuing cultural anxieties regarding the belief that gay men and lesbians prey on children were exemplified by the 2000 U.S. Supreme Court case *Boy Scouts of America v. Dale*. It provides an excellent example of how quickly anxieties can flare when homosexuals are in close proximity to children (*Boy Scouts v. Dale* 2000). In this appeal, the Boy Scouts of America challenged a ruling by the New Jersey Supreme Court that held that the New Jersey Law Against Discrimination (LAD) required the Boy Scouts to reinstate the openly gay Assistant Scoutmaster James Dale (*Dale v. Boy Scouts* 1999). The Boy

Scouts argued that the ruling violated its First Amendment associational freedoms (*Boy Scouts v. Dale* 2000).

Although the Boy Scouts never raised the concern of pedophilia directly, its pleadings offered a number of snapshots of young boys confiding in their Scoutmasters, often on overnight campouts. The Boy Scouts asserted that these "close personal relationships" involved the "transmission and cultivation of shared ideals and beliefs" that sometimes took place "far from the public gaze" (Brief for Petitioners 1999: 39). As the Boy Scouts explained, "[w]hen an 11 year-old boy away from home for the first time becomes afraid at night, skins his knee, or forgets his sleeping bag, he looks to his Scoutmaster for support" (Brief for Petitioners 1999: 41).

Amici briefs submitted by anti-gay conservative organizations such as FRC and Concerned Women for America addressed the pedophile risk directly (Brief of Amicus Curiae FRC 1999: 21-30, Brief of Amicus Curiae Concerned Women for America 1999). The FRC contended that "homosexuals account for less than 2 percent of the population, [but] ... constitute about a third of child molesters"[1] (Brief of Amicus Curiae FRC 1999: 23). After citing questionable social science research and misconstruing other research, the FRC concluded that the Boy Scouts' policy against homosexuals was part of the organization's "compelling duty to ... provide[] the greatest protection to the Scouts" (Brief of Amicus Curiae FRC 1999: 25). The FRC claimed that "the intimate association that exists between Scouts and Scout leaders has been exploited by hundreds of homosexual pedophiles to sexually abuse thousands of boys" (Brief of Amicus Curiae FRC 1999: 25–26). Ultimately, the U.S. Supreme Court decided in favor of the Boy Scouts, and the opinion did not mention pedophilia (*Boy Scouts v. Dale* 2000).

---

1   It is interesting to note that the FRC used a very conservative estimate of the number of "homosexuals" consistent with the controversy over counting discussed in Chapter 3.

Chapter 6

Homophobia and Heteronormativity among the Senior Community and Service Providers

Gay and lesbian elders express widespread fear that they will experience anti-gay bias and discrimination in the context of various senior settings, including senior centers and assisted living facilities. They are also extremely wary of encountering bias on the part of health-care and elder-care professionals. In order to avoid this perceived bias, gay and lesbian elders remain closeted in senior settings and in their dealings with service providers. As discussed in Chapter 4, the closet can exact a heavy cost on the individual level and create a barrier to effective health care. The desire to remain closeted can also cause gay and lesbian elders to underutilize essential aging resources, thereby increasing the likelihood for self-neglect and social isolation. Moreover, living life in the closet is directly contrary to the leading developmental theory of successful gay and lesbian aging (Friend 1991).

Existing research regarding homophobia and discrimination on the part of senior organizations, aging agencies, and medical and elder-care providers strongly suggests that the fears that can lead gay and lesbian elders to retreat to the closet are not misplaced. Moreover, their fears seem to be broadly shared by the younger post-Stonewall gay and lesbian Baby Boomers who also express greater anxiety about growing older than their non-gay peers. Although the last several years have seen an increased willingness on the part of mainstream senior advocacy organizations to embrace gay and lesbian concerns, there remains much to be done to improve the visibility of gay and lesbian elders and counteract their tendency toward isolation.

The Senior Community and the Non-Gay Pre-Stonewall Generation

The senior community is easily one of the most powerful constituent groups in the United States, but, until the last several years, it has not been eager to address the needs of gay and lesbian elders. Whereas the movement for gay and lesbian equality remains controversial, the agenda pressed by the senior community is decidedly mainstream and all-American. Politicians on both sides of the aisle actively court the reliable senior vote. In terms of political clout, the influence of senior voters will likely continue to grow as the population ages. In 1964, 14.9 percent of all voters in the presidential election were aged 65 or older, whereas in 2002, 23.2 percent of all voters in the presidential election were 65 or older (Sutherland 2004).

The 2005 White House Conference on Aging (WHCoA) presents an excellent example of how difficult it has been to secure a place at the table for gay and lesbian aging advocates. Under the Older Americans Act (OAA), the executive office of the president is charged with convening a White House Conference on Aging every ten years, the purpose of which is to provide input and guidance on aging policy. As required by the OAA, delegates to the conference are chosen by governors, members of Congress, and tribal authorities. Out of the approximately 1,200 delegates who attended the 2005 conference, only one delegate had been invited to represent a gay or lesbian organization. LGBT delegates and their allies argued that the WHCoA's policy committee used heavy-handed procedures to squelch any discussion of the needs of gay and lesbian elders, so they organized an alternative conference, called Make Room for All, in order to press their case (National Gay and Lesbian Task Force 2006). In the end, WHCoA 2005 included only one reference to sexual orientation in the 50 resolutions that were submitted to the president (White House Conference on Aging 2005). Sexual orientation was added to one of the implementation strategies under Resolution 34 that called for the reduction of "healthcare disparities among minorities" (White House Conference on Aging 2005: 27). Specifically, the implementation strategy recommended expanding the definition of "minority populations" to include "gays, lesbians, bisexuals, and transgenders" (White House Conference on Aging 2005: 115).

Although this was a relatively minor nod in the direction of gay and lesbian elders, the counter summit raised awareness of the issue within the aging community. Since WHCoA 2005, there has been an increasing willingness on the part of senior organizations, most notably AARP, to advance the concerns of gay and lesbian elders. For example, in 2007, the AARP launched its "Divided We Fail" initiative to support broad-based health-care reform, and it enlisted the support of the Human Rights Campaign and the National Gay and Lesbian Task Force. In 2008, AARP co-sponsored SAGE's fourth conference on aging, It's About Time: LGBT Aging in a Changing World. In addition, sexual orientation is now one of the minority categories addressed by AARP's Office of Diversity and Inclusion, and SAGE has praised the AARP as "being ahead of most straight seniors' organizations" (Friedman 2008). In 2010, the chief operating officer of AARP wrote a forward for a comprehensive advocacy report produced by SAGE, titled Improving the Lives of LGBT Older Adults (in SAGE 2010).

One explanation for the long-standing reluctance of mainstream senior organizations to endorse gay and lesbian issues is that, as an age cohort, non-gay seniors tend to view homosexuality in an unfavorable light. As noted in Chapter 3, older Americans are more likely to have negative opinions about gay men and lesbians. It is not surprising that seniors report a higher incidence of homophobia than other age groups, given that seniors are also members of the pre-Stonewall generation who came of age and developed their views on homosexuality when it was pathologized and criminalized (Cahill, South and Spade 2000: 17). A national survey by the Kaiser Family Foundation revealed stark differences between the attitudes toward homosexuality held by young people and those held by individuals age 65 and older (Kaiser Foundation 2001). When asked whether homosexuality was morally wrong, 47 percent of the 65-and-older respondents said that they "completely agreed" and another 10 percent "somewhat agreed" (Kaiser Foundation 2001). The percentage went down considerably among 18- to 29-year-olds, where only 30 percent "completely agreed" that homosexuality was morally wrong and an additional 14 percent somewhat agreed (Kaiser Foundation 2001). Splits between the age cohorts were also seen with respect to various pro-gay policy proposals, such as same-sex marriage and equal adoption rights (Kaiser Foundation 2001). Among the respondents age 65 and older, only 25 percent thought that gay men and lesbians should be able to adopt, whereas 55 percent of the respondents aged 18–29 were in favor of equal adoption rights (Kaiser Foundation 2001). Similarly, only 25 percent of the senior respondents believed that gay men and lesbians should be able to marry a same-sex partner, whereas 60 percent of the young people approved of same-sex marriage (Kaiser Foundation 2001).

The extent of anti-gay sentiment among non-gay elders can influence the policies of senior action organizations and other aging bodies, but it can also impact gay and lesbian elders on an individual basis. For example, gay or lesbian elders may feel uncomfortable or unsafe at a senior center or an assisted living facility where other seniors are openly disapproving. In 2007, *The New York Times* reported the case of Gloria Donadello, who experienced painful shunning at her assisted living facility when she came out to the other residents, whom she had considered her friends, and asked them to stop making anti-gay remarks (Gross 2007). As a result of the shunning, Gloria went into a deep depression and eventually had to move (Gross 2007). She later told the *Times* that "it was a choice between life and death" (Gross 2007). Gloria was lucky because she had the resources and the ability to move. Other seniors are not as fortunate, such as the case of the elderly gay man, discussed in Chapter 10, who was transferred to the memory ward because the other residents objected to his sexual orientation (Gross 2007). Confined with residents suffering from severe disabilities or dementia, the gay elder eventually hanged himself (Gross 2007).

The potential for peer-on-peer harassment can cause gay and lesbian elders to remain closeted and to underutilize senior services. It can also increase their feelings of vulnerability and isolation in assisted living facilities and other senior housing options. As discussed in Chapter 10, one way to address this problem is through the adoption of anti-bullying policies similar to those adopted by schools to protect LGBT students.

Elder-Care and Health-Care Professionals

Gay and lesbian elders are deeply fearful that medical and elder-care professionals will discriminate against them or abuse them on account of their sexual orientation. When viewed in conjunction with the potential for peer-on-peer harassment, it is easy to see how gay and lesbian elders can feel friendless and alone in an elder-care setting. It also explains how gay and lesbian elders can view the closet quite literally as a "survival" tactic (Starkey 2008). At the age of 61, and in declining health, Ryan Meyer of Long Beach, New York, told *Newsday* that he was dreading the prospect of becoming dependent on strangers and would likely become increasingly closeted as he grew older (Starkey 2008). Ryan explained, "It is one thing to be openly out walking around on my two feet, but when you are very vulnerable and you know that there is a prejudiced world, it can be very terrifying" (Starkey 2008).

The fact that at age 61 Ryan was already worried about whether the level of care he will receive would be compromised by homophobia reflects a disturbing finding – Baby Boomers share the fears expressed by gay and lesbian elders with respect to the ability of service providers to care for them in an unbiased manner as they age. In 2006, a national survey of 1,000 self-identified gay and lesbian Baby Boomers aged 40 to 61 showed a deep concern among these post-Stonewall Boomers that they will be subject to discrimination on account of their sexual orientation or gender identity as they age (Metlife 2006). According to the Metlife Boomer survey, even the first post-Stonewall generation to benefit from the increased gay and lesbian visibility remains fearful of encountering discrimination and homophobia in senior settings and on the part of service providers. A large percentage of the Boomers surveyed anticipate that as they age they will be treated poorly on account of their sexual identity. This expectation might explain why gay and lesbian Boomers are more fearful of growing older than are their non-gay peers. Forty-one percent of gay and lesbian Boomers reported that they were worried about growing older, whereas, in an earlier study, only 33 percent of non-gay Boomers reported concern over aging (Metlife 2006: 13).

In identifying their "greatest concerns about aging," 32 percent of the gay men and 28 percent of the lesbians cited "discrimination due to their sexual orientation" (Metlife 2006: 14). One in five responded that their greatest fear was dying alone, and 18 percent indicated that anti-gay discrimination or prejudice was their number one fear (Metlife 2006: 14). For individuals who were in relationships, the fear of discrimination increased considerably (Metlife 2006: 14). A full 33 percent of the respondents who were in relationships listed fear of discrimination as their primary concern, suggesting they are worried about the legal fragility of their partnerships, as discussed in greater detail in Chapter 8 (Metlife 2006: 14). Nineteen percent reported that they have "little or no confidence that medical personnel will treat them with dignity and respect as LGBT people in old age" (Metlife 2006: 14). This lack of confidence in the medical profession was most pronounced among lesbians, with 12 percent of the lesbians surveyed responding that they have *absolutely no* confidence in the medical profession (Metlife 2006: 14).

The existing research regarding homophobia and discrimination by senior organizations, aging agencies, and elder-care providers strongly suggests that the fears of elder, as well as older, gay men and lesbians are not unfounded. Anecdotal evidence confirmed by some limited survey data points to widespread discriminatory attitudes and practices. As Grant concludes, "Although formal survey data in this area is scarce, the anecdotal evidence is overwhelming" (Grant 2010: 47). Existing studies show that health-care and elder-care providers can be, at best, ignorant of the needs of gay and lesbian elders and, at worst, openly hostile to them. Moreover, there is some indication that elder-care service providers may actually be "more intolerant" of gay men and lesbians and "more heterosexist" than the general medical profession (Kimmel et al. 2006: 12).

A 2001 study conducted by Department of Health and Human Services confirmed that gay and lesbian elders under-utilize federally funded senior services (King and Kimmel 2006: 266). In the United States, federal aging policy is coordinated by the Agency on Aging (AoA) that is located in HHS. Created in 1965 by the Older Americans Act (OAA), the AoA oversees the implementation of most aspects of the OAA, along with the bulk of its $2 billion plus annual appropriation. The OAA authorizes the establishment of a nationwide aging network comprised of state and local agencies that provide an array of social services to older Americans. Over 650 regional area agencies for aging (AAAs) provide a range of services that are designed to make it possible for elders to remain in their homes and communities and "age in place." AAAs have primary responsibility for administering coordinating services that include meals and nutritional support, in-home care, transportation, day care, and even emergency home repair.

According to the 2001 HHS study, gay and lesbian elders are only 20 percent as likely as their non-gay peers to take advantage of the available aging services provided through AAAs, as well as other entitlements such as housing assistance and food stamps (King and Kimmel 2006: 266). As late as 1994, nearly half of the AAAs surveyed reported that gay men and lesbians would not be welcome at the senior centers in their areas if their sexual orientation were known and 94 percent of the AAAs did not provide gay-specific programming (Cahill, South, and Spade 2000: 40). Larger metropolitan areas increasingly have resources specifically for gay and lesbian seniors that are provided by LGBT organizations, but gay and lesbian elders may be unable or unwilling to access the services because many members of the pre-Stonewall generation have little contact with gay and lesbian organizations and may be reluctant to initiate such contact.

The failure of gay and lesbian elders to access essential services can lead to what gerontologists refer to as "self-neglect," which, according to the National Center for Elder Abuse, is the most commonly reported type of elder abuse (National Center for Elder Abuse 2005). Almost one-third of all reported cases of elder abuse are cases of self-neglect, and for every case of elder abuse that is reported to the authorities, it is estimated that five cases go unreported (National Council for Elder Abuse 2005). The failure of gay and lesbian elders to utilize existing support services also increases the likelihood that an elder will experience social isolation. Given the potential for peer-on-peer harassment and the demands of the closet, gay and lesbian elders are especially fearful of congregate living facilities and express a clear desire to age in place (Orel 2006: 233). Gay and lesbian elders who attempt to age in place are already disadvantaged because they often lack a cross-generational support network. However, this disadvantage is compounded when they underutilize the federally funded services that are specifically designed to help individuals age in the community, such as allowances for home health care or meal delivery.

Home health-care workers directly threaten the privacy of closeted gay and lesbian elders because a home health-care aide has to enter the one place where closeted elders are able to express themselves and display identifiably gay or lesbian books, photographs, and other memorabilia. As explained in Chapter 4, a visit from a home health-care worker requires a closeted elder to "de-gay" the house or apartment, thereby forcing the elder into hiding in his or her own home. To avoid this and the threat of potential harassment or abuse, gay and lesbian elders who manage to "age in place" may be doing so alone and without crucial support services that are provided as a matter of federal aging policy. Those gay and lesbian elders who do utilize support services do so at the risk of exposing themselves to anti-gay bias. According to a survey by the Family Caregiving Alliance, 50 percent of the LGBT elders who received institutional care or who had *in-home* health care experienced discrimination and harassment on account of their sexual orientation or gender identity (San Francisco Human Rights Commission 2003: 15). In some instances, it seems that poor health and infirmity may force gay and lesbian elders to invite their potential abusers into their homes.

The fear that health-care professionals may be disapproving, or even overtly hostile, can keep gay and lesbian elders silent and closeted. Barker notes that older lesbians are "especially wary and fearful of health care and other service providers with their power to disrupt everyday life" (Barker 2003: 54). As a result, gay and lesbian elders will put off seeing a doctor and then remain closeted when they actually do see a doctor. The silence of the closet presents a serious barrier to receiving full and effective health care because when patients do not reveal their sexual orientation, the ability to provide appropriate health care is compromised. The Gay and Lesbian Medical Association (GLMA) explained the effect of the closet on medical care in *Healthy People 2010: Companion Document for Lesbian Gay, Bisexual Transgender Health* – a publication designed to complement an HHS initiative by the same name:

> LGBT persons face documented structural, financial, personal, and cultural
> barriers when attempting to access health-care services. These barriers tend to alter
> the individual's behavior and attitudes toward health-care services, if available,
> and probably adversely affect health outcomes. Personal and cultural barriers

to health have been well researched for LGBT populations. The results from multiple studies document provider bias as to LGBT people or patients. Findings also show that, perhaps in an effort to avoid this bias or because of internalized homophobia, LGBT patients frequently withhold personal information about their sexual orientation, gender identity, practices, and behavioral risks from their health-care providers. In addition, many health-care providers may be uncomfortable, reluctant, and under-trained to take sexual histories. These barriers are of concern for LGBT individuals and providers of health care, as barriers could result in LGBT people not seeking needed preventive screening tests and preventive interventions, or delaying seeking treatment for acute health conditions or exacerbation of chronic conditions.

As the GLMA report indicates, bias and homophobia on the part of medical professionals negatively impacts the delivery of health care. A 2008 report prepared by the New York City Public Advocate found that the seven health-care networks within the New York City Health and Hospitals Corporation were ill-equipped to address the health-care needs of LGBT patients. The report concluded that "LGBT individuals experience hostility and discrimination in care" and "concerns about homophobia and transphobia keep LGBT individuals from using healthcare services" (Public Advocate of the City of New York 2008).

As explained in Chapter 10, when a gay or lesbian elder encounters hostility or discrimination in care, it is more likely than not that the elder will have no legal recourse because the majority of states do not extend anti-discrimination protection on account of sexual orientation. In addition to instances of outright hostility and discrimination, unchallenged heteronormative assumptions can also negatively impact gay and lesbian elders. For example, residential facilities often prohibit unrelated individuals from living together (Cahill, South and Spade 2000: 54). Such a restriction is not an absolute ban on gay and lesbian elders, but it would exclude any same-sex couple who reside in the vast majority of states that do not provide any recognition for same-sex relationships. The policy also disadvantages members of a chosen family group who are not recognized as being "related" for legal purposes. Although siblings or cousins might be permitted to live together, a same-sex couple or two lifelong friends would not be permitted to live together because the relationship is not legally recognized. As discussed in greater detail in Chapter 10, cultural competency training could bring to light underlying heteronormative assumptions that may otherwise seem unremarkable. Cultural competency programs have been widely deployed to address barriers to access to health care that are caused by cultural differences, such as race and ethnicity.

Anti-Gay Bias and the Closet

Discrimination and heteronormative aging policies can present obvious barriers to access and cause gay and lesbian elders to underutilize senior resources.

However, gay and lesbian elders sometimes express fears that transcend concerns over disparate treatment or targeted slights or even anti-gay slurs. As discussed in Chapter 4, gay and lesbian elders are a vulnerable population, and the anti-gay bias they fear has the potential to manifest itself as anti-gay violence and abuse. To make matters worse, individuals who work with victims of elder abuse believe that gay and lesbian elders may actually be more prone to elder abuse than their non-gay peers because gay and lesbian elders are accustomed to being treated poorly (Grant 2010: 52). Moreover, closeted gay and lesbian elders are susceptible to threats of "outing," which represents a type of abuse specific to gay men and lesbians that is also seen in the context of same-sex domestic violence. Threats of disclosure can then be used by an abuser to keep an elder silent about abuse.

Unfortunately, there are no reliable statistics on the extent of gay and lesbian elder abuse. The National Coalition of Anti-Violence Program (NCAVP) compiles statistics on violence against LGBT individuals based on reports from slightly more than a dozen local organizations located in predominantly urban areas, but its records on gay and lesbian elder abuse are woefully inadequate because the age of the victims is one of the least often collected pieces of information. For 2008, 44 percent of the recorded cases failed to report the age of the victim (NCAVP 2009: 8). With respect to gay men and lesbians generally, a Kaiser Family Foundation study of 405 randomly selected gay men and lesbians found that they had experienced high levels of anti-gay discrimination and violence (Kaiser Foundation 2001). Seventy-four percent of the respondents reported that they had experienced prejudice or discrimination on account of their sexual orientation (Kaiser Foundation 2001). Thirty-two percent reported that they had been targeted for physical violence either against their person or their property, while 74 percent had experienced verbal abuse such as name-calling and homophobic slurs (Kaiser Foundation 2001). In addition, respondents expressed concern that they would experience violence in the future. A full 39 percent said that they were either very worried (31 percent) or somewhat worried (8 percent) that they would be "physically assaulted or attacked by someone who disliked gays" (Kaiser Foundation 2001).

The D'Augelli and Grossman study of 416 gay men and lesbians age 60 and older also found high levels of anti-gay victimization (D'Augelli and Grossman 2001). As discussed in Chapter 3, the study reported that 63 percent of the respondents had experienced verbal abuse (D'Augelli and Grossman 2001: 1016). Twenty-nine percent had been threatened with violence, and the same percentage had been threatened with "outing" (D'Augelli and Grossman 2001: 1016). Sixteen percent of the respondents had been physically assaulted on account of their sexual orientation (D'Augelli and Grossman 2001: 1016). Consistent with the figures for anti-gay violence generally, men were more likely to experience physical violence and, when they did, the attack was more likely to involve weapons (Balsam and D'Augelli 2006: 119). A significant percentage of the respondents were closeted in at least some facets of their lives, with only 38 percent responding that they were out to more than 75 percent of their acquaintances (D'Augelli and Grossman

2001: 1022). The study found that the earlier the respondents "came to terms with their sexual orientation by self-identification and by disclosure to others, the more victimization they recollected" (D'Augelli and Grossman 2001: 1021). The study concluded "It may be, then, that more victimization would have been reported had more of the older adults been open with others" (D'Augelli and Grossman 2001: 1022).

The fear of violence and abuse can keep gay and lesbian elders firmly in the closet and induce others to become more closeted. As previously noted, the closet makes it difficult to assess the needs of gay and lesbian seniors, increases the likelihood of social isolation, and carries a high emotional cost. It is also directly contrary to the developmental theory of successful gay and lesbian aging advanced by Dr. Richard Friend (1991). Since the declassification of homosexuality as a mental illness, there have been a number of efforts to delineate a gay-positive theory of identity formation. These efforts have primarily involved questions around coming out and have generally not paid much attention to the senior end of the life cycle. One constant among these models is the emphasis placed on being "out" – a view that coincides with the contemporary focus on pride and openness that was discussed in Chapter 1. Todd W. Rawls explains that, as a result, there has developed "a canonical position ... in the research literature that homosexuals, of all ages, who are more 'out,' open, and actively involved in gay community contexts will enjoy higher levels of mental well-being than those who are more 'closeted' and less involved" (Rawls 2004: 119).

Friend's theory of successful aging for gay men and lesbians posits that those elders who are most open and affirming about their sexual orientation will age the most successfully (Friend 1991). According to Friend, the gay and lesbian elders who have "managed heterosexism by reconstructing what it means to be gay or lesbian into something positive" will also be able to manage aging in a superior fashion (Friend 1991). In contrast, Friend warns that "passing" gay and lesbian elders who are closeted and distant from the gay and lesbian community would experience "heightened levels of anxiety and self-consciousness generated by the possibility of being 'found out,' conditional self-acceptance and the absence of emotional support during crises and times of need" (Friend 1991: 109). If Friend's theory is accepted as the blueprint for successful gay and lesbian aging, then gay and lesbian elders are left with an impossible choice: secrecy will take its toll on the elder's emotional well-being and compromise his or her ability to age successfully. On the other hand, being "out" could expose the elder to unacceptable risks of exploitation and violence. As Berger correctly explained, "Being openly gay can be personally liberating, but it is not adaptive in every situation" (Berger 1982: 11).

PART III
Advocacy

Gay and lesbian elders are long-time survivors of homophobia and discrimination. Today, their resilience is once again being tested as they try to adapt their pre-Stonewall coping skills to a new set of challenges. As they are confronted with the inevitable frailties of aging, many gay and lesbian elders have chosen to shoulder the burdens of anti-gay bias, prejudice, and ignorance in the silence of the closet. The silence of gay and lesbian elders renders them invisible to service providers, advocates, and policy-makers. It also keeps them separate and apart from both the larger gay and lesbian community and the senior community. Acts of discrimination and intimidation can take on an especially menacing hue when directed at a closeted elder who finds herself in poor health, dependent on others, and confined to an institutional setting.

As explained in Part II, the concerns of gay and lesbian elders have been historically overlooked by advocates for gay and lesbian equality, as well as by senior advocates. Although gay and lesbian elders would certainly benefit from broader equality measures such as marriage equality, ENDA, and the repeal of DADT, these initiatives speak more directly to the interests of coupled, middle-class, able-bodied, and primarily young, gay men and lesbians. To the contrary, gay and lesbian elders present a distinct set of concerns that reflect their unique life experiences tempered by the demands of aging. Issues that more directly impact the pre-Stonewall generation include: the legal fragility of chosen families, financial insecurity, and anti-gay bias in senior settings and on the part of service providers. Unlike the three discrete policy goals articulated by the mainstream movement for gay and lesbian equality, these areas of concern are relatively broad and both require and invite numerous policy interventions on multiple levels.

This section first examines the three signature issues of the contemporary movement for gay and lesbian equality (i.e., marriage equality, ENDA, and the repeal of DADT) from the perspective of gay and lesbian elders. It then devotes the remaining three chapters to the policy areas of primary concern to gay and lesbian elders: the fragility of chosen families, financial insecurity, and anti-gay bias in senior-specific venues. The disconnect between the two sets of issues illustrates the limitations inherent in the arguments of equivalence relied upon by the contemporary movement for gay and lesbian equality. In order to address the needs of gay and lesbian elders and others who do not conform to a heteronormative model, the movement must learn to embrace the diversity of sexual identity and incorporate this diversity throughout its advocacy agenda. Only then will the mainstream movement be able to articulate policy proposals that insure equity (and dignity) in aging for gay and lesbian elders.

Chapter 7

The Contemporary Movement for Gay and Lesbian Equality

The contemporary gay and lesbian civil rights movement rests on an ethnic or identity model of homosexuality that posits sexual orientation as an immutable, unchosen, and benign characteristic. The identity model first establishes gay men and lesbians as a valid minority organized around this benign characteristic and then advances equality measures by asserting that gay men and lesbians are *the same as* their non-gay peers. The moral force behind these measures is an implied claim of equivalence – if gay men and lesbians are *the same as* everyone else, then they deserve equality of treatment and opportunity.

This model of sexual orientation fits nicely with existing equal protection jurisprudence, and seems to position gay men and lesbians as the model suspect category – politically powerless, historically disadvantaged, and united by an immutable trait. Despite numerous attempts, however, advocates for gay and lesbian equality have not convinced the courts that classifications based on sexual orientation warrant a heightened level of scrutiny. That being said, the identity model has successfully won over the hearts and minds of many gay and non-gay individuals alike and public opinion polls consistently show wide support for a biological or genetic understanding of homosexuality (E. Stein 2001). This understanding of homosexuality differs fundamentally from the liberationist model popularized in the early 1970s that stressed the role of agency and choice in the definition of sexual identity. Whereas the liberation model discussed in Chapters 1 and 2 may have changed the way society discussed sexuality and gender, the identity model has introduced the American public to a new minority who are just like them with the exception of one insignificant characteristic – sexual orientation. Other than that one minor detail, the members of this new and deserving minority are just like everyone else – they want to get married, get a good job, and serve their country.

Educating service providers, policy-makers, and the public about the needs of gay and lesbian elders requires moving beyond such arguments of equivalence because gay and lesbian elders are not the same as their non-gay peers. They are more likely than their non-gay peers to be single and live alone, and even partnered gay and lesbian elders are more likely to experience financial insecurity than their non-gay peers. As explained in Chapters 1 and 2, gay and lesbian elders survived a dark period in American history. Over the course of their lifetime, gay and lesbian elders were simultaneously labeled as mentally ill, degenerate, and criminal. Their employment options were greatly curtailed due to officially sanctioned anti-gay bias, and the closet was a fearful place where the threat of disclosure was ever present.

This chapter examines the three major equality initiatives of the contemporary gay and lesbian civil rights movement from the perspective of gay and lesbian elders to illustrate that many of their interests fall outside the mainstream advocacy agenda because gay and lesbian elders are different, and their needs demand initiatives that are targeted to address their specific concerns of being a gay or lesbian elder in a homophobic and ageist society.

Marriage Equality and Relationship Recognition

The United States has been consumed in a contentious debate over same-sex marriage since the 1990s, when advocates of marriage equality secured their first victories in state courts. Since then, gay and lesbian advocacy organizations have aggressively pushed for equal marriage rights through the state courts and legislatures, and they have been met with fierce opposition from social conservatives and conservative anti-gay organizations such as the FRC. Between 1994 and 2009, it is estimated that more than $100 billion was spent by both sides on ballot initiatives prohibiting same-sex marriage. The battle over marriage equality is a major source of anti-gay rhetoric, and, as explained in Chapter 5, much of it harkens back to the days of the American Freudians and the notion of sexual predator/pedophile. Opponents of marriage equality often focus on how same-sex marriage will affect children. In their court filings, the anti-marriage forces argue that the state has a compelling interest in preserving "traditional" marriage because different-sex marriages are optimal for raising children (Proponents' Trial Brief 2009). Their television ads opposing marriage equality exploit a deep-seated fear that children will be indoctrinated by the so-called "gay agenda." If same-sex marriage is legalized, they argue that schools will be required to teach children about gay marriage and, presumably, homosexuality (Everything to Do With Schools 2009).

With respect to gay and lesbian elders, there is no question that marriage equality is an important issue, but it is certainly no panacea. Gay and lesbian elders are considerably less likely to be partnered than their non-gay peers, and marriage equality would not address the needs of single gay and lesbian elders unless they were also surviving partners. Moreover, gay and lesbian elders rely on chosen family for a wide range of support, and marriage equality would not empower gay and lesbian elders to protect members of their chosen family. This fundamental shortcoming is discussed further in Chapter 8, along with various proposals to permit an individual to designate another as "family" for purposes of inheritance rights, health-care decision-making and a host of other rights usually reserved by statute for next of kin.

In recent years, any attempt to outline the state of relationship recognition in the United States has been quickly outdated as the map of marriage rights and marriage prohibitions has proved to be ever-changing. By 2010, the vast majority of states had either passed laws restricting marriage to a union between a man and a woman or amended their state constitutions to prohibit same-sex marriage. Some states had done both for good measure. Despite the prevalence of anti-marriage measures, more than a dozen states provided some level of recognition for same-sex relationships and, when municipalities and counties are included in the tally, an estimated 46 percent of all same-sex couples lived in a jurisdiction where they were entitled to some level of legal recognition (Kincaid 2010).

For partnered gay and lesbian elders, state-level recognition can carry with it valuable property rights and decision-making authority discussed in greater detail in Chapter 8. Types of state-wide relationship recognition range from actual marriage in Massachusetts to the limited set of rights available to "reciprocal beneficiaries" under Hawaii law. A number of states grant actual marriage or recognize same-sex marriages performed in other jurisdictions. A nearly equal number of states offer marriage equivalence and extend full marriage rights to same-sex couples under a parallel status bearing a title other than marriage, such as civil union or registered domestic partnership. To further complicate matters, the various forms of recognition do not share the same terminology nor do they provide the same benefits. For example, California grants rights to "registered domestic partners" that are equivalent to those extended to opposite-sex married couples, whereas New Jersey also provides marriage equivalence, but uses the term "civil union." Adding to the confusion, both Vermont and Connecticut had originally extended marriage equivalence under the term "civil union," but now recognize same-sex marriage. Some states offer levels of relationship recognition that fall short of the rights and obligations enjoyed by married couples, but are nonetheless important. These lesser levels of recognition include state-wide domestic partner registries and the limited granting of health-care decision-making authority. Some states restrict non-marriage relationship recognition to same-sex couples, whereas other states, such as Hawaii and New Jersey, extend the status to different-sex couples. In some cases, states started with relatively modest forms of relationship recognition, but eventually expanded the scope of recognition to provide marriage equivalence. Hawaii, however, was the first state to enact relationship recognition in 1997, and it has steadfastly resisted efforts to increase the quantum of rights afforded same-sex couples.

On the federal level, the Defense of Marriage Act (DOMA) blocks federal recognition of same-sex marriages and mandates that marriage can only be between one man and one woman for all federal purposes, including taxation, Social Security benefits, and Medicare. As a result, same-sex couples who are married in their home state are considered unmarried for all federal purposes and will not qualify for the estimated 1,138 federal benefits that attach to marital status (Shah 2004). For partnered gay and lesbian elders, the spousal benefits available under Social Security are an obvious area of concern, but, as explained in greater detail in Chapter 9, marriage recognition would be a double-edged victory for gay and lesbian elders in terms of federal benefits. It would advantage some elders with respect to taxes, Social Security benefits, and other spousal protections, but low-income partnered gay and lesbian elders may be disadvantaged because their income and assets would be aggregated in order to determine their eligibility for certain means-tested benefit programs, such as Medicaid and Supplemental Security Income (SSI).

When it was enacted in 1996, DOMA, with its arguably Orwellian name, was wholly prophylactic in nature because no state had yet legalized same-sex marriage. The 1993 Hawaii Supreme Court decision, *Baehr v. Lewin*, had earlier signaled that the judicial imposition of same-sex marriage was a clear possibility. Introduced in the Senate by presidential candidate Bob Dole during the 1996 Republican primaries, DOMA gave members of Congress the opportunity to demonize same-sex couples and the dreaded "gay agenda" just in time for the 1996 presidential election. It was another seven years before the Supreme Court of Massachusetts issued its groundbreaking opinion in *Goodridge v. Dep't of Pub. Health*, which paved the way for the first legally recognized same-sex marriages to be performed in the United States in 2004.

Prior to DOMA, marriage had been the traditional province of the states, and there was no federal definition of marriage. In questions involving federal law, the validity of a marriage was determined under the applicable state law, usually the domicile of the parties. Many state laws were drafted in gender-neutral language, but the pervasive heteronormativity of the time ensured that the very notion of a same-sex union was inconceivable. In the 1970s, several same-sex couples sued under gender neutral statutes for the right to be issued a marriage license, and the courts responded with incredulity. The cases held that the gender-neutral language in marriage statutes prohibited same-sex marriage on definitional grounds – marriage, by definition, was solely between a man and a woman (*Baker v. Nelson* 1971). Similarly, when Phyllis Schlafly suggested that the passage of the Equal Rights Amendment could lead to same-sex marriage, she was roundly ridiculed and accused of using inflammatory arguments to detract from the real debate over gender equality (Chauncey 2005: 157).

In 1993, *Baehr v. Lewin* suddenly cast serious doubt on the ability of this definitional argument to weather the changing status of same-sex relationships in the United States. Congress responded by creating a federal definition of marriage with the enactment of DOMA. In an attempt to limit the reach of any future judicial decision (or legislative action) legalizing same-sex marriage, DOMA purports to authorize states to refuse to recognize a same-sex marriage performed under the laws of a sister state. This last provision was roundly criticized when it was enacted as violating the full faith and credit clause of the U.S. Constitution, but at the time the objections were strictly academic because no state yet recognized same-sex marriage.

Taking their cue from the federal DOMA, states then began to enact so-called mini-DOMAs that defined marriage as a union between one man and one woman. When it became clear that state-level DOMAs could be invalidated under state constitutional due process, equal protection, or equal rights arguments, opponents of marriage equality began to push for state constitutional amendments that prohibited same-sex marriage. A state constitutional amendment was preferred to a statute because it would necessarily shield the marriage prohibition from a state constitutional challenge, leaving only a federal constitutional claim. In recent years, state DOMAs and state constitutional marriage prohibitions have become more aggressive, and they increasingly target not just same-sex marriage, but also the grant of any of the "incidents of marriage" to same-sex couples. These second-generation DOMAs prohibit marriage equality, as well as marriage equivalence and all limited grants of relationship recognition, including the provision of domestic partner employee benefits by public employers (*National Pride at Work v. Cox* 2008).

The state of relationship recognition in the United States is further complicated by the fact that local and municipal authorities can also provide some level of recognition. By ordinance, a county or municipality can establish the status of domestic partnership and establish a registry system to formalize the relationship. The rights conferred by such ordinances tend to be relatively meager because they are limited to those rights that the municipality has the authority to grant, which could include the right to visit a partner incarcerated at a county prison, local tax benefits enjoyed by married couples, and the ability to transfer certain municipal licenses, such as a liquor license, to a same-sex partner. Some municipalities also extended domestic partner health-care coverage to their public employees, but like all of these local benefits, the grant of employee benefits can be blocked if the state has a second-generation DOMA or state constitutional amendment with "teeth."

This confusing and conflicting state of relationship recognition weighs heavily on same-sex couples and must be especially vexing for elder same-sex couples. The lack of uniformity creates a level of uncertainty that complicates daily life in ways that different-sex couples need never consider. A couple legally married in Massachusetts who vacations in Connecticut will be legally married while on vacation. If they go to New Jersey instead, they will be considered parties to a civil union, but they will not be considered "married" because in New Jersey that term is reserved for different-sex couples. In Florida, the couple will be legal strangers, as they are for all federal purposes. In its 2004 resolution in favor of same-sex marriage, the American Psychological Association noted the extreme minority stress experienced by same-sex couples due to the absence of uniform recognition of same-sex relationships and the fact that relationship recognition granted by one jurisdiction is rarely "portable" (American Psychological Association 2004). The other APA, the American Psychiatric Association, followed suit the next year with a similar resolution (American Psychiatric Association 2005). In addition to the lack of uniformity, same-sex couples must also grapple with a deeper uncertainty because, once granted, marriage equality continues to be under assault by the traditional values movement. As evident from Proposition 8 in California and the repeal of same-sex marriage legislation in Maine in 2009, relationship recognition is not only jurisdiction-specific, it can also be fleeting. Once granted, marriage equality continues to be assaulted by the traditional values movement and it remains contested and provisional, thereby exacerbating the pre-existing minority stress.

Workplace Discrimination

On the federal level, the Employment Non-Discrimination Act ("ENDA") has been the focal point of efforts to end discrimination in the workplace on account of sexual orientation and, more recently, gender identity. ENDA has been pending before Congress in one form or another since 1994, when it was introduced by Rep. Gerry Studds (D-MA), who was the first openly gay member of Congress. In its current form, ENDA prohibits discrimination on account of sexual orientation and gender identity by all employers with 15 or more employees. It provides exemptions for religious organizations and certain tax-exempt private membership clubs. Federal executive branch employees have been covered by anti-discrimination protections since 1998, when President Clinton issued an executive order that prohibited discrimination in the executive branch on account of sexual orientation. In public opinion polls, a strong majority consistently supports non-discrimination in the workplace. A 2008 Gallup poll indicated that 89 percent of those individuals surveyed agreed that gay men and lesbians should have "equal rights in terms of job opportunities" (Gallup 2010). Despite such popular support, critics of ENDA characterize the grant of anti-discrimination protections to gay men and lesbian as "special rights."

From the perspective of gay and lesbian elders, ENDA has one obvious shortcoming in that it only applies to discrimination in the workplace. No doubt many gay and lesbian elders have experienced anti-gay discrimination in employment, but the importance of the workplace as a venue for discrimination necessarily diminishes as elders prepare to exit the workforce and enter retirement. Although a good number of young elders remain in the workforce beyond age 65, gay and lesbian elders are primarily confronted with anti-gay discrimination in the more intimate and potentially more threatening senior-specific venues such as assisted living facilities, nursing homes, and senior centers. As discussed in Chapter 10, comprehensive anti-discrimination protections for seniors will require far-reaching legislative and regulatory reform.

ENDA will continue to have significance for gay and lesbian elders who remain in the workforce, even though it fails to address the central venues for elder discrimination. Uncertain economic times, longer life expectancy, and the demise of mandatory retirement policies have combined to increase the number of workers who are 65 years of age or older and push back minimum age to qualify for Social Security benefits. An individual who turned 65 in 2007 has a life expectancy of 19 additional years. In the D'Augelli and Grossman study, 18 percent of the respondents still worked (D'Augelli and Grossman 2001: 1010). ENDA will also benefit future generations of gay and lesbian elders to the extent that it will help close the financial security gap between gay and lesbian elders and their non-gay peers.

With respect to anti-discrimination protections in the workplace, there have been considerable gains on the state level, but, as of 2010, a majority of states still have not extended anti-discrimination protections in employment to include sexual orientation and more than three-quarters of the states do not provide anti-discrimination protections based on gender identity. Public employees fare somewhat better because a number of states have executive orders or other regulatory guidance that prohibit discrimination based on sexual orientation and, by 2010, public employees were protected against anti-gay discrimination in a majority of states.

As in the case of relationship recognition, the level of anti-discrimination protections adopted by the states vary in scope. Some states limit the protections to the employment context. Others extend the protections beyond employment to prohibit discrimination in public accommodation, housing, lending, and other venues. The New Jersey statute involved in *Dale v. Boy Scouts* provides an example of an expansive anti-discrimination provision that grants broad protections and prohibits unlawful discrimination in employment, housing, places of public accommodation, credit, and business contracts. The first federal rights bill barring discrimination on account of sexual orientation was similarly broad in scope. Known as the Equality Act of 1974, the bill was introduced in Congress on the fifth anniversary of the Stonewall riots by Representatives Bella Abzug (D-NY) and Edward I. Koch (D-NY). It would have amended the Civil Rights Act of 1964 to provide broad-based anti-discrimination protections for "sexual preference," reflecting the liberationist vocabulary in use at the time.

Private industry has proved receptive to demands for non-discrimination protections and other workplace equity measures. According to the HRC, an overwhelming majority of Fortune 500 companies now have policies in place that prohibit discrimination on account of sexual orientation, and a growing number have extended these policies to include gender identity. In many instances, this policy of non-discrimination also extends to spousal employee benefits that are discussed in greater detail in Chapter 9. As of 2010, more than half of all Fortune 500 companies offered domestic partner benefits, including pension rights and health insurance benefits.

It bears noting that the very concept of a "domestic partnership" was the creation of the marketplace, necessitated when employers responded to the demand from gay and lesbian employees for health insurance benefits for their same-sex partners. In an effort to respect the concept of "equal pay for equal work," human resource managers originated the now familiar menu approach to domestic partnership. Under this approach, an employee is required to satisfy a prescribed number of relationship indicators (e.g., jointly owned property, reciprocal estate-planning documents, joint credit card). The determination provides a form of relationship verification in lieu of formal legal recognition.

Don't Ask, Don't Tell (DADT)

Along with marriage equality and ENDA, the repeal of DADT has been a major goal of the contemporary movement for gay and lesbian civil rights. Gay and lesbian elders are beyond the age of mandatory retirement for active duty and reserve duty officers and, therefore, there are not directly affected by the policy. However, the gay and lesbian elders who are veterans may feel the impact of the policy in connection with the delivery of their veterans benefits, especially health care (Cahill, South and Spade 2000: 19). The continuing official policy of discrimination mandated under DADT reinforces and condones homophobic or discriminatory opinions held by the administrators, health-care providers, and staff at the U.S. Department of Veterans Affairs (VA). It also sends a strong message about how the institution views gay and lesbian veterans, thereby posing yet another barrier to access for gay and lesbian elders who are already fearful of disclosure.

DADT was adopted in 1993 during the early years of the Clinton administration, and it generated the first sustained federal-level debate on gay and lesbian equality. During the 1992 presidential campaign, candidate Bill Clinton had promised to end discrimination in the military. Once elected, President Clinton proposed to issue an executive order banning discrimination on account of sexual orientation following the example of President Truman, who had issued his historic executive order desegregating the armed services in 1948. President Clinton's proposal was met with staunch resistance by the military establishment and led to widely publicized Congressional hearings. The overwhelmingly anti-gay sentiment expressed at the hearings, and in later Congressional debate, served as a harbinger of things to come at the DOMA hearings that would follow three years later.

DADT mandates that all gay and lesbian military personnel stay in the closet under threat of separation of service and loss of benefits (Halley 1999: 2–5). Although homosexuality per se is no longer deemed "incompatible with military service," a member of the armed services is subject to separation if the service member acknowledges that he or she is gay. Department of Defense regulations provide that "sexual orientation is considered a personal and private matter, and homosexual orientation is not a bar to continued service unless manifested by homosexual conduct." The same regulations, however, go on to define "homosexual conduct" to include any open avowal of homosexuality. Under this definition, the simple statement "I'm gay," is sufficient to warrant separation from service because it constitutes a prohibited act of homosexuality. The enforcement of DADT has been quite controversial, but public opinion polls show a strong majority favors the abolishment of the policy, and the United States now stands in the minority of Western countries that do not allow gays and lesbians to serve openly in their military. As of 2010, more than 13,500 service members have been discharged for being gay since the inception of DADT in 1993 (Servicemembers Legal Defense Network 2010).

Arguments in favor of the repeal of DADT almost always focus on the inequities imposed on active duty personnel, but the policy also has an indirect effect on the more than 25 million living veterans (Olsen 2005). Despite the ban on gays in the military, gay men and lesbians have continued to serve their country. As of 2010, it is estimated that there were approximately 66,000 gay men and lesbians serving in the U.S. military (Gates 2010: 1) and more than 1 million gay and lesbian veterans (Burke 2003, Gates 2003b). According to the census data on same-sex partnered households, women in same-sex partnered households are much more likely to report veteran status than women in different-sex marriages (Dang and Frazer 2005: 26). Eleven percent of African-American women in same-sex partnered households and 9 percent of white women in same-sex partnered households are veterans, as compared to only 1 percent of women in different-sex marriages (Dang and Frazer 2005: 26).

There are no reliable figures regarding what percentage of gay veterans are age 65 or older, but it is likely that a disproportionate number of gay and lesbian veterans are seniors given the high incidence of military service among seniors generally, the mandatory draft, and the high level of mobilization that occurred during World War II and then again during the Korean conflict. In terms of the larger population, one in four Social Security recipients is also a veteran (Olsen 2005). According to a preliminary analysis of 2000 census data on same-sex partnered households, more than 20 percent of men in same-sex partnered households who were aged 63 to 67 reported military service, as did almost 10 percent of the women in the same age cohort (Gates 2003b: 13).

One of the major advantages of military service is lifelong veterans benefits, including health care, disability compensation, survivor benefits, and burial benefits. The medical benefits are of particular value because they are more comprehensive than those available under Medicare or Medicaid. Gay and lesbian elders who received a Section VIII or blue discharge, discussed in Chapter 1, are ineligible for these benefits, as are any veterans who receive a less than honorable discharge. Today, service members who are discharged under DADT are often able to negotiate the type of discharge they receive and preserve their benefits, but a less than honorable discharge remains a possibility.

As discussed in Chapter 6, gay and lesbian elders underutilize senior and related aging resources due to fear of discrimination, but, in the case of the military, discrimination against gay men and lesbians is articulated as official policy. Despite the fact that the DADT policy does not apply directly to veterans, anecdotal evidence suggests that gay and lesbian elders who qualify for veterans benefits may think twice about using the health-care system run by the VA (Cahill, South and Spade 2000: 19). Gay and lesbian elders report that the existence of DADT provides added pressure to be closeted when interacting with VA health-care providers (Cahill, South and Spade 2000: 19). As a result, gay and lesbian elders are less likely to discuss matters involving their sexual orientation, and they are less likely to include their partners in decision-making (Cahill, South and Spade 2000: 19). They may also be less likely to access available health-care services because the services are only covered when they are dispensed by the VA health-care system. For example, despite the high cost of HIV retroviral drugs, a gay veteran may not use the VA prescription benefit because it only applies to prescriptions written by a VA provider (Cahill, South and Spade 2000: 19). The same could be true of nursing care. The VA nursing care benefit is superior to the one available under the means-tested Medicaid program, discussed in greater detail in Chapter 9. It is possible that gay and lesbian elders may choose not to utilize the benefit because they believe they would not be welcome at a VA nursing home.

The repeal of DADT will have an immediate impact for the estimated 66,000 gay men and lesbians in the military (Gates 2010), but the repeal will not automatically reinstate the VA benefits that have been forfeited over the years by service members who received less than honorable discharges on account of homosexuality. Nor will it automatically create an atmosphere of tolerance and inclusion in VA facilities. In order to secure the latter, the VA would have to adopt an affirmative policy of non-discrimination, as well as cultural competency programs for its medical providers and anti-bullying measures in its long-term care facilities as discussed in greater detail in Chapter 10.

Chapter 8
The Legal Fragility of Same-Sex Partnerships and Chosen Family

As noted in the previous chapter, over the last 15 years, same-sex marriage has become *the* signal issue in the struggle for gay and lesbian equality. The hotly contested public debate over marriage equality has highlighted the wide range of spousal benefits that attach to marriage and serve to reinforce the marital unit as a fundamental building block of society. For example, the U.S. General Accountability Office estimates that there are 1,138 federal statutory provisions under "which marital status is a factor in determining or receiving benefits, rights, and privileges" (Shah 2004). A number of these federal benefits are of particular concern to gay and lesbian elders, such as the spousal provisions of Social Security and Medicaid, as well as the rules governing pension benefits.

The debate over same-sex marriage, however, is about much more than equal access to certain spousal and survivor benefits – it is ultimately about the ability to define your family. Marriage is the only way to make a partner *family*. In the absence of relationship recognition, a partner is a legal stranger who stands behind children, parents, siblings, grandparents, aunts and uncles, cousins, and even the state in terms of priority for a host of property and decision-making rights, some of which involve highly personal and intimate choices. In the majority of jurisdictions, however, same-sex couples do not have the ability to use marriage instrumentally to create family. They must rely on an imperfect combination of contract and estate-planning documents to delineate rights and responsibilities. Whenever a same-sex partner is denied access to her dying partner's hospital room or a distant cousin swoops into town to challenge a will in favor of a surviving partner, the security of gay and lesbian families everywhere is shaken to the core. The legal fragility of gay and lesbian families may explain why such a large percentage of *partnered* gay and lesbian Baby Boomers in the Metlife Boomer survey reported that discrimination on account of sexual orientation is their greatest fear with respect to aging (Metlife 2006: 14).

For gay and lesbian elders who rely on members of a chosen family for care and support, this legal disability extends beyond their partner and includes all of their potential caregivers because an individual cannot designate her chosen family as legal family. Thus, although a same-sex partner may be considered "next of kin" in a handful of jurisdictions, the other members of a chosen family remain legal strangers in all 50 states and the District of Columbia. As a result, members of an individual's chosen family will be excluded from all of the rights and benefits afforded next of kin, including inheritance rights and decision-making authority with respect to who serves as a guardian, who has the authority to make medical treatment decisions, and who can authorize organ donation. The exercise of such decision-making authority is particularly critical for gay and lesbian elders and plays an essential role in any elder-care or estate plan. Although some of these rights and benefits can be secured through private contract and estate-planning documents, even the most comprehensive legal drafting cannot make someone "next of kin."

Property Rights

Despite the changing face of the American family, the law continues to privilege those relationships defined by blood, marriage, or adoption. Family members are automatically included as heirs for purposes of intestate succession, and they have standing to bring wrongful death actions (Culhane 2001: 953–54). When a person dies without a will, the distribution of his estate is governed by the rules of intestate succession that are designed to approximate the result most decedents would have directed had they written a will. A surviving same-sex partner who resides in a state that does not recognize same-sex relationships has no legal right to his or her partner's property upon death. If a same-sex partner dies without a will, the rules of intestate succession will generally distribute the partner's property to the partner's closest relatives in the following priority: children, parents, siblings, nieces and nephews, grandparents, aunts and uncles, first cousins, and so on (Uniform Probate Code). The bulk of the estate is reserved for the surviving spouse, but the spouse's share is reduced if the decedent is survived by parents, children who are not also the children of the surviving spouse, or stepchildren who are the children of the surviving spouse. If an individual is not survived by any relatives within the prescribed degrees of relationship, all property escheats to the state.

The rules of intestate succession are often described as a default setting in that they mandate the distribution of probate assets in the absence of a will. They are intended to approximate what most people would have wanted had they thought about it. Given that an estimated two-thirds of all people die without a will, however, the rules of intestate succession are much more than a default setting because they actually direct the distribution of the majority of estates in the United States. Some states now include same-sex partners as spouses or spousal equivalents in the rules of intestate succession, but no state includes close friends. Accordingly, an individual who wishes to leave his or her estate to someone other than her intestate heirs must leave a valid will in order to protect the intended beneficiary. For gay and lesbian elders, this presents an obvious transaction cost. Beyond the question of cost, however, gay and lesbian elders must be aware that they need planning documents in the first place, and they must have access to a legal professional. For different-sex married couples, estate-planning documents may represent a tying up of loose ends and the responsible thing to do, but for same-sex couples estate-planning documents are an essential component of relationship formation.

The case of Frank Vasquez and Robert Schwerzler provides an example of what can happen when same-sex couples fail to execute estate-planning documents and the survivor is faced with the rules of intestate succession and incredulous in-laws. Frank and Robert had been together for 28 years when Robert died at age 78 without a will. Frank quickly learned that the entire $230,000 estate – their house, their two cars, and their furniture – was titled in Robert's name (King 2001). Frank and Robert ran a burlap bag recycling business in Puyallup, Washington, where they shared a modest three-bedroom house (King 2001). If Frank and Robert had been married, the fact that Robert died intestate would have mattered little. As a surviving spouse, Frank would have received 100 percent of the estate because Robert was not survived by children or parents. In the absence of marriage or other statutory recognition, however, Frank was a mere legal stranger and was not entitled to receive anything under the rules of intestate succession. As his next of kin, Robert's siblings asserted their rights to the property that was titled in his name. According to Frank's lawyer, the siblings "literally wanted to put Mr. Vasquez out on the street with nothing" (Skolnik 2001). Although not required to legally, the siblings justified their claim to Robert's estate, including the home he had shared with Frank, by asserting that the two men were not partners. With respect to whether the two men were gay, Robert's brother testified that "[c]ertainly, there was nothing being done in public" (King 2001). In the eyes of Robert's family, Frank was really more like a housekeeper or a boarder who just happened to stick around for 28 years. With this argument, Robert's next of kin were able to use the closet against Frank while at the same time claiming publicly that their actions were not borne of animus toward gays. As far as they were concerned, their dearly departed brother, Robert, was not gay and Frank was not a surviving partner. The Washington Supreme Court ultimately awarded the estate to Frank on an equitable theory akin to the doctrine of equitable adoption, but Frank was able to secure this resolution only after several years of litigation and publicity (*Vasquez v. Hawthorne* 2001).

The rules of intestate succession have influence beyond inheritance because the basic priority ordering of relationships outlined in the rules of intestate succession is used in a variety of settings, ranging from pensions to tort claims, to identify the class of individuals eligible to receive benefits. In some instances, a decedent does not have the power to opt out and designate another beneficiary, and the rules of intestate succession operate to require a compulsory schedule of distribution. This type of compulsory distribution occurs in the case of certain pension benefits and other employment-related death benefits discussed in Chapter 9. The continued use of distribution schemes that exclusively benefit family members defined solely by marriage, blood, and adoption illustrates the inability of private contract or testamentary documents to grant a surviving same-sex partner or a member of a chosen family the rights enjoyed by surviving spouses or surviving next of kin.

The rules of intestate succession also operate to give intestate heirs standing to challenge a will, provided the heirs would benefit financially if the will were set aside. This means that in states without equal marriage rights or marriage equivalence, a decedent's next of kin are automatically empowered to challenge a will made in favor of a same-sex partner. They would have standing to contest the will on a number of grounds, including lack of testamentary capacity, undue influence, fraud, and duress. In all states, however, a decedent's next of kin would have standing to challenge a will in favor of a member of the decedent's chosen family.

One way to avoid a will contest is adult adoption (Turnipseed 2010). If an individual adopts his or her intended beneficiary, then the next of kin will not have standing to challenge the will, assuming the next of kin are not surviving children or a spouse. In the 1898 Massachusetts case of *Collamore v. Learned*, Justice Holmes declared that it was a "perfectly proper" to use adult adoption in order to secure inheritance rights, but, more recently, some courts have disallowed adult adoptions where there is a sexual relationship between the parties on public-policy grounds. For example, in 1984, New York's highest court disallowed the application of a 57-year-old gay man to adopt his 50-year-old male partner (*In re Adoption of Robert Paul P.* 1984). The court held that the proposed adoption was "a patently incongruous application of our adoption laws," and the sexual nature of the relationship between the parties was "repugnant" to the parent-child dynamic (*In re Adoption of Robert Paul P.* 1984). This last point underscores the fact that parties considering this step must also investigate the applicability of state criminal incest laws. More importantly, however, adult adoption cannot be entered into lightly because, unlike marriage, adoption is forever – a parent cannot divorce his or her child.

In terms of will challenges, gay and lesbian elders may be especially susceptible to claims that they lack the necessary mental capacity to execute a will. Elders generally must be concerned about claims relating to capacity from disappointed heirs, given the incidence of dementia discussed in Chapter 4. For this reason, estate planners dealing with elderly clients will often go to great lengths to memorialize and substantiate their clients' capacity. In the case of gay and lesbian elders, the disappointed next of kin can point to the non-normative disposition to a surviving partner or chosen family member as proof that the elder lacked capacity. Similar claims were used during the first wave of the HIV/AIDS epidemic to challenge the wills of gay men who died from HIV/AIDS because, at the time, a high percentage of persons with HIV/AIDS developed dementia or other neurological conditions (Maier 1988).

The doctrine of undue influence can also be an exceptionally effective tool in the hands of next of kin who are seeking to void a testamentary plan in favor of a same-sex partner in a jurisdiction without marriage or marriage equivalence. The doctrine of undue influence voids a will where the beneficiary induced the testator to favor that beneficiary over the next of kin, whom the law considers to be the natural objects of the decedent's bounty (Madoff 1997). In many states, undue influence is easier to prove where the beneficiary and the testator were in a non-marital sexual/romantic relationship because it is considered to be a "confidential relationship," and the burden shifts to the beneficiary to disprove the existence of undue influence. Thus, a same-sex partner in a non-marriage jurisdiction would always be in a "confidential relationship" with the testator and, therefore, would be required to justify the inner dynamics of their relationship. As evident from the case of Frank Vasquez and Robert Schwerzler, the closet can greatly complicate relations between the same-sex partner and the decedent's next of kin. The fact that a couple was closeted can help bolster a claim of undue influence because the secrecy that surrounded the relationship can be seen as fertile ground for victimization and exploitation, as was argued successfully in the Sharon Kowalski case discussed in Chapter 4.

The closet played an aggravating role in the unreported case of Ms. H and Ms. F. At the time of Ms. H's death from cancer, the two women had lived together secretly for 32 years. They went to great lengths to hide their relationship from Ms. H's family to the extent that her family believed that Ms. H lived alone. Ms. F was estranged from her own family. Ms. H and Ms. F had no interaction as a couple with family or heterosexual friends. Ms. F left the house whenever Ms. H's family visited, and Ms. F spent holidays alone. Ms. H worked in the family business and was the main breadwinner. Ms. F cared for the house. Ms. H and Ms. F had reciprocal wills that left everything to the other and they often joked that their secret would be out when one of them died. When Ms. H died, her surviving sister and brother contested the will alleging undue influence and, arguing in the alternative, that Ms. F forged the signature or made Ms. H sign under duress when she was in a weakened state from chemotherapy. Under the doctrine of undue influence, the burden was on Ms. F to disprove impropriety due to the existence of a confidential relationship. Ms. F had to prove her relationship with the decedent, as did Frank Vasquez and countless other surviving partners who are outed by the death of a partner. The case ultimately settled, Ms. F received the house she had shared with Ms. H and one-third of the remainder of the estate, but she did not receive all that had been promised to her under Ms. H's will.

Decision-Making Authority

For gay and lesbian elders, medical decision-making issues are obviously a central feature of any estate plan. Advances in medical technology have greatly increased the likelihood that individuals will experience a period of incapacity prior to death. A durable power of attorney and advance directive are now essential elements of any estate plan. When an individual is incapable of expressing his or her wishes regarding medical care, such estate-planning documents can make sure that an individual's wishes are respected by service providers. An individual can appoint a surrogate to act on his or her behalf in the event of incapacity, designate a guardian, or direct the terms of end-of-life care. In the absence of these documents, the law looks to next of kin to make the necessary decisions and provides another series of default settings that generally follow the rules of intestate succession and rank next of kin in descending order of priority. Sometimes next of kin are given preference to the exclusion of all others, such as hospital visitation policies that limit visitors to "immediate family members." In other instances, a third party, such as a funeral director or a cemetery company, may simply refuse to honor the directions of the surviving same-sex partner or a chosen family member, especially when the directions are contrary to the wishes of the next of kin. When this occurs, a same-sex surviving partner may be forced to resort to litigation. If litigation is the only choice, closeted gay and lesbian elders may not be willing to pursue their case in court. Even those partners who are willing to consider legal action may find out that litigation simply offers too little too late.

Burial and cemetery arrangements are an especially emotional subject, and they can be a frequent source of friction between next of kin and surviving same-sex partners or chosen family members. As noted in the cases of Robert Schwerzler and Ms. H, the closet can greatly complicate matters because family members may be surprised to learn that not only was the deceased family member gay, but he or she had a romantic partner and an entire chosen family. If the deceased family member was closeted due to the family's anti-gay and homophobic attitudes, then the surprise may be tinged with hostility and the surviving same-sex partner may be in for an especially rough time. The disapproving family may blame the surviving partner or the decedent's chosen family and may be hostile and resentful.

Although not involving elders, the case of Sherry Barone provides an example of the types of disputes that can arise over burial issues when the next of kin and a surviving same-sex partner do not see eye to eye. Sherry Barone and Cynthia Friedman had been partners for 13 years when Cynthia died from cancer at age 35. Cynthia left a will appointing Sherry as executor and expressly authorizing Sherry to make the burial arrangements. Notwithstanding the clear language of the will, the cemetery refused to follow Sherry's direction with respect to the inscription on Cynthia's headstone because Cynthia' parents objected. It took Sherry three years and a federal lawsuit to get the cemetery to inscribe the headstone with the epitaph "Beloved life partner, daughter, granddaughter, sister and aunt" because Cynthia's parents objected to the use of the term "beloved life partner" (Dubin 1997a). Not surprisingly, the parents preferred a slightly different ordering that stressed Cynthia's traditional family ties. Their version read: "Beloved daughter, sister, granddaughter, and loving friend" and neatly recast the nature of Cynthia's relationship with Sherry as that of "friend" (Ginanni 1997).

This case illustrates how difficult it can be to force third parties to respect the wishes of same-sex partners (or chosen family) even when the parties plan ahead and execute the required legal documents. As executor, Sherry was expressly authorized to "arrange for the disposition" of Cynthia's remains and yet the cemetery refused to honor Sherry's directions because Cynthia's parents, who had no legal right to represent the estate, objected (Dubin 1997a). It is difficult to know whether there was anything else that Sherry and Cynthia could have done that would have been sufficient to safeguard Cynthia's wishes. Attorneys who specialize in estate planning for gay and lesbian families routinely draft supplemental documents to express the testator's intent where the legal force of the documents remain unclear, such as hospital visitation authorization forms and burial instructions. Even with this level of formality, it is still possible that the cemetery would choose to follow the wishes of the parents and ignore the document. It is this element of third-party choice that is at the heart of the fragility of gay and lesbian families. In the absence of statutory rights for same-sex partners or chosen family, there are many instances where third parties can choose to respect the wishes of next of kin over those of a same-sex partner or a chosen family member, and next of kin can choose whether to assert priority even when there is a valid will.

Hospital Visitation Policies

Sherry Barone's ordeal was no doubt horrific, but the agony a same-sex partner endures when she is denied the opportunity to be with and comfort her dying partner in the hospital because she is not considered "family" represents the final indignity, and a same-sex partner's worst nightmare. In these situations, there often is no time to hire a lawyer and file a complaint. Indeed, that was exactly what a hospital social worker told Janice Langbehn as her partner of 18 years, Lisa Pond, was dying alone, in restraints, in a hospital trauma ward in Florida (*Langbehn v. Memorial Hospital* 2009). After explaining that they were in an "anti-gay city and state," the social worker added that it would be days before Janice would be able to get a court order because it was a holiday weekend (*Langbehn v. Memorial Hospital* 2009: 1332). For Janice and Lisa, and the three children they had adopted together, there was simply no time. Despite the fact that Janice provided the hospital with a copy of Lisa's power of attorney authorizing Janice to act on her behalf and appointing Janice as the guardian of her person, the hospital staff kept Janice and the children waiting for eight hours as they watched other families come and go (Parker-Pope 2009). When Lisa's sister and brother-in-law arrived at the hospital, they were immediately treated like family and given an update on Lisa's condition. In the absence of marriage or marriage equivalence, Janice and Lisa – like all same-sex couples – had to hope that hospital staff would choose to recognize their relationship and grant them the privileges afforded to other families.

Despite the fact that an estate plan for a gay or lesbian testator now routinely includes a hospital visitation authorization form and a health-care power of attorney with specific language granting visitation rights, some health-care providers feel free to ignore even the most detailed authorizations. It is also not clear whether the documents are legally sufficient to require a hospital with a visitation policy limited to "immediate family" to admit a same-sex partner or chosen family member. Janice later sued the Florida hospital and the doctors involved for negligence, negligent infliction of emotional distress, intentional infliction of emotional distress, and breach of a fiduciary relationship. In 2009, the U.S. District Court of the Southern District of Florida granted the hospital's motion to dismiss the case for failure to state a cause of action (*Langbehn v. Memorial Hospital* 2009). In other words, the judge determined that, even assuming that every fact Janice alleged were true, Florida law could not provide her any relief. Judge Aldaberto Jordan concluded:

> If the plaintiffs' allegations are true, which I assume they are when deciding the defendants' ... motion to dismiss, the defendants' lack of sensitivity and attention to Ms. Lanbehn, Ms. Pond and their children caused them needless stress at a time of vulnerability. The defendants' failure to provide Ms. Langbehn and her children frequent updates on Ms. Pond's status, to allow Ms. Langbehn and the children to visit Ms. Pond after emergency medical care ceased; to inform Ms. Langbehn that Ms. Pond had been moved to the intensive care unit, and to provide Ms. Langbehn with Ms. Pond's medical records as she requested, exhibited a lack of compassion and was unbecoming of a renowned trauma center like Ryder. Unfortunately, no relief is available for these failures based on the allegations plead in the amended complaint (*Langbehn v. Memorial Hospital* 2009: 1347).

A similar case was brought in state court in Maryland by Bill Flanigan, who was denied access to his dying partner, Robert Daniel, despite the fact that they were registered domestic partners in their hometown of San Francisco and despite the fact that Bill held Robert's health-care power of attorney (*Flanigan v. University of Maryland Medical Center* 2001). The suit alleged negligence and intentional infliction of emotional distress, but the jury found for the hospital. The partners had been on a cross-country trip when Robert became seriously ill, and he was admitted to the hospital's trauma center. The staff refused to allow Bill to see Robert, and, like Janice, Bill had to watch as other family members arrived at the emergency room and were quickly escorted to see their loved ones. It was only much later, when Robert's mother got there, that Bill was allowed to see his partner. By that time, Robert was unconscious and had been connected to life support without consulting Bill and against Robert's previously expressed wishes. The complaint stated: "Defendant Hospital blocked any communication between [Robert] and [Bill] as [Robert] slipped into unconsciousness, alone and without comfort, support and solace, during his final hours. The two partners were unable to speak with each other before [Robert's] death" (*Flanigan v. University of Maryland Medical Center* 2001).

Bill was barred from Robert's hospital room because he did not qualify as "family" according to the hospital's visitation policy. Under Maryland law, Bill and Robert were legal strangers, and the hospital had no duty to expand its policy to include same-sex partners. The fact that Bill and Robert were registered as domestic partners under a San Francisco ordinance did not carry any weight with the hospital staff in Maryland. The hospital staff also chose to disregard the health-care power of attorney that Bill presented in an attempt to establish his decision-making authority and, instead, waited for Robert's mother to arrive. Bill and Robert had done everything possible to insure that their relationship would be respected, but they could not control for attitudes of third parties. Luckily, Bill was on good terms with Robert's mother. If not, Bill might not have gotten to see his partner before he died because it was Robert's mother who ultimately gave Bill permission to visit her dying son (*Flanigan v. University of Maryland Medical Center* 2001).

In 2008, a hospital visitation case survived a motion to dismiss in a Washington State court, suggesting that hospitals may have a duty in that state to provide patients access to visitors of their choosing (*Reed v. ANM Health Care* 2008). The facts of the case, however, are slightly different because they involve a single employee who was acting contrary to the attending physician's instruction. Still, the case of Sharon Reed and Jo Ann Ritchie illustrates how even the most detailed planning can be undermined by the actions of a single gatekeeper who, for whatever reason, chooses not to recognize the validity of a same-sex partnership. In the lawsuit, Sharon alleges that a night nurse from a temporary staffing agency kept her from seeing her dying partner, Jo Ann, until the next morning when Jo Ann was drugged and non-responsive (*Reed v. ANM Health Care* 2009). The power exercised by the night nurse, and Sharon's inability to get around her orders, is a stark example of the vulnerabilities and skewed power dynamics existing in hospitals and health-care facilities – something that has particular resonance for gay and lesbian elders.

Again, it is not clear what Sharon and Jo Ann could have done differently. Jo Ann had been ill for several years with liver disease before she died and wanted to make sure that Sharon, her partner of 17 years, would be treated as "family" for hospital visitation purposes. Jo Ann's durable power of attorney was very explicit and authorized Sharon "[t]o provide for companionship for me and to be accorded the status of a family member for purposes of visitation" and "to provide for such companionship for me as will meet my needs and preferences at a time when I am disabled or otherwise unable to arrange for such companionship" (*Reed v. ANM Health Care* 2009: 266). When Jo Ann was admitted to the hospital in the final stages of her illness, Sharon and other family members were allowed to visit without restriction, but the disapproval of one nurse was sufficient to bar Sharon from Jo Ann's bedside the night before she died. Earlier that evening, Jo Ann had been transferred to an intensive care unit, and she told Sharon, "I'm afraid of dying. Don't leave me alone" (Parker-Pope 2009).

In 2010, President Obama issued a presidential memorandum to the Secretary of Health and Human Services to initiate rulemaking "to ensure that hospitals that participate in Medicare or Medicaid respect the rights of patients to designate visitors." The memorandum further provides "that participating hospitals may not deny visitation privileges on the basis of race, color, national origin, religion, sex, sexual orientation, gender identity, or disability." This proposed regulatory reform has the potential to protect same-sex partners from being denied access to the partner's hospital room, but much remains to be seen regarding implementation and the extent to which hospitals can impose restrictions based on medical necessity. Chapter 9 discusses some additional examples of recent regulatory reform.

The Luxury of Grief

It also bears mentioning that the lack of legal standing experienced by surviving partners and grieving chosen family members is often compounded by a lack of social or community standing. Remarking about the aftermath of the September 11 attacks, Tom Miller, whose partner, Seamus O'Neal, was killed in the North Tower, explained: "I did not have the luxury of grieving without having to defend myself and prove who I am and who we were" (Knauer 2005). A public or community acknowledgement of grief can be sustaining for those grappling with a major loss. The status of being a widow or widower carries with it social meaning and social position that both embraces the survivor and honors the relationship. For closeted gay and lesbian elders, the loss of a partner can be devastating, and further increases their risk of social isolation. Those relying on chosen family are also disadvantaged. Whereas a surviving partner can assert that he or she should be treated like a widower or widow, there is no ready template to express how a surviving member of a chosen family should be treated. What does it mean to say that you lost someone who was "like family"? How should that loss be honored?

It is from this place of unacknowledged grief that survivors are often forced to litigate. Although Frank Vasquez and other surviving partners have achieved some victories, chosen family members do not seem to have not pursued analogous litigation. The reasons might reflect the lack of a ready comparison for how they should be treated. For purposes of the rules of intestate succession, a surviving same-sex partner can demand to be treated as a spouse, but what about a chosen family member? Even though friends may be "like family," the law tends to be more specific. Is a chosen family member more like a sibling? Or an aunt? Or maybe a cousin? Or is a chosen family member something else entirely?

Legal Options for Choosing Family

In the states with same-sex marriage or marriage equivalence, same-sex partners can choose to make each other family. Until the repeal of DOMA and universal same-sex marriage or equivalence, however, relationship recognition will remain local and may not necessarily be portable. This fact will disadvantage same-sex couples when they move or even when they vacation, as was the case with Janice Langbehn and Lisa Pond. In advance of the 2010 annual meeting of the Association of American Law Schools (AALS) that was held in New Orleans, the chief executive officer of the AALS issued a statement warning meeting attendees of the potential consequences of traveling to a jurisdiction with a second-generation DOMA provision in its state constitution (Prager 2009). Specifically, the AALS offered free legal assistance in the event "any attendee or guest of an attendee experience[d] a hospital refusing access (to the patient) to the patient's partner, or refusing the partner access to the patient's hospital doctors, or if hospital personnel are reluctant to recognize a power of attorney" (Prager 2010). The statement noted that the AALS had received assurances from the New Orleans Convention and Visitors' Bureau and the Tulane Medical Center that powers of attorneys and health-care directives held by same-sex partners would be recognized. Still, the AALS decided that precautions were warranted in light of "reports of hospital personnel who will not allow same-sex partners visitation accorded family members, or who may even attempt to make the exercise of a health care power of attorney difficult" (Prager 2009).

The fact that the AALS thought this sort of warning was necessary is especially disturbing because the membership of the AALS is overwhelmingly comprised of lawyers – individuals who are much more suited to advocate their case than the surviving partners discussed in the prior sections. If a professional organization of legal scholars is intimidated by impending travel to a jurisdiction with a second-generation DOMA, then imagine the burden imposed on a same-sex partner who finds herself forced to advocate for her rights and her partner's rights from the waiting room of a hospital emergency room.

Short of marriage equality, there are a number of ways that states could statutorily extend at least some of the property rights and decision-making authority discussed in this chapter to same-sex partners and chosen family. As Justice Louis Brandeis famously said, federalism allows a state to "serve as a laboratory and to try novel social and economic experiments" (*New State Ice Co. v. Liebmann* 1932). In the area of gay and lesbian families, states have done just that, adopting conflicting and contradictory recognition and non-recognition schemes for same-sex partners. Looking outside the box of marriage equality, states have also enacted statutory measures that provide some forms of recognition that are not designed to approximate marriage or even approach marriage. Some of these initiatives are very broad, such as the Colorado Designated Beneficiary Agreement Act. Others are more narrowly tailored, such as the recently enacted Rhode Island law that authorizes a "domestic partner" to claim his partner's remains.

Legislative proposals such as these are sometimes controversial because there is a perception among some members of the gay and lesbian community that anything less than full marriage equality represents a defeat. They are viewed as disingenuous attempts on the part of the legislature to derail demands for marriage equality by granting same-sex couples insignificant low-cost rights or by extending such rights to different-sex unmarried couples and, as a result, making them cost prohibitive. Although these observations may be valid, it should be clear from the stories briefly detailed in this chapter that even a grant of limited rights can greatly improve the lives of gay men and lesbians – not to mention that any grant of recognition carries the secondary benefit of normalizing homosexuality.

Incremental reform need not inscribe inequality, and it may be possible to advocate for piecemeal reform while not losing sight of the larger goals of marriage equality and obtaining greater protections for chosen family. From a pragmatic standpoint, partial recognition may be a more attainable step in the short term because marriage equality may be quite a long time coming in the states with anti-marriage amendments. In these states, marriage equality will require either a remedial state constitutional amendment or a U.S. Supreme Court decision affirming marriage rights. Also, the immediate interests of gay and lesbian elders may be better served by some of the more limited laws that cover non-partners and leave room for chosen family – something marriage equality does not do.

The Rhode Island burial legislation is an example of a limited grant of rights that is not restricted to same-sex partners, but also does not easily apply to chosen family members. It extends the right to make burial decisions to "domestic partners" who have to satisfy two out of four relationship indicators, all of which require a level of economic interdependence (e.g., partnership agreement, joint ownership, beneficiary designations). The Rhode Island law adds the category of "domestic partner" to the traditional list of next of kin who are authorized to make burial arrangements and gives them equal priority with spouses. It does not require partners to register or designate each other in advance, but instead allows the surviving partner to prove his or her relationship after the fact.

The Rhode Island law was prompted by the 2008 case of Mark Goldberg, who struggled through bureaucratic red tape for four weeks before he was eventually able to claim the remains of his partner of 17 years, Ron Hanby (Edgar 2009). Mark was not permitted to claim Ron's remains despite the fact that they had been legally married in Connecticut, and Ron left no surviving next of kin. In 2009, the governor of Rhode Island vetoed the burial legislation because he saw it as part of "a disturbing trend" that furthers the "erosion of the principles surrounding traditional marriage" (Carcieri 2009). The legislature overrode the governor's veto by an overwhelming margin (Edgar 2009).

The successful enactment of the Rhode Island legislation came at a time when the legislature was unwilling to pursue a marriage equality bill, and it illustrates that some of the "incidents of marriage" are more easily obtainable and much less controversial than marriage equality. For example, prior to President Obama's 2010 presidential memorandum on hospital visitation, there was strong public opinion in favor of granting same-sex partners hospital visitation rights. A 2008 Newsweek poll conducted by the Princeton Survey Research Associates International showed that 86 percent of the respondents favored hospital visitation rights for same-sex partners and only 10 percent opposed such rights (Newsweek 2008). The issue of hospital visitation (along with employment non-discrimination) was considered sufficiently uncontroversial that then-candidate Barrack Obama referred to it in his acceptance speech at the 2008 Democratic National Convention as an example of a place where people with differing opinions could come together on the issue of relationship recognition. Obama said, "I know there are differences on same-sex marriage, but surely we can agree that our gay and lesbian brothers and sisters deserve to visit the person they love in the hospital and to live lives free of discrimination" (Obama 2008).

The Colorado Designated Beneficiary Agreement Act is open to all unmarried adults regardless of whether they are in a romantic relationship and, therefore, applies to chosen family. The Colorado Act is similar to the concept of a "designated family relationship" advocated by Professor Nancy Polikoff (Polikoff

2009: 133–135). It authorizes an individual to designate the person he or she wants to hold certain property rights and decision-making authority usually reserved for family members. Adopting a menu approach, the law prescribes a form that an individual fills out and then files in the county clerk's office. The form allows an individual to check "yes" or "no" with respect to 15 different rights, including pension benefits, hospital visitation, and burial rights. The law also has similarities to the Hawaii Reciprocal Beneficiary Law that was enacted in 1997 as an attempt to forestall court-imposed same-sex marriage. The Colorado Act, however, is more flexible than the Reciprocal Beneficiary Act because it does not require *reciprocal* designations.

In some states, inheritance rights and medical decision-making authority were the first rights extended to same-sex couples. Both California and New Jersey initially granted domestic partners only certain rights, but now offer full marriage equivalence. The District of Columbia provides a case in point. In 1992, D.C. adopted a domestic partnership law that extended relatively modest rights to same-sex couples, including visitation rights in publicly operated facilities such as hospitals and jails. The law was expanded seven times over the years to provide full marriage equality by 2008. In 2009, D.C. began recognizing out-of-state same-sex marriages, and in 2010 it began to issue marriage licenses to same-sex couples. This sort of trajectory, however, is not inevitable, as noted earlier with respect to Hawaii's reciprocal beneficiary law that has not been augmented to extend additional rights.

In the absence of legal recognition for same-sex partners and chosen family, gay and lesbian elders have to rely on the less-than-perfect alternative of private contract and, simply, hope for the best. Unlike traditional families, partners and chosen family cannot rely on the family-friendly default settings that permeate the law, nor can they necessarily count on the goodwill of third parties. Contract and estate planning are the only legal tools with which gay and lesbian elders can constitute their families in the absence of marriage equality, but these tools are necessarily incomplete and ineffective to reach every eventuality. In recent years, even this right to contract has come under attack. Virginia has taken steps to strip away the ability of same-sex couples to use private contract to define their rights and responsibilities. The Virginia Marriage Affirmation Act that was enacted over the governor's veto in 2004 provides:

> A civil union, partnership contract or other arrangement between persons of the same sex purporting to bestow the privileges or obligations of marriage is prohibited. Any such civil union, partnership contract or other arrangement entered into by persons of the same sex in another state or jurisdiction shall be void in all respects in Virginia and any contractual rights created thereby shall be void and unenforceable (Virginia Code Annotated §20–45.3 (2005)).

Chapter 9

Financial Insecurity and Legal Barriers to Equality

For many gay and lesbian elders, financial insecurity further complicates the uncertainty surrounding the property rights and decision-making authority discussed in the preceding chapter. The reduction of poverty among the elderly has been one of the great social policy success stories of the 20th century. Largely through the efforts of federal Social Security programs, the poverty rate among senior citizens has decreased from one-third in 1959 to slightly more than 10 percent in 2001 (Pratt 2007: 339). This success has not been enjoyed equally by gay and lesbian elders, who are significantly more likely to live in poverty and more likely to receive government assistance than their non-gay peers. According to census data, elder same-sex partnered households lag behind their non-gay peers in terms of important financial indicators, such as income, retirement savings, and home ownership.

To some extent, the financial insecurity experienced by gay and lesbian elders may represent the inevitable effect of a lifetime of discrimination, limited career options, and state-sponsored anti-gay bias. This effect would naturally be compounded in the case of lesbian elders and elders with intersecting racial or ethnic identities who experience multiple planes of discrimination. Financial insecurity, however, is also exacerbated by the affirmative legal barriers that prohibit the recognition of same-sex relationships, such as DOMA, and those laws and policies that insist on a narrow definition of family, such as federal Family Medical Leave Act (FMLA).

This chapter discusses the financial insecurity experienced by gay and lesbian elders in light of those legal barriers to equality and to full participation in federal programs designed to assist seniors. It makes the disturbing conclusion that marriage equality may actually disadvantage some of the most vulnerable gay and lesbian elders with respect to their entitlement for certain benefit programs. The apparent connection between sexual orientation and financial insecurity firmly refutes the myth of gay affluence that was popularized by anti-gay conservative organizations during the Culture Wars of the 1990s (Herman 1997: 118). It also suggests that issues of poverty reform are highly relevant to the gay and lesbian community despite the fact that they are rarely incorporated in the mainstream gay and lesbian civil rights agenda.

Financial Insecurity

Although there is no comprehensive data on the financial status of gay men and lesbians, census data on self-reporting same-sex partnered households provides a partial view of the economic situation of gay men and lesbians. As discussed in Chapter 3, this data is necessarily incomplete because it is unclear what percentage of same-sex couples actually self-identify on the census, and the census tends to underreport marginalized groups. Moreover, gay and lesbian elders are much less likely to be partnered than their non-gay peers. As a result, census data restricted to partnered households may not be representative of gay and lesbian elders more generally. To the contrary, the census data may actually overstate the financial well-being of gay and lesbian elders because the elders who are not reflected in the data may very well be the ones who are at the highest risk of poverty – single elders with intersecting identities.

As outlined in Chapter 3, elder same-sex partnered households have less income, less retirement savings, and are less likely to own their home than their different-sex married peers. The disparity between gay and lesbian elders and their non-gay peers is most striking at the lower rungs of the economic ladder. Elder same-sex partnered households are more likely to live in poverty than their non-gay peers and elder female same-sex partnered households are almost twice as likely to live in poverty (Albelda et al. 2009: 11). Same-sex partnered households are also more likely to receive public assistance (Albelda et al. 2009: 14). Elder female same-sex partnered households have almost 20 percent (nearly $12,000) less income than different-sex married couples (Goldberg 2009: 7). They also rely more heavily on Social Security income as a percentage of their overall income, and receive, on average, 15 percent less in Social Security benefits than different-sex married couples (Goldberg 2009: 7–9). Elder female same-sex partnered households have considerably less income from retirement plans or accounts, and they are 21 percent less likely to have any income from interest, rentals, and dividends (Goldberg 2009: 10).

Given this rather bleak picture, it is not surprising that older gay men and lesbians report significant concerns with respect to their future financial security. For example, the Metlife Boomer study found that "[i]n planning for their own future care needs, LGBT baby boomers' most serious worries are financial, with one-third reporting that how to pay for [future] care is of most concern" (Metlife 2006: 12).

Caregiving Burdens

Aging policy in the United States assumes that the majority of caregiving will be provided by informal caregivers rather than paid professionals. As noted in Chapter 3, the fact that 80 percent of all caregiving is by informal caregivers has implications for gay and lesbian elders who rely on a single-generational chosen family for support and may be estranged from their family of origin. As individuals age, they are more likely to require assistance, and it is this assistance that will allow them to age in place. Within a single-generational chosen family, support obligations are often mutual, such that gay and lesbian elders are more likely to be providing caregiving support to one of their peers as well as receiving support.

Federal policy recognizes the importance of informal caregiving through the FMLA and the National Family Caregivers Support (NFCS) Program, but chosen family caregivers, including same-sex partners, only qualify under the NFCS Program. Created in 2000 as part of the reauthorization of the OAA, the NFCS Program awards grants to the states to support the efforts of informal "family caregivers" by providing "information and assistance services, individual counseling, organization of support groups and caregiver training, respite services to provide families temporary relief from caregiving responsibilities, and supplemental services (such as home care and home adaptations) on a limited basis to complement care provided by family and other informal caregivers." The 2006 amendments to the OAA expanded the definition of "family caregiver" to include any individual who is "an informal provider of in-home and community care to an older individual."

As a result of this amendment, same-sex partners and chosen family qualify for the services that are available under the NFCS Program. The AoA estimates that the NFCS Program provided services to more than 600,000 caregivers in 2008, including more than 9.3 million hours of respite care in the form of in-home care and adult day care. Because data on sexual orientation is not recorded, it is not possible to know how many of these 600,000 caregivers who took advantage of NFCS in 2008 were gay or lesbian or how many were caring for gay or lesbian elders. As explained in Chapter 3, however, studies suggest that gay and lesbian elders are often reluctant to utilize senior services due to their fear of discrimination. They are only 20 percent as likely as their non-gay peers to access senior-specific programs and services (King and Kimmel 2006: 266).

In contrast, the FMLA does not take an expansive view of family. The FMLA mandates that all public-sector employers and all private employers with 50 or more employees must grant their employees up to 12 weeks of unpaid leave per year to care for a spouse, child, or parent who has with a serious health condition. The command of DOMA makes it clear that a "spouse" for purposes of the FMLA does not include a same-sex spouse, much less a same-sex partner or a chosen family member. Although the FMLA would not be widely applicable to gay and lesbian elders because it is a workplace initiative, it would apply to those elders who are still working or who have a younger partner or younger chosen family member who would want to apply for an FMLA leave to care for the elder.

Spousal Benefits and DOMA

DOMA mandates that same-sex couples who are married in their state of residence are ineligible for federal spousal benefits. As a result, same-sex married couples in Massachusetts are entitled to file their state income taxes jointly, but they must file their federal income taxes separately and calculate their tax liability under the rates that apply to "unmarried" taxpayers. Same-sex couples who live in states that do not recognize same-sex marriage are unmarried for both state and federal purposes, regardless of their degree of financial interdependence. Advocates for marriage equality have just begun to quantify the "costs" of the legal barriers erected by DOMA (Bennett and Gates 2004). Even though a large percentage of gay and lesbian elders are not partnered, DOMA remains a significant legal barrier for partnered gay and lesbian elders with respect to federal spousal benefits, such as Social Security benefits, the Medicaid "spend down" rules, survivor veterans benefits, favorable tax treatment, and pension benefits.

Social Security

Administered by the Social Security Administration, an independent federal agency, Social Security is the largest federal entitlement program. Social Security is a vast safety net that provides a major source of income for the majority of seniors. In 2008, it paid nearly $650 billion in benefits to approximately 60 million retired and disabled workers, their spouses, former spouses, widows, and children. As of 2005, 71 percent of seniors relied on Social Security payments for at least half of their income, whereas 40 percent of elders relied on Social Security for 90 percent of their income or more (Sidor 2005: 24). For 26 percent of seniors, Social Security was their *only* source of income (Sidor 2005: 24).

The amount that a worker is entitled to receive under Social Security is generally a function of how long the individual worked and how much he or she earned. In order to be considered "fully insured," an individual must have worked a specified number of quarters (42 U.S.C. §414(a) 2010). The amount of an individual's Social Security payments is then determined by the individual's reported wages and self-employment income (42 U.S.C. §403(a) 2010). Accordingly, periods of unemployment or underemployment will adversely impact the amount of an individual's benefits. This consideration is particularly important for gay and lesbian elders whose earning potential and employment options over the years may have been compromised by homophobia and discrimination.

Under the Social Security program, there are a number of different spousal benefits: retirement benefits, disability benefits, and survivor's benefits. These benefits account for one-fifth of all federal spending. Upon retirement, the spouse of the retired worker is entitled to up to 50 percent of the worker's retirement benefit. This amount is in addition to the worker's benefit. Even divorced spouses are eligible for a spousal retirement benefit provided the marriage lasted at least 10 years and the non-worker divorced spouse has not remarried. The amount a divorced spouse receives does not reduce the amount a current spouse receives, which means that a worker can generate more than one spousal retirement benefit. When a worker is entitled to receive Social Security disability insurance, the worker's spouse is qualified to receive a payment equal to up to one half of the worker's disability benefit, if the spouse is 62 or older or is caring for the worker's child who is less than 16 years of age or is disabled. As with the retirement benefit, a divorced spouse may also qualify for the benefit provided the marriage lasted 10 years.

Social Security survivor benefits provide additional financial security to a traditional different-sex married couple where the wife did not work outside the home or worked at lower-paying jobs with greater periods of nonemployment due to childrearing responsibilities. In the case of a traditional different-sex marriage, it is more likely that the husband will predecease due to a combination of the longer life expectancy for women and the higher age at first marriage for men (Zernike 2006). When a worker dies, the surviving spouse and/or a divorced former spouse are entitled to a survivor's benefit equal to the worker's full retirement benefit. The spousal survivor benefits operate to increase the amounts that otherwise would be paid to the non-worker spouse, and the non-worker spouse is entitled to receive whichever benefit is greater – the survivor's benefit or the benefit the non-worker would be entitled to in his or her own right. Thus, Social Security survivor benefits insure that a widow will be maintained at a rate that is based on her husband's (presumably more lucrative) employment history.

As a result of DOMA, same-sex partners are not entitled to any Social Security spousal benefits, even if the partners are legally married under state law. In 2000, it was estimated that the exclusion of surviving same-sex partners costs gay and lesbian elders $124 million annually in forgone benefits (Cahill, South and Spade 2000: 43). A more recent Congressional Budget Office (CBO) report estimated that 30 percent of same-sex couples would receive higher benefits if federal law recognized same-sex marriage and if all partnered same-sex couples married (Congressional Budget Office 2004: 7). The CBO report estimated that by 2014 this would amount to $350 million annually (Congressional Budget Office 2004: 7). The disparity in treatment between same-sex couples, including those legally married under the law of their domicile, and different-sex married couples raises obvious questions of equity and uniformity because the spousal benefits are determined by the amount the worker paid into the program. A worker in a same-sex marriage who pays the same amount as a similarly situated worker in a different-sex marriage is entitled to fewer benefits because his or her partner is not eligible for survivor benefits.

Medicare/Medicaid

Medicare provides health insurance coverage for individuals who are 65 years of age or older. Originally created in 1965, it is now administered by the Centers for Medicare and Medicaid within the Department of Health and Human Services and is second only to Social Security in terms of its outlays. In 2008, Medicare provided health-care coverage for approximately 46 million Americans, and it is the largest single-payor health-care provider in the United States. Despite Medicare's breadth of coverage, it is not free, and millions of low-income seniors are unable to pay the out-of-pocket costs associated with required premiums, deductibles, and co-payments. Seniors who cannot afford these costs can turn to Medicaid, a program jointly run by the states and the federal government. Medicaid provides health insurance for low-income and disabled individuals regardless of age, and it has traditionally covered some expenses not eligible for Medicare reimbursement, such as long-term care and prescription drugs. For example, before Medicare added prescription drug coverage in 2006, many seniors could not afford the high cost of prescription medications. Seniors reported that they regularly skipped doses to keep the cost down and some resorted to having their prescriptions filled in Canada or Mexico, where the costs are considerably lower. In the case of gay and lesbian elders, the issue of prescription drug coverage was especially relevant because of the high incidence of HIV/AIDS among older gay men and the high cost of the complex drug "cocktail" required to keep the HIV virus in check (Waysdorf 2002: 55, 75). These elders were able to turn to Medicaid only after they had exhausted their savings because Medicaid is means tested.

Currently, Medicare does not cover the cost of long-term care in a skilled nursing facility or nursing home. The extremely high cost of long-term care has made Medicaid the only viable payment option for many middle-income seniors who did not purchase long-term care health insurance (Miller 2004). The income and asset thresholds imposed by Medicaid have given rise to a new and controversial method of middle-class estate planning, referred to as the Medicaid "spend down," where individuals have to spend or transfer their assets in order to qualify under the asset and income limitations imposed by the regulations (Miller 2004). The spousal impoverishment rules are an important exception to the Medicaid asset limits and the "spend down" provisions. Designed to avoid impoverishing the healthy spouse, these rules allow the healthy spouse to keep a portion of the income and assets of the institutionalized spouse. They also allow the healthy spouse to keep the marital home, regardless of its value, until his or her death. The spousal impoverishment rules do not apply to same-sex partners, and Medicaid does not aggregate their income and assets. If their home is owned by the institutionalized partner, a Medicaid lien will attach in order to recover payment of expenses. In the case of a surviving spouse, this lien is not recovered until his or her death, but in the case of a same-sex partner, recovery occurs after the death of the institutionalized spouse, thereby dispossessing the survivor.

As discussed below, marriage equality and the aggregation of spousal income and assets may actually have a negative effect on some gay and lesbian elders with respect to Medicaid coverage, as well as other forms of public assistance. This unintended consequence could result in considerable hardship given the already high level of poverty present among gay and lesbian elders.

Veterans Benefits

Gay and lesbian elders who are also veterans are entitled to veterans health benefits as explained more fully in Chapter 7. The continuation of the DADT policy, however, may make gay and lesbian elders reluctant to take advantage of these benefits, especially for HIV/AIDS-related treatment (Cahill, South and Spade 2000: 19). Spouses of disabled veterans, surviving spouses, and other dependents are also entitled to a host of benefits, ranging from a substantial grant of free health care to "no fee" passports for trips to visit a loved one's grave on foreign soil. In addition, surviving spouses of certain disabled veterans are entitled to a pension. Surviving spouses can also participate in the VA Loan Guaranty Program, and surviving spouses of service members killed while on active duty are entitled to a "death gratuity" of $100,000. The death gratuity would presumably be only of historical interest to gay and lesbian elders due to the mandatory retirement age of 62, but it provides an example of a death benefit that is only payable to a narrowly prescribed set of relatives, similar to some of the pension benefits discussed below. With respect to the military "death gratuity," if there is no surviving spouse, the amount must be paid to surviving children and, if there are no children, then it must be paid to surviving parents or siblings according to a statutorily prescribed schedule. The service member can allocate the payment among his or her parents and siblings, but the service member is not allowed to designate a non-relative beneficiary, subject to a limited exception for guardians.

Taxation

Traditionally, the federal tax code looked to state law to determine the validity of a marriage, but that changed with the enactment of DOMA in 1996. With respect to the federal income tax, the major issue affecting gay and lesbian taxpayers is that of filing status. As noted earlier, DOMA dictates that a same-sex couple legally married under state law may file their state income taxes jointly, but they will be considered "unmarried" for all purposes of federal law, including their Form 1040. As an increasing number of states recognize same-sex marriage or provide some form of marriage equivalence, the costs associated with being required to keep two sets of books and prepare two different sets of returns will add to what *The New York Times* has referred to as the high cost of being a gay couple (Bernard and Lieber 2009).

For some taxpayers, being considered "unmarried" for federal income-tax purposes may actually be a benefit, but for others it can be quite costly. Generally, upper income couples with relatively equal incomes incur a tax penalty when they marry because their combined tax bill will increase due to the progressive rate structure. Equal earners in the lower tax brackets do not incur a tax penalty upon marriage because, over the years, Congress has taken steps to alleviate the penalty for lower-income taxpayers. Couples with disparate income levels receive a marriage bonus when they get married because their combined tax burden goes down upon marriage, also due to the progressive rate structure. The 2004 CBO report estimated that the federal recognition of same-sex marriage would result in a net increase in federal tax revenues, meaning that, at the end of the day, marriage equality would cost same-sex couples an estimated $400 million in additional federal taxes for 2010 and an estimated $700 million annually from 2011 through 2014 (Congressional Budget Office 2004: 3). The fact that many same-sex couples would experience a tax penalty rather than a tax bonus if their partnership were recognized at the federal level makes sense because their salaries are not cross-effected by gender. In other words, both partners in a female same-sex couple are disadvantaged by the persistent gender inequality in wages. A female worker still makes approximately 76.5 cents for every dollar earned by a male worker (DeNavas-Walt et al. 2005). Accordingly, female same-sex couples would be less likely to have partners with disparate income levels. The same is true, but in reverse, for a gay male couple where neither partner is disadvantaged by gender. In the case of different-sex couples, the wage disparity is a structural feature of the gender difference that frames the relationship, thereby making the current marriage bonus/marriage penalty system that rewards disparate earners uniquely suited to benefit different-sex couples.

Despite the overall net revenue effect projected by the CBO, there are number of instances where the tax code clearly disadvantages same-sex partners, such as the taxation of employer-provided domestic partner health benefits. These instances remain important in the lives of individuals and as a general matter of equity and uniformity. Domestic partner health benefits are included in the employee-partner's gross income, unless the employee's partner also qualifies as a dependent. Employer-provided spousal benefits, on the other hand, are excluded from gross income. The rules determining who can qualify as a dependent are sufficiently broad to include same-sex partners and members of a chosen family because the rules allow even unrelated members of a household to qualify. A partner or member of a chosen family can qualify as a dependent, provided he or she is a member of the taxpayer's household, makes less than the exemption amount, and the taxpayer provides over one-half of his or her support (IRC §152(d)(2)(H)). Social Security payments count toward total support, which might make it difficult for a gay and lesbian elder to qualify as a dependent. If a partner or chosen family member qualifies, a taxpayer can claim an additional personal exemption. Even where a partner qualifies as a dependent, however, the supporting partner is not entitled to compute his or her taxes using the "head of household" rate schedule and still must file as "unmarried." Additionally, a same-sex partner is not entitled to file as a "surviving spouse" and take advantage of the more favorable tax rates applicable to that status (IRC §2(b)(3)(B)(i)).

Upper-income and wealthy same-sex partners are greatly disadvantaged under the federal estate and gift tax because they do not qualify for the marital deduction.[1] The unlimited marital deduction treats a husband and wife as a single taxable unit for transfer tax purposes, such that the vast majority of transfers between spouses never give rise to transfer tax liability. The unlimited marital deduction defers transfer taxation of marital assets until the death of the surviving spouse. The deduction is granted in the estate of the first spouse to die with the view that the property qualifying for the deduction will be included in the estate of the survivor, absent consumption. There is also an unlimited gift tax deduction, such that spouses can transfer property to each other during their lifetimes with no gift tax consequences. The unlimited marital deduction means that, for most high-asset married couples, it is relatively easy to avoid paying transfer tax until the death of the survivor. A surviving same-sex partner, however, cannot take advantage of this opportunity for tax deferral. There will be tax in the estate of the first to die, unless the decedent did not have sufficient assets (when combined with taxable gifts) to trigger estate tax. Assuming that there is estate tax in the estate of the first to die, the survivor will have fewer assets to enjoy during his or her lifetime and will not get the benefit of tax deferral. In addition, some states have inheritance taxes that burden even relatively modest estates. Pennsylvania, for instance, has a hard-hitting inheritance tax that does not provide an exemption for non-spousal transfers. As a result, in Pennsylvania all transfers to surviving partners and members of a chosen family are taxed at a rate of 15 percent.

Pensions and Retirement Plans

The Department of Labor estimates that approximately 60 percent of all full-time workers in the United States participate in an employer-sponsored retirement plan. For survivors, pension and retirement fund benefits often provide a significant source of financial support. Benefits payable under retirement plans are considered nonprobate assets, which means that they do not pass under the employee's will nor are they subject to the rules of intestate succession if the employee dies intestate. As a result, they are immune from the types of claims discussed in Chapter 7 that can be brought by family members. One major drawback, however, is that a worker does not always have power to designate a beneficiary of his or her own choosing. A number of recent cases have called attention to the fact that some plans limit permissible beneficiaries to spouses or close family members, thereby making it impossible for a surviving same-sex partner or other member of the employee's chosen family to receive the retirement benefit.

The Employee Retirement Security Act of 1974 (ERISA) regulates employer-sponsored retirement funds, (both defined benefit and defined contribution

---

1   When this book went to press in 2010, the federal estate and gift tax was in a period of unprecedented flux. This discussion reflects the application of the federal estate and gift tax prior to 2010 and beginning again in 2011.

plans), as well as the welfare plans that provide health insurance and disability benefits. Demands for marriage equity and workplace equity have mostly focused on employer-provided domestic partner health insurance. The issue of health benefits is extremely important because employer-provided health insurance is the manner by which the non-indigent non-retiree, non-veteran population gets health insurance in the United States. Efforts to secure workplace equity, however, do not always address the issue of retirement funds that are also under the province of ERISA. This failure seems to illustrate, once again, that contemporary gay and lesbian equality claims focus on the interests of younger able-bodied gay men and lesbians.

Defined benefit plans are the classic type of pension plan under which an employee is guaranteed a certain payment for life upon working for a set number of years. They are typically offered by large public employers and employers with unionized workforces. In recent years, defined benefit plans have declined in popularity in favor of more flexible defined contribution plans where employees can direct their own investment accounts that are funded with a mix of employer and employee contributions. Notwithstanding their declining popularity, defined benefit plans continue to provide a significant source of retirement funds.

With respect to the distribution of benefits, the combination of a lack of flexibility and a strong focus on the welfare of surviving spouses can leave surviving same-sex partners out in the cold. This problem occurs when the plan document provides that a surviving spouse is the only permissible beneficiary. Given DOMA, there remains a question as to whether a valid same-sex marriage would allow a surviving same-sex partner to qualify as a "spouse." Where a plan restricts the beneficiary to a spouse, then a covered employee who is married to a different-sex spouse at retirement receives a Qualified Joint and Survivor Annuity that pays out over the lifetimes of the employee and his spouse. If an employee is considered unmarried at retirement, then the employee receives a single life annuity that expires on the employee's death. For example, when Rep. Gerry Studds died in 2006, he was survived by his husband whom he had legally married under the laws of Massachusetts, the state that he had represented in Congress. Despite being legally married under state law, Rep. Studds' surviving spouse did not qualify for any federal spousal survivor benefits. Representative Studds' widower is currently a plaintiff in a federal lawsuit challenging DOMA, *Gill v. OPM.*

The greatest potential for hardship occurs where the covered employee dies before retirement. If the employee is survived by a different-sex spouse, the surviving spouse is entitled to a Qualified Pre-Retirement Survivor Annuity that pays out the accrued retirement funds over the spouse's life expectancy. If the employee is not married, there is no requirement that the defined benefit plan must pay out the accrued amount, although a plan *may* authorize the payment of the accrued amount to a designated beneficiary or certain enumerated family members. Where a plan limits the class of beneficiaries in such a way to exclude same-sex partners or chosen family, the only option for a plan participant is to urge the employer to amend the terms of the plan.

This is exactly what happened in 2006, when Laurel Hester, a police lieutenant in Ocean County, New Jersey, successfully lobbied the county board of freeholders to pass a resolution allowing county law enforcement officers to designate someone other than their spouse as the beneficiary of their pension funds. Laurel had been a police investigator with the Ocean County Prosecutor's Office for 25 years (Cave 2006). When she was diagnosed with terminal cancer, Laurel realized that, unlike a spouse, her partner of six years, Stacee Andree, would not receive her accrued pension benefits. Laurel further realized that without those funds, Stacee would not be able to keep the house they had bought together. For over a year, Laurel urged the county freeholders to pass the resolution. At that time, New Jersey had a registered domestic partnership law. State law specifically authorized local authorities to extend benefits to registered domestic partners, but it did not require that they do so. As Laurel's condition worsened, she garnered support from other law-enforcement officers and gay and lesbian organizations. When Laurel was too weak to attend a meeting of the board of freeholders, she videotaped her message to the board and asked them "to make a change for good ... a change in the lives of so many people who have dedicated themselves to county government" (Cave 2006). After watching Laurel's video, the freeholders again rejected the request, but reversed themselves only seven days later after public pressure in support of Laurel and Stacee intensified. Laurel died a little over three weeks later on January 20, 2006, at the age of 49. Stacee received her pension benefits, and a film about the ordeal, titled *Freeheld*, received the Academy Award for best short documentary in 2008.

A similar situation arose a year earlier, in 2005, when William (Bill) Swensor died unexpectedly at the age of 66 and was survived by his partner of 51 years, Marvin Burrows (Grant 2010: 56). Bill and Marvin had started dating when they were just 15 and 17, respectively. As a teenager, Bill was kicked out of his home when his father found out about the relationship, and Bill moved in with Marvin and his mother. Bill and Marvin were registered domestic partners and were married in San Francisco in 2004 during a brief period of civil disobedience when the city had issued marriage licenses to same-sex couples. Bill was a member of the International Longshore and Warehouse Union (ILWU) and worked the graveyard shift in a warehouse for 38 years. When Marvin applied to receive Bill's health and pension benefits, his request was denied. Two years later, the union was able to re-negotiate the terms of its contract to provide pension benefits for domestic partners, and the new contract made the coverage retroactive to Bill's date of death. During that two-year period, Marvin struggled financially, and lost the house that he had shared with Bill for 35 years. When he was notified about the contract change, Marvin remarked, "finally ... my 51 years with Bill will mean something to others, not just to me" (National Center for Lesbian Rights 2007).

In both of these cases, the plan did not offer the covered employee the option of designating a beneficiary other than a spouse. However, even when a plan authorizes the employee to designate a beneficiary, there will always be employees who, for whatever set of reasons, procrastinate and fail to fill out the beneficiary designation. Typically, in the absence of a beneficiary designation, the plan will provide an order of distribution that tracks the rules of intestate succession with the final recipient being the employee's estate. Unless the plan specifically includes same-sex partners, a surviving partner would have to depend on the generosity of the deceased partner's family. However, as discussed in prior chapters, relations between surviving partners and next of kin can be strained by homophobia, disbelief, disapproval, opportunism, or perhaps a sincere belief that "family" should come first. It is unclear which motivation was at play in the case of the family of Tampa police officer Lois Marrero, who was killed at age 40 in the line of duty by a suspect in a bank robbery in 2001 (Mcleod 2002). Lois' partner of 11 years, Detective Mickie Mashburn, tried to convince the city of Tampa that she should be treated as a 'spouse' over the objections of Lois' family because Lois had failed to designate Mickie as the beneficiary of a $50,000 lump sum death benefit. If Mickie had been Lois' legal spouse, she would have automatically received one-half of Lois' salary for life (Herdy 2001b). The Tampa pension board voted 7-1 to reject Mickie's request and the board awarded a lump sum payment of $50,000 to Lois' relatives (Herdy 2001b).

In addition to the limitations inherent in some of the plans themselves, non-spouse beneficiaries are also subject to less favorable federal tax treatment for amounts received from a decedent's retirement fund and, until recently, the rules governing hardship withdrawals did not take into account hardships encountered by non-relatives. The Pension Protection Act of 2006 (PPA) addressed both of these concerns. The PPA made two changes to federal pension rules that have improved the situation for gay and lesbian elders, but the rules are still a long way from treating same-sex partners as spouses. The reforms do not expressly reference same-sex partners, but instead allow for a non-related designated beneficiary. Although this does not embrace marriage equality, it has the added benefit of making room for chosen family.

The first change under the PPA involved hardship withdraws. Under prior law, a taxpayer was only entitled to make a hardship withdraw from a retirement plan to alleviate the financial hardship of the covered employee, the employee's spouse, and the employee's dependents. The PPA amended ERISA to allow a withdrawal for financial hardship encountered by any beneficiary designated under the plan, thereby potentially including a same-sex partner or a member of a chosen family. The provision is permissive only, and it does not require plans to provide hardship withdrawals.

The second change altered the tax treatment of non-spousal distributions from retirement plans. Prior to the PPA, any non-spousal distribution from a tax-deferred retirement plan was immediately subject to income tax, whereas distributions to a surviving spouse did not trigger immediate taxation. As a result, a surviving same-sex partner (or other non-spousal beneficiary) had to pay a considerable percentage of the original principal in income tax, thereby producing less income going forward. Spousal distributions, on the other hand, retain their tax-deferred character, and the surviving spouse is permitted to "roll over" the distribution to his or her retirement fund. The surviving spouse only incurs income taxation as distributions are made from the fund and continues to earn income on a principal amount that has not been diminished by a large tax bite.

Under the new law, a non-spousal lump sum distribution is not immediately subject to income tax, but instead can be "rolled over" into a special retirement account that bears the name of the deceased employee. Non-spousal beneficiaries must either withdraw funds within five years of the death of the plan participant or start taking the funds immediately over the life expectancy of the deceased participant or that of the beneficiary. In contrast, a spousal beneficiary can wait until age 70½ before receiving distributions and, therefore, is entitled to a much longer period of tax deferral.

Means-Tested Entitlements: Unintended Consequences of Marriage Equality

As with the case of the federal income tax laws, there are several instances where DOMA may actually advantage married gay and lesbian elders. These cases involve instances where entitlements are means tested. The current refusal to count the other partner's income may help explain the relatively large proportion of gay men and lesbian elders who are receiving some form of public assistance relative to their non-gay peers. If the federal government recognized same-sex marriage, then the income and assets of the elder's same-sex spouse would be included to determine whether the elder qualified for a number of public benefits, such as Medicaid and SSI. Both Medicaid and SSI are means-tested entitlement programs that are available to the elderly and the disabled. In order to qualify for SSI, the program counts a spouse's income and assets. In 2004, the CBO estimated that the recognition of same-sex marriage would save the federal government approximately $100 million annually in SSI payments by 2014. To put this another way, individuals in same-sex partnerships would receive $100 million less a year in SSI. The CBO concluded that the same was true for Medicaid. Even with the added protection that a same-sex couple would receive for their home, the CBO determined that the net result would be a loss for same-sex couples. The CBO estimated that the recognition of same-sex marriage would translate into total annual Medicaid savings of $350 million, meaning that married same-sex couples would receive $350 million less a year in medical benefits.

Beyond DOMA

With respect to federal benefits, DOMA stands as the most obvious barrier to equality – at least for same-sex partners. The state-by-state strategy that marriage advocates have pursued can yield only partial victories so long as DOMA remains in place. By the same token, however, the legislative repeal of DOMA would only provide full marriage equality for those same-sex couples who reside in states that recognize same-sex marriage. In the absence of DOMA, the question of whether a couple was legally married for federal purposes would be determined by the law of the couple's domicile. Individuals in states that recognize same-sex marriage would qualify as married for all federal purposes, including taxation, Social Security, the FMLA, and pension laws, but the repeal of DOMA would not help same-sex couples in non-marriage states. For some gay and lesbian elders, federal marriage recognition would produce a net benefit, but for the most vulnerable – those living at or near the poverty level – marriage recognition could produce a penalty that would make them lose even more ground.

The vast majority of states, however, do not recognize same-sex marriage, and, to further complicate matters, the majority of states have amended their state constitutions to expressly prohibit same-sex marriage. Marriage equality in these states will require not just the repeal of DOMA, but the adoption of state constitutional amendments authorizing same-sex marriage. Comprehensive marriage equality for all same-sex couples would require a U.S. Supreme Court ruling along the lines of the 1967 landmark case *Loving v. Virginia*, where the Court invalidated a Virginia statute that criminalized inter-racial marriage on both equal protection and due process grounds. At the time, 16 states had criminal miscegenation laws. For comparison purposes, it is interesting to note that a 1968 Gallup Poll, taken the year after the *Loving* decision, reported that 73 percent of the public disapproved of interracial marriages. It was not until 1994 that a majority of those polled approved of interracial marriage. In contrast, a 2009 Gallup Poll showed that only 57 percent of the public disapproved of same-sex marriage, and a much larger percentage approve of a marriage-equivalent status such as civil unions.

It is difficult to assess the likelihood that a direct constitutional challenge to the prohibition of same-sex marriage would be successful.[2] Marriage advocates had actively discouraged litigation that would ultimately raise the federal question because they thought it was prudent to wait until more states had embraced same-sex marriage. The case arising out of Proposition 8, *Perry v. Schwarzenegger*, has the potential to mandate nationwide marriage equality, but the case was very controversial among the marriage-equality advocates who had favored a state law approach. The court challenge was orchestrated by the unlikely duo of Ted Olson, the former solicitor general under President George Bush, and David Boies, the liberal ace litigator. The pair had represented opposite sides in the case that decided the 2000 presidential election between George Bush and Al Gore. In 2010, the

---

2   It is also possible to challenge DOMA on "full faith and credit" grounds. At the time of DOMA's enactment, constitutional law scholars testified before Congress and questioned its validity under the full faith and credit clause of the U.S. Constitution with respect to Congress' ability to grant the states authority to refuse to recognize a marriage performed in a sister state. The same concerns were voiced when the Senate considered an amendment to the Constitution to prohibit same-sex marriage, the Federal Marriage Amendment, in 2004. At the time, several senators who supported the amendment asserted that the clarifying amendment was necessary because DOMA could not withstand a constitutional challenge.

Federal District Court for the Northern District of California ruled that Proposition 8 violated both the due process clause and the equal protection clause of the 14th Amendment.

In the event that same-sex marriage became available nationwide, the 2004 CBO report estimates that the recognition of same-sex marriage on the federal level would actually have a net positive effect on revenue. When comparing increased costs, such as spousal benefits under Social Security, to the revenue that would be raised in the tax and entitlements areas, the CBO estimates a net revenue increase of between $500 million and $700 million annually. The estimate includes the cost of extending employee benefits to the same-sex spouses of current and retired federal employees. The CBO report concluded that recognizing same-sex marriage would "improve the budget's bottom line to a small extent." Despite the fact that the figures sound high and will doubtless result in some individual hardship, the CBO report characterized the change as "small" because the amounts represent less than 0.01 percent of all revenue.

An alternative way to provide equal access to federal spousal benefits would be to institute marriage equivalence on the federal level. This way, a couple could qualify for federal spousal benefits regardless of the law of their domicile. For the same-sex couples in states without relationship recognition, this reform would create a reverse lack of uniformity whereby the couple would be married for federal purposes, but unmarried for state purposes. A federal scheme of marriage equivalence would require a federal definition of marriage and presumably some sort of registration mechanism whereby a couple could record their partnership for federal purposes. Such a proposal is distinct from the concept embodied in the Domestic Partnership and Benefits Obligations Act (DPBOA) that would extend spousal employment benefits to both the same-sex and different-sex domestic partners of federal employees.

Finally, in terms of pension reform, there is a role for individual employers who can make a big difference by amending their retirement plans to provide benefits to same-sex partners to avoid the results encountered by Laurel Hester and Bill Swensor. Employers may balk at the potential for increased cost, but the Williams Institute reports the cost to employers would be negligible. On the other hand, the benefit to a survivor's well-being may be immeasurable. The Board of Freeholders of Ocean County. hid behind the issue of higher costs for more than a year as it resisted Laurel's request on behalf of her partner. One freeholder said the cost would be too high and another used a slippery-slope argument, saying that including domestic partners was unfair because it did not let siblings or other relatives who lived together qualify for pension benefits (Cave 2006). This last argument is frequently used to undermine the demand for domestic partner benefits because the addition of siblings or friends or unmarried different-sex couples can significantly raise the costs of benefits, especially health insurance. For example, the DPBOA that would extend federal benefits to the registered domestic partners of federal employees has a very high price tag because it includes coverage for different-sex couples, and the CBO estimates that 83 percent of the individuals who would register for the coverage would have different-sex partners (Congressional Budget Office 2004: 10).

Chapter 10
Fear of Discrimination and Anti-Gay Bias

The fear of encountering discrimination and prejudice prevents gay and lesbian elders from taking advantage of a wide variety of senior services, as well as medical assistance, and makes them extremely wary of service providers generally. The D'Augelli and Grossman nationwide study of gay men and lesbians 60 years of age and older found a high level of victimization, with one in five respondents reporting that they had experienced harassment or discrimination at work (D'Augelli and Grossman 2001). With this in mind, it is easy to see how the financial difficulties reported by many gay and lesbian elders outlined in the prior chapter may have roots in the prevailing homophobia of the time in which they came of age and entered the workforce, combined with the forces of racism and sexism in the case of those elders with intersecting identities. For the pre-Stonewall generation, however, homophobia and discrimination are not relics of the past. Anti-gay bias continues to figure prominently in the lives of gay and lesbian elders. Its primary venue for expression is no longer the office or the loading dock, but instead it is the senior center, the doctor's office, the assisted living facility, and the nursing home – spaces that are far more private and intimate than the workplace. An individual who experiences anti-gay bias and harassment at work still gets to go home at the end of the day, but there is no refuge for gay and lesbian elders who can face bias where they live and, with respect to the threat posed by home health aides, may be forced to invite their abusers into their homes.

Anti-discrimination measures, such as ENDA, that focus primarily on the workplace, will not be sufficient to address the fear expressed by gay and lesbian elders, and overcoming their fear is essential to facilitating successful aging and minimizing social isolation. Countering the fear and discrimination experienced by gay and lesbian elders requires broad-based statutory reforms on both the state and local levels in public accommodations and housing. Because heteronormative assumptions and anti-gay bias are so entrenched in certain sectors, a comprehensive plan to protect gay and lesbian elders should also include cultural competency programs and anti-bullying measures. Finally, as in the case of employee benefits, the private sector can also take positive steps to minimize the potential for discrimination against gay and lesbian elders.

Intimate Senior-Specific Venues

For the pre-Stonewall generation, the closet was a non-negotiable fact of life, and the risks that accompanied being outed were considerable, including loss of job, civil commitment, and estrangement from friends and family. Today, the decision of many gay and lesbian elders to be closeted is not motivated by some quaint attachment to modesty or an old-fashioned sense of privacy or even shame. The members of the pre-Stonewall generation believe that they once again face considerable risks on account of their sexual orientation. Older gay men and lesbians report a very high level of anti-gay victimization and a concern that they will experience victimization in the future.

The National Family Caregiving Alliance advises caution when weighing the pros and cons of whether to disclose sexual orientation to an elder-care provider. Under Frequently Asked Questions, the organization offers the following advice in response to a question asking whether an elder same-sex couple should come out to the employees of an AAA because the health of one partner has deteriorated:

> This is clearly one of the most delicate—and important—questions you can face. Unfortunately, there is no easy answer, no cut-and-dried formula to follow. How you proceed may well depend upon whether state and local laws where you live protect LGBT individuals from discrimination. You may decide it is best to be open with service agencies from the start, especially if you have learned from acquaintances or local LGBT resources which organizations are likely to maintain an open attitude. Or you may adopt a step-by-step approach, confiding in individual care providers whom you have come to trust or raising concerns only when you feel your needs are not being fully met.

As the response continues, it becomes clear that the organization is advising gay and lesbian elders on how to remain closeted while dealing with elder care service providers:

> The importance of having the proper documents in place before a loved one becomes ill and can no longer make decisions cannot be stressed enough. This will allow you the greatest flexibility in developing a network of available services and grant you, your partner, or a close friend the legal right to act in each other's behalf without having to offer anyone—biological family members, service organizations, government agencies—in-depth explanations about your relationship. As the person with legal authority, you do not need to define your relationship. If you prefer, *you can simply say you are a good friend* [emphasis added] who has the legal authority to make decisions on her/his behalf.

The notion that the National Family Caregiving Alliance is giving partnered gay and lesbian elders tips about how to conceal their relationships is troubling given that contemporary models of gay and lesbian identity formation maintain that openness about one's sexual orientation is an essential part of becoming a well-adjusted and fully integrated individual (Friend 1991). The fact that expert advice offered by a national caregiving organization runs contrary to the best advice for successful aging speaks to the extent of the dilemma encountered by gay and lesbian elders. "You can simply say you are a good friend," seems like cold comfort, but it also illustrates the use of the closet as an adaptive device to avoid bias and harassment.

All individuals, regardless of their sexual orientation or gender identity, report considerable anxiety when faced with the prospect of becoming dependent on others as they age. Although only 4 percent of all seniors aged 75 and older live in nursing homes, the nursing home remains a powerful symbol in the popular imagination, where it is associated with dependency, neglect, and sadness (AoA 2009d). Objectively, gay and lesbian elders face significant disadvantages in the aging process, including their lack of multi-generational support networks, financial insecurity, and the legal fragility of chosen families. They also have to face the reality that anti-gay bias persists and that, as elders, they are vulnerable to discrimination, as well as abuse, harassment, and exploitation. According to the Metlife Boomer survey, however, older gay and lesbian elders report more anxiety about aging than do their non-gay peers (Metlife 2006: 13).

In an attempt to shield themselves from anti-gay bias, gay and lesbian elders report that they affirmatively choose to be closeted in institutional settings or when dealing with health-care providers (Gross 2007). Anti-gay bias can manifest itself in a variety of ways in the eldercare setting, ranging from intentional discriminatory treatment to policies that disadvantage gay and lesbian elders due to unspoken heteronormative assumptions. But it is important to remember that abuse and violence are always potential outcomes when discriminatory attitudes are directed at a vulnerable population. Thus, when gay and lesbian elders evaluate the cost of the closet, they are weighing the possibility that they will be subject to abuse or violence, not simply that they will be subject to some form of economic discrimination or that they will be denied access to housing. Their fear is much more visceral. Gay and lesbian elders fear that they will be subject to abuse and mistreatment on account of their sexual orientation while in an institutional setting or in their home. They are worried that health-care workers will hurt or neglect them on account of their sexual orientation. Simply put, they fear for their safety and, as discussed in Chapter 6, studies suggest that fear is not misplaced.

Federal and State Legislative and Regulatory Reform

The current focus on ENDA as a means of combating anti-gay discrimination is obviously inadequate to address the needs of gay and lesbian elders who are more likely to encounter discrimination in housing and public accommodations than in the workforce. As noted in Chapter 7, the first federal gay rights bill that was introduced in Congress in the 1974 was a broad-based bill that would have provided protection from discrimination in employment, housing, and public accommodation. A return to a broad-based anti-discrimination platform would advance the interests of gay and lesbian elders and underscore the unpleasant fact that anti-gay discrimination permeates all aspects of individual's life – not merely the workforce. Following the existing outline of the Civil Rights Act of 1964 and the Fair Housing Act of 1968, federal legislation could prohibit discrimination in privately owned public accommodations, state and municipally owned facilities, and housing. With respect to public accommodations, the legislation would have to include a definition of public accommodation that was more expansive than the one in Title II of the Civil Rights Act of 1964 in order to cover areas of specific concern to seniors. In this regard, the definition of public accommodation under the American with Disabilities Act could provide a useful starting point. It specifically includes senior centers, health-care providers, and hospitals, whereas the definition of public accommodation in the Civil Rights Act of 1964 encompasses the venues associated more directly with the struggle that led to its enactment: lunch counters, gas stations, and theaters.

An often-overlooked provision of the Civil Rights Act of 1964 is Title VI, which prohibits discrimination by any agency receiving federal funding. Comprehensive anti-discrimination prohibitions would go a long way to furthering equity (and dignity) in aging for gay and lesbian elders and perhaps increase the rate at which gay and lesbian elders utilize federally funded senior services. Amending Title VI (or enacting separate legislation) to add anti-discrimination protection on account of sexual orientation would have an extremely wide reach because senior centers and senior-specific programs across the country receive federal funding under the OAA and hospitals and nursing homes receive Medicare/Medicaid funding. The OAA, in particular, sponsors a broad array of community-based services and resources through the AAAs, many of which are designed to maximize the ability of seniors to age in place within their communities. The OAA also established the National Eldercare Locator Service, which creates an ombudsmen program to investigate and resolve complaints of residents in long-term care facilities and safeguard seniors from elder abuse. The ombudsmen program requires states to undertake activities to educate the public regarding elder abuse. For gay and lesbian elders, the ombudsmen program could serve as a valuable ally, assuming elder abuse was defined to include mistreatment on account of sexual orientation. Finally, the OAA also provides funding for research on aging and the inclusion of sexual orientation would help to fill in the gaps with respect to the missing data on gay and lesbian elders.

Short of amending Title VI of the Civil Rights Act of 1964, it would be possible to secure the protection and inclusion of gay and lesbian elders through targeted legislative and regulatory changes in federal aging policy. For example, the 2005 White House Conference on Aging recommended that the AoA add sexual orientation and gender identity in the definition of "minority populations" for purposes of certain research, and the AoA reluctantly complied. Although that concession was controversial and hard fought, the advent of a new administration in Washington created some further momentum for change. As discussed in Chapter 3, HHS announced in 2009 that it would award a three-year grant to SAGE for the development of a resource center on LGBT aging. That same year, the Department of Housing and Urban Development announced its intention to clarify the term "family" to include otherwise eligible LGBT individuals and couples for purposes of the eligibility rules for public housing and the Housing Choice Voucher programs. This change does not solely benefit gay and lesbian elders, but it does represent the power of regulatory change to introduce and impose anti-discrimination protection.

In addition to these federal initiatives, there are many opportunities on the state level to address the concerns of gay and lesbian elders. Although nearly half of the states prohibit discrimination in employment on the basis of sexual orientation, considerably fewer states extend that nondiscrimination protection to public accommodations and housing. California is currently the only state with specific legislation designed to protect gay and lesbian elders. The Older Californians Equality and Protection Act enacted in 2006 requires the California Department of Aging to incorporate LGBT elders in its area needs assessment and related activities. It further mandates LGBT-specific cultural competency training for individuals who work and volunteer for state aging programs. A second California law passed in 2008 now requires LGBT cultural competency training for nurses and other health-care professionals.

The Promise of Cultural Competency Programs

In the field of health care, the importance of cultural competency is widely acknowledged, at least with respect to racial and ethnic minorities. In 1994, Congress mandated the Office of Minority Health (OMH) in HHS to address cultural and linguistic barriers to health care and the resulting health disparities caused by miscommunication. The following year, OMH created the Center for Linguistic and Cultural Competence in Health Care to enhance the ability of the health-care system to deliver linguistically appropriate and culturally competence services to populations with limited English proficiency. The California law is an example of how such programs can be expanded to include gay and lesbian elders. This expansion recognizes that the barriers encountered by gay and lesbian elders are sufficiently deep to be explained in terms of cultural differences. The pre-Stonewall generation shares a unique and formative history that continues to influence their behavior and beliefs, especially with respect to their relationship with health-care providers. The tools developed to bridge cultural differences can also be adapted to improve access for gay and lesbian elders to senior services and elder-care resources.

The goal of cultural competency training is to empower individuals to communicate cross-culturally. As a starting point, this requires an individual to have an awareness of his or her own cultural frame of reference. In the case of gay and lesbian elders, an elder-care service provider would be urged to recognize the pervasiveness of heteronormativity and anti-gay bias and examine his or her attitude toward these subjects. Service providers would also learn about the specific concerns and challenges faced by gay and lesbian elders and consider how existing practices and policies may present a barrier to access. Cultural competency programs can be mandated or voluntarily adopted by elder-care providers, as well as government agencies. For example, in Boulder, Colorado, the County Aging Service runs Project Visibility, which is designed to educate and train service providers regarding the needs and concerns of gay and lesbian elders (Grant 2010: 99).

Assessment tools suggest that cultural competency training can be highly effective in addressing the treatment of gay and lesbian elders. The 2008 training assessment conducted for Project Visibility surveyed elder-care providers who had been trained in LGBT elder cultural competency. It found that 83 percent of the respondents agreed with the statement that "I understand the fears of LGBT elders better than I did before" (Project Visibility 2008). In terms of dealing directly with elders, 89 percent of the respondents agreed with the statement that "I don't make assumptions about any elder's marital status or life experiences" (Project Visibility 2008). Only 29 percent reported that they had not made any changes in their workplace as a result of the training (Project Visibility 2008). The respondents reported that they had taken various positive steps, such as: displaying non-discrimination posters, providing additional employee training, and revising admission material and forms. Most importantly, 15 percent responded that they believed patients and potential patients had come out to them on account of the changes prompted by the training (Project Visibility 2008). This finding is consistent with a study of older gay men and lesbians where 34 percent of the respondents believed that hiding their sexual orientation would be necessary if they had to enter an assisted living facility, but 93 percent of the same group believed that providing diversity training for the staff and administrators could help ease their transition (Johnson et al. 2005).

At a minimum, education regarding gay and lesbian elders, their experience, and the challenges they face may help eliminate the many instances where gay and lesbian elders are inadvertently treated poorly or subjected to disparate treatment. For example, many retirement facilities have policies that unmarried individuals cannot live together. In states without marriage equality, same-sex partners are always unmarried and, therefore, partnered gay and lesbian elders would be perpetually barred under such a policy. If the exclusion of same-sex couples is unintended, then cultural competency training would reveal the policy's heteronormative bias and the facility could easily change the policy to accommodate same-sex partners. Cultural competency thus encourages service providers to be proactive because gay and lesbian elders affected by the policy may be reluctant to challenge it. In fact, gay and lesbian elders may interpret the existence of the policy as a sign of affirmative hostility where none is intended. Cultural competency can help correct such unintended signaling.

On the other hand, cultural competency training has a much more difficult task when the participants are actively anti-gay. In those instances, education regarding pre-Stonewall history and the contemporary isolation of gay and lesbian elders may not be sufficient to reform a homophobic heart. Obviously, in these cases, anti-discrimination protections, as well as an accessible ombudsman structure, are essential to safeguarding the welfare of gay and lesbian elders. Where cultural competency training is not adequate to overcome entrenched homophobia, anti-discrimination protection can empower gay and lesbian elders to challenge the offending policy or practice – even when the facility is privately owned. For example, when Shelia Ortiz-Taylor, a professor of literature and a well-known author, and her partner Joy Lewis, a librarian, applied to purchase a unit in the Westminster Oaks Retirement Community in Tallahassee, Florida, their application was denied because the community had a policy against two unrelated individuals living together (National Center for Lesbian Rights 2008). Sheila and Joy had entered into a civil union in Vermont, but there was no relationship recognition available under Florida law. The couple sued the national chain of retirement communities under a county anti-discrimination ordinance that barred discrimination in housing on the basis of sexual orientation and marital status. The case ultimately settled. Although the terms of the settlement are confidential, the women have stated that they are looking forward to becoming members of the retirement community and that they were pleased that the community had clarified that its services were open to all on equal terms.

Cultural competency programs are designed to reach elder-care providers and administrators and staff, but, as explained in Chapter 6, other seniors can also be a source of anti-gay bias. To avoid conflicts among residents, some nursing homes will move gay and lesbian elders (or elders perceived to be gay or lesbian) out of the general population, thereby accommodating the fears and prejudices of the other residents. In 2007, the *New York Times* reported that in one instance this practice had a tragic result (Gross 2007). A nursing home moved an elderly gay man, who had neither family nor friends because there had been complaints from the residents and their family members (Gross 2007). The man was moved to a floor for patients with dementia because the administration knew the patients on that floor would not complain about his perceived sexual orientation (Gross 2007). The gay senior, however, did not have dementia. He was perfectly aware of his surroundings and later hanged himself (Gross 2007).

Stories such as this indicate that anti-discrimination protections and educational programs must also be directed toward non-gay seniors. As explained in Chapter 6, the majority of individuals 65 and older view homosexuality unfavorably. Widespread anti-gay sentiment in congregate living facilities and senior centers can make gay and lesbian elders feel unwelcome, and possibly subject them to ostracism, harassment, and violence. One solution may be the imposition of anti-bullying rules for residents that are similar to those that have been enacted as part of the "Safe Schools" initiatives and campaigns. Although some of these measures specifically prohibit bullying on account of sexual orientation, others are directed at generic bullying. For example, in 2008, the Florida legislature enacted anti-bullying legislation for all primary and secondary schools (Florida Statute 2008a). The legislation defines "bullying" as "systematically and chronically inflicting physical hurt or psychological distress on one or more students" (Florida

Statute 2008b). The statute provides that the prohibited behavior includes: teasing; social exclusion; threats, intimidation; stalking; physical violence; theft; sexual, religious, or racial harassment; public humiliation; or destruction of property (Florida Statute 2008b).

Market-Based Solutions

In the short term, it is unlikely that even the best anti-discrimination laws and the most thorough cultural competency training will be sufficient to quell the fears of gay men and lesbians regarding senior housing and the dangers presented by home health aides. Gay and lesbian elders consistently report a preference for senior housing options that cater to gay and lesbian elders. In one study, 67 percent of the participants stated that they would prefer to live in an "LGBT- only retirement communit[y]" (Orel 2006: 233). Nancy Orel notes that "the primary reason ... was the belief that if their sexual orientation were known, they would not be welcomed in existing retirement communities" (Orel 2006: 233).

Not surprisingly, the market has responded to this demand with a number of proposals for gay-friendly retirement facilities. These proposals have received considerable media attention, but remarkably few of them have turned out to be viable. It is estimated that between two and three dozen projects never advanced beyond predevelopment stage (Grant 2010: 101). At least three others opened briefly, but then closed (Grant 201: 101). It is possible that the initial optimism surrounding these projects was based at least in part on the myth of gay affluence. There are approximately eight gay-friendly retirement communities in operation today with another 20 in development. Only one of the facilities offers affordable housing and only one includes assisted living options. Even if all of the projects that had been in production over the last several years actually opened, the demand for gay-friendly housing would still outstrip supply.

Just as employers have increasingly adopted policies that promote workplace equity for their gay and lesbian employees, senior housing facilities can also play a role in providing a welcoming atmosphere for gay and lesbian elders. As more elder-care providers become sensitive to the needs of gay and lesbian elders and more attuned to the potential for anti-gay bias and harassment, there is an opportunity for accreditation agencies to institute standards that mandate equal treatment of gay and lesbian elders. For example, in 2002, a major accreditation organization, the Joint Commission on the Accreditation of Healthcare Organizations (JCAHO), added "respect" for sexual orientation to its accreditation standards for assisted living facilities and nursing homes. Specifically, the standard now calls for respect for "residents' habits and patterns of living (including lifestyle choices related to sexual orientation)." Although this represents a step in the right direction, the accreditation standard, as presently written, is vague and lacks a clear enforcement mechanism. Moreover, it is phrased in the pejorative language of anti-gay politics that insists on describing homosexuality as a "lifestyle."

An organic home-grown alternative to senior housing is the concept of the Naturally Occurring Retirement Community (NORC) that is currently gaining in popularity. NORCs are a much less expensive substitute for the traditional assisted living facility or retirement home and, in many ways, are tailor-made for gay and lesbian elders who have a single-generational chosen family and a strong preference for aging in place. A NORC develops when individuals who are aging in place within the community choose to live in close proximity to one another. This proximity provides social and emotional support, but it also facilitates the coordination of aging services and supportive programs. SAGE currently sponsors an LGBT NORC in Harlem. With funding from the State of New York, SAGE established a community drop-in center to serve the residents of the NORC. The drop-in center offers numerous health programs, HIV screening and counseling, workshops on topics such as "Safety & the Law," cultural programming, book clubs, outings to local places of interest, and old-fashioned social mixers.

Conclusion

For many gay and lesbian elders, the acceptance of their non-normative sexuality was a long and difficult process. They came of age at a time when homosexuality was criminalized and classified as a severe mental illness. Many accepted the prevailing scientific view that homosexuality was a sickness and attempted a "cure" through psychotherapy and other more intrusive means. At this time, the closet was a way of life, and there was no public counter-narrative of gay pride. Estranged from their families of origin, they formed chosen families and cautiously navigated the multitude of hazards that were associated with being a homosexual in pre-Stonewall America. Today, even those elders who later embraced the post-Stonewall discourse of pride and openness report that, as they have advanced in years, they have retreated to the closet in search of safety and security. As a result, many gay and lesbian elders are spending their final years frightened and closeted.

Although gay men and lesbians currently enjoy an unprecedented degree of social and political acceptance, this acceptance does not yet translate to formal legal equality. In the vast majority of states, gay and lesbian elders are not permitted to marry nor are they covered by anti-discrimination protections. On the federal level, there are no anti-discrimination laws, and DOMA denies gay and lesbian elders federal recognition, regardless of whether they are legally married under state law. Moreover, homosexuality remains stigmatized and politicized while anti-gay bias, harassment, and violence persist as part of the social fabric. Studies show that, over the course of their lifetimes, older gay men and lesbians have experienced high levels of victimization on account of their sexual orientation. They have also been subject to decades of government-sponsored discrimination in the workplace, leaving many gay and lesbian elders financially insecure.

For these reasons, today's gay and lesbian elders are extremely vulnerable. In their senior years, they are struggling to protect themselves (and their chosen family) from homophobic service providers and the prejudices of their non-gay peers. Without financial resources or legal protections, gay and lesbian elders predictably turn to the closet as an adaptive strategy. Although the closet may minimize the immediate threat of anti-gay bias, being closeted about one's sexual orientation is contrary to the existing developmental models for successful gay and lesbian aging, and the individual costs involved in maintaining the level of secrecy necessitated by the closet are quite high (Friend 1991). Nevertheless, many gay and lesbian elders continue to conclude that the closet is their only option.

Efforts to guarantee equity in aging for gay and lesbian elders must center on the development of a livable alternative to the closet. Models for successful gay and lesbian aging advocate openness and involvement with the gay and lesbian community, but it is unrealistic (and perhaps dangerous) to urge gay and lesbian elders to adopt out-and-proud personas without equipping them with the tools to address the perils they face daily. The first step toward this livable alternative is to acknowledge that gay and lesbian elders differ from the post-Stonewall generations and their conceptions of self and perceptions of others are still influenced by pre-Stonewall views on homosexuality. They are living examples of the historical contingency of gay and lesbian identity.

The second step is to recognize that the interests of gay and lesbian elders have not been well-represented by mainstream gay and lesbian advocacy efforts because gay and lesbian elders present a distinct set of interests and concerns. The existing gay and lesbian identity model and advocacy agenda stresses that gay and lesbian individuals are *the same as* non-gay individuals. Deploying arguments of equivalence, the advocacy agenda has focused on three main issues: marriage equality, employment non-discrimination, and the repeal of DADT. As illustrated in Part III, each of these policy areas fails to address the specific interests of gay and lesbian elders. Of more immediate concern to gay and lesbian elders is the legal fragility of chosen families, financial insecurity, and the potential for anti-gay bias and harassment by service providers and peers in much more intimate venues than the workplace.

Addressing the unmet needs of gay and lesbian elders demands a more holistic approach to gay and lesbian identity *and* advocacy – one that acknowledges the differences among gay and lesbian individuals, as well as the fact that, in some instances, gay and lesbian individuals are indeed different from their non-gay peers. These points of difference need not be points of division nor should the fact of difference serve to invalidate claims for equality. From a strategic standpoint, the reliance on claims of equivalence in the early stages of a civil-rights struggle has its definite advantages, but there are times when the moral force of a claim for equity is not grounded in sameness. Approximation to the majority culture may make a minority more familiar and less politically threatening, but it is not what makes a minority deserving.

Gay and lesbian elders are a deserving minority because their life choices are constrained by the social meaning attached to a characteristic that does not otherwise impair their ability to contribute to society or experience love or loss or rejection. They bear the scars from the days when sexual orientation was pathologized and criminalized and that experience sets them apart from the post-Stonewall generations with respect to their family relationships, financial opportunities, and coping stratagems. In this way, policy interventions on their behalf need to focus on their points of difference and seek recognition for their chosen families, compensation for decades of state-sponsored discrimination in the workplace, and the eradication of anti-gay bias in senior-specific venues through competency training and legal protections.

The contemporary gay and lesbian civil rights movement has successfully introduced mainstream America to a new minority – gay men and lesbians – who are united by a single insignificant characteristic and who share the hopes and dreams of all Americans to grow up, get a good job, and serve their country. The next challenge is to explain how the social meaning attached to this one insignificant characteristic can derail those shared dreams by limiting opportunity and placing entire populations at risk. In the case of gay and lesbian elders, their family patterns, financial difficulties, and fear of encountering bias all trace their roots to that single insignificant characteristic of sexual orientation. It has stigmatized them and set them apart from their non-gay peers. Advocacy on their behalf must openly acknowledge this difference while asserting that gay and lesbian elders are nonetheless entitled to equal treatment and opportunity.

There is much to be celebrated about the determination and creativity of today's gay and lesbian elders. From their marginalized position, they created new types of family and new ways to form life-long connections in the absence of legally recognized relationships defined by blood, marriage, or adoption. As this example illustrates, the view from the margin can be a source of great innovation and insight, but there is no reason to valorize life on the margin for its own sake. It is possible to value the perspective offered by marginalized groups while also working to ensure that individuals are no longer relegated to live at the margins of society. Policy arguments based on difference can honor the multiplicity of gay and lesbian lives without attempting to mold them into a heternormative simulacrum of the majority culture, and thereby target existing disparities without sacrificing diversity.

References

Albelda, R. et al. 2009. *Poverty in the Lesbian, Gay, and Bisexual Community* [Online: The Williams Institute]. Available at: http://www.law.ucla.edu/williamsinstitute/pdf/LGBPovertyReport.pdf [accessed: 30 March 2010].

Alderman, J.H. 2008. Gray gay housing becomes smart business. *Columbia News Service* [Online: 5 March]. Available at: http://m.naplesnews.com/news/2005/mar/17/ndn_senior_housing_for_gray_gays_becomes_smart_bus/ [accessed: 30 March 2010].

Alliance Healthcare Foundation. 2004. *The San Diego County LGBT Senior Healthcare Needs Assessment. LGBT Seniors – Proud Pioneers* [Online]. Available at: http://www.sage-sd.com/SeniorNeedsAssessment [accessed: 30 March 2010].

Altman, A. 2006. *The NORC Supportive Service Program* [Online: United Jewish Appeal Federal of New York]. Available at: http://www.wcjcs.org/QC2007/Materials/The%20NORC%20Supportive%20Service%20Program%20-%20Anita%20Altman.pdf [29 March 2010].

Amicus Curiae Brief, Family Research Counsel No. 99-699. 1999. *Dale v. Boy Scouts of America*, 160 N.J. 562.

Anetzberger, G.J. et al. 2004. Gray and gay: A community dialogue on the issues and concerns of older gays and lesbians. *Journal of Gay and Lesbian Social Services*, 17, 23.

AoA. 2009a. *A Statistical Profile of Black Older Americans Ages 65+* [Online: Department of Health and Human Services Administration on Aging]. Available at: http://www.aoa.gov/AoARoot/Aging_Statistics/minority_aging/Facts-on-Black-Elderly-plain_format.aspx [accessed: 30 March 2010].

AoA. 2009b. *A Statistical Profile of Asian Older Americans Ages 65 or Older* [Online: Department of Health and Human Services Administration on Aging]. Available at: http://www.aoa.gov/AoARoot/Aging_Statistics/minority_aging/Facts-on-API-Elderly2008-plain_format.aspx [accessed: 30 March 2010].

AoA. 2009c. *A Statistical Profile of Hispanic Older Americans Ages 65+* [Online: Department of Health and Human Services Administration on Aging]. Available at: http://www.aoa.gov/AoAroot/Aging_Statistics/minority_aging/Facts-on-Hispanic-Elderly.aspx [accessed: 30 March 2010].

A Profile of Older Americans: 2009 [Online: Department of Health and Human Services Administration on Aging]. Available at: http://www.aoa.gov/AoARoot/Aging_Statistics/Profile/2009/3.aspx [accessed: 30 March 2010].

AoA. 2009d. *Profile of Older Americans* [Online: Department of Health and Human Services Administration on Aging]. Available at: http://www.aoa.gov/AoARoot/Aging_Statistics/Profile/index.aspx [accessed: 30 March 2010].

AoA 2009e. *Projected Future Growth of the Older Population* [Online: Department of Health and Human Services Administration on Aging]. Available at http://www.aoa.gov/AoARoot/Aging_Statistics/future_growth/future_growth.aspx [accessed: 30 March 2010].

AoA. 2005. *2005 White House Conference on Aging* [Online: United States Department of Health and Human Services, Administration on Aging]. Available at: http://www.whcoa.gov/about/about.asp [accessed: 30 March 2010].

APA. *Resolution on Sexual Orientation and Marriage: Research Summary* [Online: American Psychological Association]. Available at: http://www.apa.org/about/governance/council/policy/gay-marriage.pdf [accessed: 30 March 2010].

APA. 2004. *Same Sex Marriage Resource Document* [Online: American Psychiatric Association]. Available at: http://archive.psych.org/edu/other_res/lib_archives/archives/200417.pdf [accessed: 30 March 2010].

ASA Connection. 2007. *Housing Options for LGBT Elders: Snapshots of Projects Nationwide* [Online: American Society on Aging]. Available at: http://www.asaging.org/asav2/asaconnection/enews/07june/top2.cfm [accessed: 30 March 2010].

Associated Press. 1989. Musician's death at 74 reveals he was a woman. *The New York Times*, 3 February, A18.

Badgett, M.V.L. 2001. *Money, Myths and Change: The Economic Lives of Lesbians and Gay Men*. 1st edition. Chicago: University of Chicago Press.

Badgett, M.V. and Rogers, M.A. 2003. Left out of the count: Missing same-sex couples in census 2000. *Institute for Gay and Lesbian Strategic Studies*.

Balsam, K.F. and D'Augelli, A.R. 2006. The victimization of older LGBT adults: Patterns, impact and implications for intervention, in *Lesbian, Gay, Bisexual, and Transgender Aging: Research and Clinical Perspectives*, edited by D. Kimmel, T. Rose and S. David. New York: Columbia University.

Bannerman, L. 2008. The camp that "cures" homosexuality. *The Times*, 7 October.

Barker, J.C. 2004. Lesbian aging: An agenda for social research, in *Gay and Lesbian Aging: Research and Future Directions*, edited by G. Herdt and B. De Vries. New York: Springer.

Baumle, A.K. and Romero, A.P. 2009. *Elder Gays, Lesbians, and Bisexuals: New Demographic and Policy Analyses*, unpublished manuscript.

Bayer, R. 1987. *Homosexuality and American Psychiatry: The Politics of Diagnosis*. Princeton, N.J.: Princeton University Press.

Beemyn, B. and Eliason, M. 1996. *Queer Studies: A Lesbian. Gay, Bisexual, and Transgender Anthology*. New York: New York University Press.

Benker, K.B. 1869. An open letter to the Prussian Minister of Justice, in *We are Everywhere: A Historical Sourcebook of Gay and Lesbian Politics*, edited by M. Blasius and S. Phelan. London: Routledge, 67–78.

Bennett, K.C. and Thompson, N.L. 1991. Accelerated aging and male homosexuality: Australian evidence in a continuing debate, in *Gay, Midlife and Maturity*, edited by J.A. Lee. New York: Haworth Press, 65–76.

Bennett, L. and Gates, G.J. 2004. *The Cost of Marriage Inequality to Lesbian, Gay and Bisexual Seniors* [Online: Human Rights Campaign Foundation Report]. Available at: https://www.hrc.org/documents/cost_of_marriage.pdf [accessed: 30 March 2010].

Berger, R.M. 1996. *Gay and Gray: The Older Homosexual Man*. 2nd edition. New York: Haworth Press.

Bergler, E. 1951. *Neurotic Counterfeit-Sex; Impotence, Frigidity, "Mechanical" and Pseudosexuality, Homosexuality*. New York: Grune & Stratton.

Berling, T. 2004. *Reeling in the Years: Gay Men's Perspectives on Age and Ageism*. New York: Southern Tier editions.

Bernard, T.S. and Lieber, R. 2009. The high cost of being a gay couple. *The New York Times*, 30 March.

Berube, A. 2000. *Coming Out Under Fire*. Tampa, Florida: Free Press.

Berzon, B. 2002. *Surviving Madness: A Therapist's Own Story*. Wisconsin: University of Wisconsin Press.

Birch, S. 2001. Out of the closet. *Guardian* [Online: 25 July]. Available at: http://www.guardian.co.uk/society/2001/jul/25/guardiansocietysupplement3 [accessed: 28 March 2010].

Blackstone, W. 1765–1769. *Commentaries on the Laws of England*. 1st edition. Oxford: Clarendon Press.

Boulder County Aging Services. 2006. *Evaluation of Project Visibility Training: Outcomes and Satisfaction 2006* [Online: Project Visibility]. Available at: http://www.bouldercounty.org/cs/ag/programs/Project_Visibility/PV_Training_Evaluation.pdf [accessed: 28 July 2008].

Bonauto, M.L. *Overview of the Rights of Gay, Lesbian, and Bisexual Teachers* [Online: GLSSEN]. Available at: www.glsen.org/cgi-bin/iowa/all/library/record/192 [accessed: 28 March 2010].

Boris, E. and Honey, M. 1988. Gender, race and the policies of the labor department. *Monthly Labor Review*, 111, 28–9.

Branson, M.B., et al. 2006. *Revised Recommendations for HIV Testing* [Online: CDC]. Available at: http://www.cdc.gov/mmwr/preview/mmwrhtml/rr5514a1.htm [accessed: 30 March 2010].

Bravmann, S. 1997. *Queer Fictions of the Past: History, Culture, and Difference*. Cambridge: Cambridge University Press.

Bray, A. 1988. *Homosexuality in Renaissance England*. London: Gay Men's Press.

Brief of Amicus Curiae, Concerned Women for America. 1999. *Boy Scouts v. Dale*. 2000. [530 U.S. 640.]

Brief of Amicus Curiae, Family Research Council. 1999. *Boy Scouts v. Dale.* 2000. [530 U.S. 640.]

Brief for Petitioners. 1999. *Boy Scouts v. Dale.* 2000. [530 U.S. 640.]

Brotman, S., Ryan, B. and Cormier, R. 2002. The health and social service needs of gay and lesbian elders and their families in Canada. *The Gerontological Society of America*, 43(2), 192–202.

Brown, L.B. et al. 1997. *Gay Men and Aging (Garland Studies on the Elderly in America)*. New York: Routledge.

Browne, D. et al. 2008. *Improving Lesbian, Gay, Bisexual, and Transgender Access to Healthcare at New York City Health and Hospital Corporation Facilities* [Online: Public Advocate for the City of New York]. Available at http://sageconnect.net/uploads/LGBThealthrecs%20report%20final%20_pdf.pdf [accessed: 30 March 2010].

Brozan, B. 1989. Woman's hospital visit marks gay rights fight. *The New York Times*, 8 February, D25.

Brozan, N. 1988. Gay groups are rallied to aid 2 women's fight. *The New York Times*, 7 August, 26.

Buchanan, W. 2006. How AIDS changed us. *SF Gate*, 4 June, E1.

Burgess, A.W. et al. 2000. Sexual abuse of nursing home residents. *Journal of Psychosocial Nursing and Mental Health Services*, 38(6), 10–8.

Burke, G. 2003. A call for eternal equality; seeking acceptance, gay veterans group pushes for memorial at SE cemetery. *The Washington Post*, 13 September, C01.

Butler, S.S. and Hope, B. 1999. Health and well-being for late middle-aged and old lesbians in a rural area. *Journal of Gay and Lesbian Social Services*, 9(4), 27–46.

Cahill, S., South, K. and Spade, J. 2000. *Outing Age: Public Policy Issues Affecting Gay, Lesbian, Bisexual, and Transgender Elders* [Online: Policy Institute of the National Gay and Lesbian Task Force Foundation]. Available at: http://www.thetaskforce.org/reports_and_research/outing_age [accessed: 28 March 2010].

Campbell, A.L. 2005. *How Policies Make Citizens: Senior Activist and the American Welfare State*. Princeton: Princeton University Press.

Capeloto, A. and Ellis, R. 2000. *In the Family: A Magazine for Lesbians, Gays, and Their Relations*, vol. 6, Autumn.

Carcieri, D.L. 2009. *Veto Message* [Online]. Available at: http://www.projo.com/news/2009/pdf/veto_s0195_funeral_directors.pdf [accessed: 30 March 2010].

Cascio, J. *Cancer Risks in the Trans Community* [Online: Trans-Health.com]. Available at: http://www.trans-health.com/displayarticle.php?aid=26 [accessed: 29 March 2010].

Casta-Kaufteil, A. 2003/2004. The old and the restless: mediating rights to intimacy for nursing home residents with cognitive impairments. *Michigan State Journal of Medicine and Law*, 8, 69.

Cave, D. 2006. Dying officer again turned down on benefits for companion. *The New York Times* [Online: 19 January]. Available at: http://www.nytimes. com/2006/01/19/nyregion/19benefits.html [accessed: 30 March 2010].

CDC. 2009. *What CDC is Doing* [Online: Department of Health and Human Services. Centers for Disease Control and Prevention]. Available at: http:// www.cdc.gov/hiv/topics/over50/cdc.htm [accessed: 30 March 2010].

Census 2000 Special Reports. 2003. *Married-Couple and Unmarried-Partner Households: 2000* [Online]. Available at: http://www.census.gov/prod/ 2003pubs/censr-5.pdf [accessed: 28 March 2010].

Chauncey, G. 2005. *Why Marriage? The History Shaping Today's Debate*. New York: Basic Books.

Chauncey, G. 1995. *Gay New York: Gender, Urban Culture, and the Making of the Gay Male World, 1890–1940*. New York: Basic Books.

Classen, C. 2005. *Whistling Women: A Study of the Lives of Older Lesbians*. New York: Haworth Press.

Cohen, S.L. 2007. *The Gay Liberation Youth Movement in New York: "An Army of Lovers Cannot Fail."* New York:Routledge.

Cohler, B.J. 2003. A night at the tubs: age cohort and social life at the local gay bath, in *Gay and Lesbian Aging: Research and Future Directions*, edited by G. Herdt and B. De Vries. New York: Springer Publishing Company, 211.

Cohler, B.J. and Galatzer-Levy, R.M. 2000. *The Course of Gay and Lesbian Lives: Social and Psychoanalytic Perspectives*. 1st edition. Chicago: University of Chicago Press.

Coleman, B. and Pandya, S.M. 2002. *Family Caregiving and Long-Term Care* [Online: AARP Public Policy Institute]. Available at: http://assets.aarp.org/ rgcenter/il/fs91_ltc.pdf [accessed: 28 March 2010].

Comerford, S.A. et al. Crone songs: voices of lesbian elders on aging in a rural environment. *Affilia*, 19(4), 418–36.

Committee on Homosexual Offences and Prostitution 1964. *Report on the Committee on Homosexual Offences and Prostitution*. New York: Lancer Books.

Connidis, I.A. 2009. *Family Ties and Aging*. 2nd edition. California: Pine Forge Press.

Cory, D. W. 1951. *Homosexual in America: A Subjective Approach*. New York: Greenburg.

Cover, S.M. 2009. AG: Gay marriage law irrelevant to schools. *Kennebec Journal*, 16 October [Online]. Available at: http://findarticles.com/p/news-articles/ kennebec-journal/mi_8137/is_20091016/ag-gay-marriage-law-irrelevant/ai_ n50949947/ [accessed: 29 March 2010].

Cruz, J.M. 2003. *Sociological Analysis of Aging: The Gay Male Perspective*. New York: Haworth Press.

Culhane, J.G. 2001. "Clanging silence:" same-sex couples and tort law. *Chicago-Kent Law Review*, 89, 953–54.

Cummings, S.M. and Galambos, C. 2005. *Diversity and Aging in the Social Environment*. New York: Haworth Press, Inc.

Dang, A. and Frazer, S. 2005. *Black Same-Sex Households in the U.S.* [Online: National Gay and Lesbian Task Force]. Available at http://www.thetaskforce. org/reports_and_research/blackcouples_census [accessed: 30 March 2010].

D'Augelli, A.R. and Grossman, A.H. 2001. Disclosure of sexual orientation, victimization and mental health among lesbian, gay, bisexual older adults. *Journal of Interpersonal Violence*, 16, 1015.

D'Augelli, A.R. and Patterson, C.J. 1995. *Lesbian, Gay, and Bisexual Identities over the Lifespan: Psychological Perspectives*. New York: Oxford University Press.

Daughters of Bilitis. 1995. Statement of purpose, reprinted in *We are Everywhere: A Historical Sourcebook of Gay and Lesbian Politics*, edited by M. Blasius and S. Phelan. New York: Routledge.

Davidson, J.W. 2007. *Celebrating Recent LGBT Legislative Advances* [Online: Lambda Legal]. Available at: http://www.lambdalegal.org/our-work/ publications/facts-backgrounds/recent-lgbt-advances.html [accessed: 27 March 2010].

Del Martin and Phyllis Lyon Wedding Video. 2008 [Online]. Available at: http:// groundspark.org/del-and-phyllis [accessed: 30 March 2010].

D'Emilio, J. 1983. *Sexual Politics, Sexual Communities: The Making of a Homosexual Minority in the United States, 1940–1970*. Chicago: University of Chicago Press.

D'Erasmo, S. 1999. Out of the closets and into the streets. *The New York Times*, 4 April, 7–8.

DeNavas-Walt, C., Proctor, P.D. and Lee, C.H. 2005. U.S. Census Bureau, Current population reports. *Income, Poverty, and Health Insurance Coverage in the United States: 2004* [Online: U.S. Census Bureau], 60–229. Available at http:// www.census.gov/prod/2005pubs/p60-229.pdf [accessed: 30 March 2010].

Department of Defense. 2008. *Department of Defense Directive Number 1332.14* [Online: 28 August]. Available at: http://www.dtic.mil/whs/directives/corres/ pdf/133214p.pdf [accessed: 29 March 2010].

Department of Health and Human Services: Administration on Aging (AOA). *Projected Future Growth of the Older Population* [Online]. Available at: http:// www.aoa.gov/AoARoot/Aging_Statistics/future_growth/future_growth. aspx#age [accessed: 28 March 2010].

Devlin, P. 1965. *The Enforcement of Morals*. London: Oxford University Press.

De Vries, B. and Blando, J.A. 2004. The study of gay and lesbian aging: 3 lessons for social gerontology, in *Gay and Lesbian Aging: Research and Future Directions*, edited by G. Herdt and B. De Vries. New York: Springer Publishing Company, 3–28.

Dick, L. The impact of Medicaid estate recovery on nontraditional families. *Florida Journal of Law and Public Policy*, 15, 15.

Domestic Partner Registries [Online: Alternatives to Marriage Project]. Available at: http://www.unmarried.org/dp-registries.html [accessed: 30 March 2010].

Duberman, M.B. 1991. *Cures: A Gay Man's Odyssey*. New York: Dutton Adult.

Duberman, M.B. 1993. *Stonewall*. New York: Plume.

Dubin, M. 1997a. Late woman's parents, 'life partner' wage legal battle over headstone inscription. *Philadelphia Inquirer*, 30 June.

Dubin, M. 1997b. Dispute involving headstone epitaph now a federal case. *Philadelphia Inquirer*, 26 June, C01.

Dwight, M. 2004. Searching for the sample: researching demand for senior housing in the LGBT community. *Outward*, 11(2), 2–8.

Edgar, R. 2009. Lack of funeral rights turns mourner into gay activist. *The Providence Journal* [Online: 15 November]. Available at: http://www.projo.com/news/content/GOLDBERG_FUNERAL_RIGHTS_11-15-09_S4GE9HC_v189.3988db7.html [accessed: 30 March 2010].

Ellis, A. 1965. *Homosexuality: Its Causes and Cure*. New York: L. Stuart.

Ellis, A.L. 2001. *Gay Men at Midlife, Age before Beauty*. New York: Harrington Park Press.

Ellis, H. and Symond, J.H. 1897. Sexual inversion, in *Nineteenth-Century Writing on Homosexuality: A Sourcebook*, edited by C. White. New York: Routledge, 66–67.

El Nasser, H. 2007. Fewer seniors live in nursing homes. *USA Today* [Online: 27 September]. Available at: http://www.usatoday.com/news/nation/census/2007-09-27-nursing-homes_N.htm [accessed: 27 March 2010].

Epstein, R.H. 2002. Some retirees look abroad for prescription drugs. *The New York Times*, 24 September, F5.

Eskridge, W.N. 1999. *Gaylaw: Challenging the Apartheid of the Closet*. Cambridge: Harvard University Press.

Eskridge, W.N. and Hunter, N.D. 1997. *Sexuality, Gender and the Law*. West Publishing Company.

Evans, D. 2007. *HIV Rates Declining in Some Older Americans* [Online]. Available at: http://www.aidsmeds.com/articles/hiv_seniors_older_2131_13622.shtml [accessed: 29 March 2010].

Faderman, L. 1991. *Odd Girls and Twilight Lovers*. New York: Penguin Books.

Family Research Council. For HHS, a Senior Moment [Online: FRC]. Available at: http://www.frc.org/get.cfm?i=WU09J18&f=RF07B06 [accessed: 28 March 2010].

Family Research Council. 2009. *FRC Launches Stop Kevin Jennings Campaign* [Online: FRC]. Available at: http://www.frc.org/get.cfm?i=PR09F06 [accessed: 30 March 2010].

Family Caregiver Alliance. *About FCA* [Online: FCA]. Available at: http://www.caregiver.org/caregiver/jsp/content_node.jsp?nodeid=349 [accessed: 30 March 2010].

Frazer, S.M. 2009. *LGBT Health and Human Services Needs in New York State* [Online: Empire State Pride Agenda Foundation]. Available at: http://www.

prideagenda.org/Portals/0/pdfs/LGBT%20Health%20and%20Human%20Se rvices%20Needs%20in%20New%20York%20State.pdf [accessed: 28 March 2010].

Freud, S. 1920. The psychogenesis of a case of homosexuality in a woman. *International Journal of Psycho-Analysis*. 1, 125–49.

Friedman, S. 2008. Gray matters: AARP flexes its muscle on Medicaid, support for gays. *Newsday*, 16 August.

Friend, R.A. 1991. Older lesbian and gay people: a theory for successful aging, in *Gay, Midlife and Maturity*, edited by J.A. Lee. New York: Haworth Press, 99–119.

Foucault, M. 1978. *The History of Sexuality Vol. 1*. New York: Vintage Books.

Funders for Lesbian and Gay Issues. 2006. *Aging in Equity: LGBT Elders in America* [Online]. Available at: www.workinggroup.org/files/AgingInEquity. pdf [accessed: 29 March 2010].

Galanis, T.P. 2002. Aging and the nontraditional family. *University of Memphis Law Review*, 32, 607.

Gallo, M.M. 2007. *Different Daughters: The History of the Daughters of Bilitis and the Rise of the Lesbian Rights Movement.* Emeryville, California: Seal Press.

Gallup. 2010. Gay and Lesbian Rights [Online: Gallup]. Available at: http://www. gallup.com/poll/1651/gay-lesbian-rights.aspx. [accessed: 19 August 2010].

Garnets, L. and Peplau, L.A. 2006. Sexuality in the lives of aging lesbian and bisexual women, in *Lesbian, Gay, Bisexual, and Transgender Aging: Research and Clinical Perspectives*, edited by D. Kimmel, T. Rose, and S. David. New York: Columbia University Press.

Gates, G.J. 2003a. Gay and lesbian families in the census: gay and lesbian seniors. *The Urban Institute* [Online]. Available at: www.urban.org/url.cfm?ID=900627 [accessed: 29 July 2009].

Gates, G.J. 2003b. Gay veterans top 1 million. *The Urban Institute* [Online]. Available at: http://www.urban.org/publications/900642.html [accessed: 30 March 2010].

Gates, G.J. 2004a. 26,000 gay men and women in the U.S. military estimates from census, 2000. *The Urban Institute* [Online]. Available at: www.urban.org/ UploadedPDF/411069_GayLesbianMilitary.pdf [accessed: 29 March 2010].

Gates, G.J. 2004b. Gay men and women in the U.S. military: estimates from the census 2000. *Urban Institute* [Online]. Available at: http://www.urban.org/ UploadedPDF/411069_GayLesbianMilitary.pdf [accessed: 30 March 2010].

Gates, G.J. 2007. Geographic trends among same-sex couples in the Census and the American Community Survey. *The Williams Institute* [Online]. Available at http://www.law.ucla.edu/williamsinstitute/publications/ACSBriefFinal.pdf [accessed: 30 March 2010].

Gates, G.J. 2009. Same-sex couples in the 2008 American Community Survey. *The Williams Institute* [Online]. Available at: http://www.law.ucla.edu/

williamsinstitute/pdf/ACS2008_WEBPOST_FINAL.pdf [accessed: 30 March 2010].

Gates, G.J. 2010. Lesbian, gay, and bisexual men and women in the US military: Updated estimates. *The Williams Institute* [Online]. Available at: http://www.law.ucla.edu/williamsinstitute/pdf/GLBmilitaryUpdate.pdf [accessed: 30 March 2010].

Gates, G.J. and Ost, J. 2004. *The Gay & Lesbian Atlas*. Washington, D.C.: Urban Institute Press.

Gerassi, J.G. 2001. *The Boys of Boise: Furor, Vice and Folly in an American City*. Washington: University of Washington Press.

Ghaziani, A. 2008. *The Dividends of Dissent: How Conflict and Culture Work in Lesbian and Gay Marches on Washington*. Chicago: University of Chicago Press.

Ginanni, C.N. 1997. Cemetery to inscribe headstone, pay $15,000. *The Legal Intelligencer*. 8 September, 5.

Gist, Y.J. and Hetzel, L.I. 2004. *We the People: Aging in the United States* [Online: U.S. Census Bureau]. Available at http://www.census.gov/prod/2004pubs/censr-19.pdf [accessed: 30 March 2010].

Goldman, R. 1996. Who is that Queer? Exploring norms around sexuality, race and class in queer theory, in *Queer Studies, a Lesbian, Gay, Bisexual and Transgender Anthology*, edited by B. Beemyn and M. Eliason. New York: New York University Press, 169.

Goldberg, N.G. 2009. The impact of inequality for same-sex partners in employer-sponsored retirement plans. *The Williams Institute.* [Online]. Available at: http://escholarship.org/uc/item/0pn9c1h4?query=same sex couples in employer sponsored pension plans [accessed: 30 March 2010].

Gordon, R. 2008. Lesbian rights pioneer Del Martin dies at 78. *San Francisco Chronicle*, 28 August.

Gorman, E.M. and Nelson, K. 2003. From a far place: Social and cultural considerations about HIV among midlife and older men, in *Gay and Lesbian Aging: Research and Future Directions*, edited by G. Herdt and B. De Vries. New York: Springer, 73–96.

Grant, J.M. 2010. *Outing Age 2010. Public Policy Issues Affecting Lesbian, Gay, Bisexual and Transgender Elders* [Online: National Gay and Lesbian Task Force Policy Institute]. Available at: http://www.thetaskforce.org/downloads/reports/reports/outingage_final.pdf [accessed: 28 March 2010].

Graves, K.L. 2009. *And they were Wonderful Teachers: Florida's Purge of Gay and Lesbian Teachers*. Illinois: University of Illinois Press.

Gregg. K. 2009a. Carciere vetoes bill allowing partners to plan funerals. *The Providence Journal* [Online: 11 November]. Available at: http://www.projo.com/news/content/Carcieri_vetoes_11-11-09_KFGDHKT_v15.3b3baf2.html [accessed: 30 March 2010].

Gregg, K. 2009b. Update: R.I. governor vetoes "domestic partners" burial bill. *The Providence Journal* [Online: 10 November]. Available at: http://newsblog.

projo.com/2009/11/ri-gov-carcieri-vetoes-domesti.html [accessed: 30 March 2010].

Gross, J. 2007. Aging and gay and facing prejudice in twilight. *The New York Times*, 9 October, A1.

Grossman, A.H. 2006. *Physical and Mental Health of Older Lesbian, Gay, and Bisexual Adults* in *Lesbian, Gay, Bisexual, and Transgender Aging: Research and Clinical Perspectives* edited by D. Kimmel, T. Rose and S. David. New York: Columbia University Press.

Grossman, A.H. et al. 2000. Social support networks of lesbian, gay and bisexual adults 60 years of age and older. *Journal of Gerontology: Psychological Sciences*, 55(3), 171–179.

Haber, D. 2009. Gay aging. *Gerontology & Geriatrics Education*. 30(3), 267–80.

Hall, R. 1990. *The Well of Loneliness*. Knopf Doubleday Publishing Group.

Halley, J.E. 1993. Reasoning about sodomy: Act and identity in and after Bowers v. Hardwick. *Virginia Law Review*, 79, 1721.

Halley, J.E. 1999. *Don't: A Reader's Guide to the Military's Anti-Gay Policy*. North Carolina: Duke University Press.

Halley, J.E. 1994. Sexual orientation and the politics of biology: A critique of the argument of immutability. *Stanford Law Review*, 46(3), 503–68.

Hammonds, E. 1997. Black (w)holes and the geometry of black female sexuality, in *Feminism Meets Queer Theory*, edited by E. Weed and N. Schor. Indiana: Indiana University Press, 136–56.

Hartlaub, P. 2001. Same-sex partner can sue for damages; wrongful-death claim in dog-mauling case. *San Francisco Chronicle*, 28 July, A1.

Hart, H.L.A. 1963. *Law, Liberty, and Morality*. Stanford, California: Stanford University Press.

Hayaski, E. 2007. For gays, a generation gap grows. *LA Times*, 18 May, 1A.

Henry 8. 1533. *Buggery Statute*. 25 Henry 8 Chapter 6.

Herdt, G., Beeler, J., and Rawls, T.W. 1997. Life course diversity among older lesbians and gay men: A study in Chicago. *Journal of Gay, Lesbian, and Bisexual Identity*, 2.

Herdt, G. and De Vries, B. 2004. Introduction in *Gay and Lesbian Aging: Research and Future Directions*, edited by G. Herdt and B. De Vries. New York: Springer Publishing Company.

Herdy, A. 2001a. Partner denied Marrero pension. *St. Peter Times*, 29 August, 1A.

Herdy, A. 2001b. Woman details relationship with Marrero. *St. Peter Times*, 4 September, 1A.

Heredia, C. 2001. Dog mauling victim's partner to test wrongful death law. *San Francisco Chronicle*, 19 February, A13.

Herman, D. 1997. *The Antigay Agenda: Orthodox Vision and the Christian Right*. Chicago: University of Chicago Press.

Heron, M. et al. 2009. Deaths: Final data for 2006. *National Vital Statistics Report* [Online: Centers for Disease Control and Prevention], 57(14), 1–135. Available at: http://www.cdc.gov/nchs/data/nvsr/nvsr57/nvsr57_14.pdf [accessed: 28 March 2010].

Herring, J. 2009. *Older People in Law and Society*. New York: Oxford University Press.

Herszenhorn, D. 2007. House backs broad protections for gay workers, *The New York Times*, 7 November, A1.

Hill, J.L. 2000. *Clinical Perspectives on Elderly Sexuality*. New York: Plenum Publishers.

Hillman, J.L. 2000. *Clinical Perspectives on Elderly Sexuality (Issues in the Practice of Psychology)*. New York: Springer Publishing Co.

Hirschfeld, M. 1897. Petition to the Reichstag, in *We Are Everywhere: A Sourcebook of Gay and Lesbian Politics*, edited by M. Blasius and S. Phelan. London: Routledge, 135–37.

Hobbs, F.B. The Elderly Population [Online: U.S. Census Bureau]. Available at: http://www.census.gov/population/www/pop-profile/elderpop.html [accessed: 17 August 2010].

Holleran, A. 2008. *Chronicle of a Plague, Revisted: AIDS and its Aftermath*. Cambridge, Massachusetts: DaCapo Press.

Hollibaugh, A. 2010. The post-Stonewall/Baby Boomer generations' impact on aging in gay, lesbian, bisexual and transgender communities, in *National Gay and Lesbian Task Force* [Online]. Available at: http://www.thetaskforce.org/downloads/reports/reports/outingage_final.pdf [accessed: 30 March 2010].

Honan. W.H. 1999. Peter Wildeblood, 76, writer who fought Britain's laws against homosexuality. *The New York Times*, 21 November.

Hooker, E. 1957. The adjustment of the male overt homosexual. *Journal of Projective Techniques*, 21, 18–31.

Horan, J.E. 1999. "When sleep at last has come": Controlling the disposition of dead bodies for same-sex couples. *Journal of Gender, Race and Justice*, 2, 423.

Hostetler, A.J. 2003. Old, gay, and alone? in *Gay and Lesbian Aging: Research and Future Directions*, edited by G. Herdt and B. De Vries. New York: Springer, 143–76.

Howard Brown Health Center [Online]. Available at: http://www.howardbrown.org/hb_aboutus.asp?id=153 [accessed: 29 March 2010].

Human Rights Campaign. 2010. *Statewide School Laws and Policies* [Online: 27 August]. Available at: http://www.hrc.org/documents/school_laws.pdf [accessed: 30 March 2010].

Hunter, S. 2005. *Midlife and Older LGBT Adults: Knowledge and Affirmative Practices for the Social Services*. New York: Haworth Press.

Hutchinson, D.L. 1997. Out yet unseen, a racial critique of gay and lesbian legal theory and political discourse. *Connecticut Law Review*, 29, 516.

Jacobs, M.B. 2002. Micah has one mommy and one legal stranger: Adjudicating maternity for nonbiological lesbian coparents. *Buffalo Law Review*. 50, 364–68.

Jacobson, S.A. and Grossman, A. 1996. Older lesbians and gay men: Old myths, new images, and future directions, in *The Lives of Lesbians, Gays and Bisexuals: Children to Adults*, edited by R.C. Savin-Williams and K.M. Cohen. Fort Worth, Texas: Harcourt Brace.

Jagose, A. 1996. *Queer Theory: An Introduction*. New York: New York University Press.

Johns, A.F. 1999/2000. Three rights make strong advocacy for the elderly in guardianship: Right to counsel, right to plan, and right to die. *South Dakota Law Review*, 45, 492.

Johnson, D.K. 2006. *The Lavender Scare: The Cold War Persecution of Gays and Lesbians in the Federal Government*. Chicago: University of Chicago Press.

Johnson, M.J., Jackson, N.C., Arnette, J.K. and Koffman, S.D. 2005. Gay and lesbian perceptions of discrimination in retirement care facilities. *Journal of Homosexuality*, 49(2), 83–102.

Jones, A.S. 2009. *Losing the News: The Future of the News that Feeds Democracy*. New York: Oxford University Press.

Jordan, J. 2008. First look: Ellen & Portia's wedding album. *People* [Online: 19 August]. Available at: http://www.people.com/people/article/0,,20220057,00.html [accessed: 30 March 2010].

Kaiser Family Foundation. 2001. *Inside-OUT: A Report of the Experiences of Lesbians, Gays and Bisexuals in America and the Public's Views on Issues And Policies Related to Sexual Orientation*. Menlo Park: California.

Kalinowsky, L.P. 1952. *Shock Treatments, Psychosurgery, and Other Somatic Treatments in Psychiatry*. New York: Grune and Stratton.

Kamel, H. 2003. Sexuality in the nursing home, part 2: Managing abnormal behavior-legal and ethical issues. *Journal of American Medical Directors Association*, 4, 204–05.

Kameny, F. 1965. Does research into homosexuality matter, in *We are Everywhere: A Historical Sourcebook of Gay and Lesbian Politics*, edited by M. Blasius and S. Phelan. London: Routledge, 335–38.

Kanapaux, W. 2003. Homosexual seniors face stigma. *Geriatric Times*, November/December.

Katz, J.N. 1976. *Gay American History: Lesbians and Gay Men in the U.S.A.* Crowell.

Kehoe, M. 1989. *Lesbians over 60 Speak for Themselves (Research on Homosexuality, No 18)*. New York: Routledge.

Kelly, J. 1977. The aging male homosexual: myth and reality. *The Gerontologist*, 17(4), 328–332.

Kennedy, E. and David, M. 1993. *Boots of Leather and Slippers of Gold: History of a Lesbian Community*. New York: Routledge.

Kertzner, R., Meyer, I. and Dolezal, C. 2004. Psychological well-being in midlife and older gay men, in *Gay and Lesbian Aging: Research and Future Directions*, edited by G. Herdt and B. De Vries. New York: Springer.

Kimmel, D. and Lundy Martin, D. 2001. *Midlife and Aging in Gay America: Proceedings of the SAGE Conference 2000*. New York: Haworth Press, Inc.

Kimmel, D. 2004. Issues to consider in studies of midlife and older sexual minorities, in *Gay and Lesbian Aging: Research and Future Directions*, edited by G. Herdt and B. De Vries. New York: Springer, 265–84.

Kimmel, D., Rose, T. and David, S. 2006a. *Lesbian, Gay, Bisexual, and Transgender Aging: Research and Clinical Perspectives*. New York: Columbia University Press.

Kimmel, D. et al. 2006b. Historical context for research on lesbian, gay, bisexual, and transgender aging, in *Lesbian, Gay, Bisexual, and Transgender Aging: Research and Clinical Perspectives*, edited by D. Kimmel, T. Rose, and S. David. New York: Columbia University Press.

Kincaid, T. 2010. Nearly half of all Americans live where there is some recognition of same-sex couples [Online: Box Turtle Bulletin]. Available at: http://www.boxturtlebulletin.com/2010/03/03/20758 [accessed: 19 August 2010].

King, M. 2001. Should companion get deceased's estate? *Seattle Times*, 23 January, A1.

King, M.A., Sims, A. and Osher, D. *How is Cultural Competency Integrated in Education* [Online: Center for Effective Collaboration and Practice]. Available at: http://cecp.air.org/cultural/Q_integrated.htm#def [accessed: 20 March 2010].

King, E. and Kimmel, D. 2006. SAGE: New York City's pioneer organization for LGBT elders, in *Lesbian, Gay, Bisexual, and Transgender Aging: Research and Clinical Perspectives* edited by D. Kimmel, T. Rose, and S. David. New York: Columbia University Press.

Knauer, N.J. 1998. Domestic partnership and same-sex relationships: A marketplace innovation and a less than perfect institutional choice. *Temple Political and Civil Rights Law Review*, 7, 337.

Knauer, N.J. 1999. Same-sex domestic violence: Claiming a domestic sphere and risking negative stereotypes. *Temple Political and Civil Rights Law Review*, 8, 325.

Knauer, N.J. 2000. Homosexuality as contagion: From *The Well of Loneliness* to the Boy Scouts. *Hofstra Law Review*, 29, 401.

Knauer, N.J. 2001. "Simply so different": The uniquely expressive character of the openly gay individual after Boy Scouts of America v. Dale. *Kentucky Law Review*, 89, 1039.

Knauer, N.J. 2002. The September 11 attacks and surviving same-sex partners: Defining family through tragedy. *Temple Law Review*, 75, 31.

Knauer, N.J. 2003a. Defining capacity: Balancing the competing interests of autonomy and need. *Temple Political & Civil Rights Law Journal*, 12, 321.

Knauer, N.J. 2003b. Science, identity, and the construction of the gay political narrative. *Law and Sexuality*, 12, 64–66.

Knauer, N.J. 2005. The recognition of same-sex relationships: Comparative institutional analysis, contested social goals, and strategic institutional choices. *University of Hawaii Law Review*, 28, 23.

Knauer, N.J. 2005. The September 11 relief efforts and surviving same-sex partners: Reflections on relationships in the absence of uniform legal recognition, *Women's Rights Law Reporter*, 26, 79.

Knauer, N.J. 2008. Same-sex marriage and federalism. *Temple Political & Civil Rights Law Journal*, 17, 421.

Knauer, N.J. 2009. LGBT elder law: Toward equity in aging. *Harvard Journal of Law and Gender*, 32, 1.

Kosciw, J.G., Diaz, E.M., and Greytak, E.A. 2008. The 2007 national school climate survey: The experiences of lesbian, gay, bisexual, and transgender youth in our nation's schools [Online: *GLSEN*]. Available at: http://www. glsen.org/binary-data/GLSEN_ATTACHMENTS/file/000/001/1290-1.pdf [accessed: 30 March 2010].

Krafft-Ebing, R.V. 2006. *Psychopathia Sexualis, with Special Reference made to the Antipathic Sexual Instinct, a Medico-Forensic Study.* Montana: Kessinger Publishing.

Lambda Legal. Summary: *Flanigan v. University of Maryland Medical System Corporation* [Online]. Available at: http://www.lambdalegal.org/in-court/cases/flanigan-v-university-of-maryland.html [accessed: 29 March 2010].

Lambda Legal. 2002. *Flanigan v. University of Maryland Medical Center* [Online]. Available at: http://www.lambdalegal.org/in-court/cases/flanigan-v-university-of-maryland.html [accessed: 19 August 2010].

Lee, J.A. 1991. *Gay Midlife and Maturity.* New York: Harrington Park Press.

Letter from Members of the United States Congress to United States President Barack Obama re: Jennings. 2009 [Online]. Available at: http://downloads. frcaction.org/EF/EF09J02.pdf [accessed: 30 March 2010].

LeVay, S. 1996. *Queer Science: The Use and Abuse of Research into Homosexuality.* Cambridge, Massachusetts: MIT Press.

Lewin, E. and Leap, W.L. 2002. *Out in Theory: The Emergence of Lesbian and Gay Anthropology.* Illinois: University of Illinois Press.

Lewin, T. 1991. Disabled woman's care given to lesbian partner. *The New York Times*, 18 December, A26.

Lewis, G.B. 2001. Barriers to security clearances for gay men and lesbians: Fear of blackmail or fear of homosexuals? *Journal of Public Administration Research and Theory*, 11, 539.

Lindau, S.T. et al. 2007. A study of sexual and health among older adults in the United States. *The New England Journal of Medicine*, 357(8), 762–74.

Lisker, J. 1969. Homo nest raided: Queen bees are stinging mad. *New York Daily News*, 6 July.

Lorde, G.A. 1984. *Sister Outsider: Essays and Speeches.* 1st edition. Berkeley: Crossing Press.

Madoff, R.D. 1997. Unmasking undue influence. *Minnesota Law Review*, 81, 578.

Maier, T.J. 1988. AIDS victims' bitter legacy; lovers and relatives battle for estates in disputes over wills. *Newsday*, 2 October.

Mann, T. 2009. *Death in Venice.* Translated by M.C. Doege. Boston: MobileReference.

Marech, R. 2005. Retirement homes without closets. *San Francisco Chronicle*, 14 January, A1.

Martin, D. and Lyon, P. 1972. *Lesbian/Woman.* New York: Bantam Books.

Masotti, P.J. 2006. Healthy naturally occurring retirement communities: A low-cost approach to facilitating healthy aging. *American Journal of Public Health*, 96(7), 1165–70. Available at: http://ajph.aphapublications.org/cgi/content/full/96/7/1164?maxtoshow=&HITS=10&hits=10&RESULTFORMAT=&author1=Masotti&searchid=1&FIRSTINDEX=0&sortspec=relevance&resourcetype=HWCIT [accessed: 28 March 2010].

Mayer, K.H. et al. 2008. Sexual and gender minority health: What we know and what needs to be done. *American Journal of Public Health*, 98(6), 989–95.

Mays, V.M. et al. 1998. African American families in diversity: Gay men and lesbians as participants in family networks. *Journal of Comparative Family Studies*, 29(1), 73–87.

McFadden, R.D. 2008. State court recognizes gay marriages from elsewhere. *The New York Times*, 2 February, 1B.

McGreevey, J.E. 2007. A prayer for Larry Craig. *The Washington Post*, 3 September.

McKinley, J. 2008. A landmark day in California as same-sex marriage begins to take hold. *The New York Times,* 17 June, A19.

Mcleod, M. 2002. Law closes eyes to gay partners; a slain police officer's companion has been denied a spousal pension. *Orlando Sentinel*, 1 January, A1.

McMahon, E. 2003. The older homosexual: current concepts of lesbian, gay, bisexual, and transgender older Americans. *Clinics in Geriatric Medicine*, 19(3), 587–93.

Metlife. 2006. *Out and Aging: The Metlife Study of Lesbian and Gay Baby Boomers* [Online]. Available at: http://www.metlife.com/Applications/Corporate/WPS/CDA/PageGenerator/0,4773,P8899,00.html [accessed: 29 March 2010].

Meyer, I.H. 2003. Prejudice, social stress, and mental health in lesbian, gay, and bisexual populations: conceptual issues and research evidence. *Psychological Bulletin*, 129(5), 674–97.

Miller, J.A. 2004. Voluntary impoverishment to obtain government benefits. *Cornell Journal of Law and Public Policy*, 13 (81).

Miller, N. 2002. *Sex Panic Crime: A Journey to the Paranoid Heart of the 1950s.* New York: Alyson Books.

Minkel, J.R. 2007. *Confirmed: The U.S. Census Bureau Gave Up Names of Japanese-Americans in WW II* [Online: Scientific American]. Available at:

http://www.scientificamerican.com/article.cfm?id=confirmed-the-us-census-b [accessed: 28 March 2010].

Minter, S. 2002/2003. *Legal and Public Policy Issue for Transgender Elders* [Online]. Available at: www.nclrights.org/site/DocServer/transelder. pdf?docID=1121 [accessed: 29 July 2009].

Minton, H.L. 2001. *Departing from Deviance: A History of Homosexual Rights and Emancipatory Science in America.* Chicago: University of Chicago Press.

Mock, S.E., Taylor, C.J. and Savin-Williams, R.C. 2006. Aging together: the retirement plans of same-sex couples in *Lesbian, Gay, Bisexual, and Transgender Aging: Research and Clinical Perspectives* edited by D. Kimmel, T. Rose, and S. David. New York: Columbia University Press.

Morello, C. 2009. Census count of same-sex couples to stir policy fights. *Washington Post*, 13 September.

Murphy, D.E. 2004a. Bid to stop San Francisco from letting gays marry. *The New York Times*, 14 February, A10.

Murphy, D.E. 2004b. San Francisco married 4,037 same-sex pairs from 46 states. *The New York Times*, 18 March, A2.

National Association of Area Agencies on Aging (n4a) [Online]. Available at http://www.n4a.org/about-n4a/ [accessed: 30 March 2010].

National Alliance for Caregiving. 2009. *Caregiving in the U.S.: A Focused Look at: Those Caring for the 50+* [Online]. Available at: http://www.caregiving. org/data/FINALRegularExSum50plus.pdf [accessed: 30 March 2010].

National Center for Lesbian Rights. *Case Docket: Joy Lewis and Sheila Ortiz-Taylor v. Westminster Oaks Retirement Community* [Online]. Available at: http://www.nclrights.org/site/PageServer?pagename=issue_caseDocket_lewis [accessed: 2 November 2008].

National Center on Elder Abuse. 1998. *The National Elder Abuse Incidence Study* [Online]. Available at: http://www.aoa.gov/AoARoot/AoA_Programs/Elder_ Rights/Elder_Abuse/docs/ABuseReport_Full.pdf [accessed: 30 March 2010].

National Center on Elder Abuse. 2005. *Fact Sheet: Elder Abuse Prevalence and Incidence* [Online]. Available at: http://www.ncea.aoa.gov/ncearoot/Main_ Site/pdf/publication/FinalStatistics050331.pdf [accessed: 30 March 2010].

National Coalition of Anti-Violence Programs. 2009. Hate Violence Against Lesbian, Gay, Bisexual, and Transgender People in the United States 2008 [Online]. Available at: http://www.avp.org/documents/ 2008HVReportDraft3smallerfile.pdf [accessed: 17 August 2010].

National Gay and Lesbian Task Force. *Fact Sheet, The Many Faces of Aging: Lesbian, Gay, Bisexual and Transgender Older Persons* [Online]. Available at: http://www.thetaskforce.org/issues/aging [accessed: 29 March 2010].

National Gay and Lesbian Task Force. 2000. *Legislating Equality: A Review of Laws Affecting Gay, Lesbian, Bisexual, and Transgendered People in the United States* [Online]. Available at: http://www.thetaskforce.org/reports_and_ research/legislating_equality [accessed: 29 March 2010].

National Gay and Lesbian Task Force. 2006. *Make Room for All: Diversity, Cultural Competency & Discrimination in an Aging America* [Online]. Available at: www.thetaskforce.org/reports_and_research/make_room_for_ all [accessed: 29 March 2010].

Newsweek Poll. *Election 2008* [Online: Princeton Survey Research Associates International]. Available at: http://www.psrai.com/filesave/ 0713%20ftop%20w%20methodology.pdf [accessed: 30 March 2010].

Newton, E. 1995. *Cherry Grove Fire Island: Sixty Years in America's First Gay and Lesbian Town*. Boston: Beacon Press.

Nicolosi, J. 1991. *Reparative Therapy of Male Homosexuality: A New Clinical Approach*. New York: Jason Aronson.

Noble A. 1981. Domestic news, *United Press International*, 28 June.

Norton, R. 1992. *Mother Clap's Molly House: The Gay Subculture in England 1700–1830*. United Kingdom: GMP Publishers.

Nussbaum, M.C. 2002. Millean liberty and sexual orientation: A discussion of Edward Stein's "The mismeasure of desire." *Law and Philosophy*, 21(3), 317– 34.

Obama, B. 2010. Presidential memorandum: Hospital visitation [Online: The White House]. Available at: http://www.whitehouse.gov/the-press-office/ presidential-memorandum-hospital-visitation [accessed: 19 August 2010].

Obama, B. 2008. Remarks of Senator Barrack Obama: The American Promise [Online: Organizing for America]. Available at: http://www.barackobama. com/2008/08/28/remarks_of_senator_barack_obam_108.php [accessed: 19 August 2010].

Obama, Barack. 2008. Speech. *Denver DNC* [Online]. Available at: http://www. denverdnc2008.com/ [accessed: 30 March 2010].

Olsen, A. 2005/2006. Military veterans and social security. *Social Society Bulletin* [Online], 66(2). Available at: http://www.ssa.gov/policy/docs/ssb/v66n2/ v66n2p1.html [accessed: 30 March 2010].

Orel, N. 2006. Community needs assessment: documenting the need for affirmative services for LGB older adults, in *Lesbian, Gay, Bisexual, and Transgender Aging: Research and Clinical Perspectives,* edited by D. Kimmel, T. Rose and S. David. New York: Columbia University Press.

O'Rourke, R. 1989. *Reflecting on the Well of Loneliness*. New York: Routledge.

Over 1000 daily papers announce gay wedding*s*. *The Advocate* [Online: 1 September 2008]. Available at: http://www.advocate.com/news_detail_ ektid59625.asp [accessed: 29 March 2010].

Painton, P. et al. 1993. The shrinking ten percent. *Time* [Online]. Available at: http://www.time.com/time/magazine/article/0,9171,978345,00.html[accessed: 28 March 2010].

Palms of Manasota [Online]. Available at: www.palmsofmanasota.com [accessed: 28 March 2010].

Palo Stroller, E. and Campbell Gibson, R. 1999. *Worlds of Difference: Inequality in the Aging Experience*. 3rd edition. California: Pine Forge Press.

Parker-Pope, T. 2009. Kept from a dying partner's bedside. *The New York Times*, 18 May.

Parisex, H.G. 1932. In Defense of Homosexuality, reprinted in *We are Everywhere: A Historical Sourcebook of Gay and Lesbian Politics*, edited by M. Blasius and S. Phelan. New York: Routledge.

Petitioner's Brief No. 99-699. 1999. *Dale v. Boy Scouts of America*, 160 N.J. 562.

Perlin, M.L. 1993/1994. Hospitalized patients and the right to sexual interaction: Beyond the last frontier. *New York University Review of Law and Social Change*. 20, 530.

Pillard, R.C. 1997. The search for a genetic influence on sexual orientation, in *Science and Homosexualities*, edited by V.A. Rosario. New York, Routledge.

Plaintiff's Complaint. 2002. *Flanigan v. University of Maryland Medical System Corporation* [Online]. Available at: http://data.lambdalegal.org/pdf/118.pdf [accessed: 28 March 2010].

Plaintiffs' Trial Brief. 2009. *Perry v. Schwarzengger.* 2010. [2010 U.S. Dist. LEXIS 78816]. Available at: http://www.scribd.com/doc/23882710/Plaintiff-s-Trial-Brief-Challenging-Prop-8 [accessed: 17 August 2010].

Polikoff, N. 2009. *Beyond Straight and Gay Marriage.* Boston: Beacon Press.

PollingReport.com. *Law and Civil Rights* [Online]. Available at: http://www.pollingreport.com/civil.htm [accessed: 29 March 2010].

Poverty Guidelines. 2009. [Online: U.S. Department of Health and Human Services. Available at: http://www.aspe.hhs.gov/poverty/09poverty.shtml [accessed: 30 March 2010].

Prager, S.W. 2009. *Message to Annual Meeting Attendees.* Personal correspondence. 28 December.

Pratt, D. 2007. The new Medicare Part D prescription benefit. *Albany Law Journal of Science and Technology.* 17, 339.

Press Release. 2010. *Assembly Overrides Veto of Domestic Partners' Funeral Rights* [Online: 5 January]. Available at: http://www.rilin.state.ri.us/news/pr1.asp?prid=6043 [accessed: 30 March 2020].

Pride at: Work. 2007. Longshoreman grant retroactive pension benefits to surviving domestic partner [Online: 23 August]. Available at: http://www.prideatwork.org/page.php?id=533 [accessed: 30 March 2010].

Project Visibility. 2008. *Evaluation of Project Visibility Outcomes and Training* [Online]. Available at: http://www.bouldercounty.org/cs/ag/pdfs/PVEval2008Presentation.pdf [accessed: 30 March 2010].

Proponents' Trial Brief. 2009. *Perry v. Schwarzenegger.* 2010. [2010 U.S. Dist. LEXIS 78816]. Available at: http://www.scribd.com/doc/23892014/Trial-Brief-of-Prop-8-Proponents-Filed-12-07-09 [accessed: 19 August 2010].

Quam, J.K. 1997. *Social Services for Senior Gay Men and Lesbians.* New York: Routledge.

Richter, J. 2008. Bay area gay senior housing closer to reality. *San Francisco Chronicle*, 30 March, K8.

Rabner, S. Attorney General of the State of New Jersey. 2007. *Formal Opinion No. 3-2007* [Online]. Available at: http://www.nj.gov/oag/newsreleases07/ag-formal-opinion-2.16.07.pdf [accessed: 29 March 2010].

RainbowVision Properties, Inc. [Online]. Available at: www.rainbowvisionprop.com [accessed: 28 March 2010].

Rawls, T.W. 2004. Disclosure and depression among older gay and homosexual men: findings from the Urban Men's Health Study, in *Gay and Lesbian Aging: Research and Future Directions*, edited by G. Herdt and B. De Vries. New York: Springer: 177–210.

Rothaus, S. 2008. Pioneering lesbian activist Del Martin dies in San Francisco at: 87. *Miami Herald Blog* [Online]. Available at: http://miamiherald.typepad.com/gaysouthflorida/2008/08/pioneering-lesb.html [accessed: 30 March 2010].

Rupp, L.J. 1999. *A Desired Past: A Short History of Same-Sex Love in America*. Chicago: University of Chicago Press.

Russell, G.M. and Bohan, J.S. 2005. The gay generation gap: Communicating across the LGBT divide. *The Policy Journal for the Institute for Gay and Lesbian Strategic Studies*, 7 (2).

Ryan, C. 2009. *Helping Families Support their Lesbian, Gay, Bisexual and Transgender (LGBT) Children* [Online]. Available at: http://www11.georgetown.edu/research/gucchd/nccc/documents/LGBT_Brief.pdf [accessed: 30 March 2010].

Ryan, C. et al. 2009. Family rejection as a predictor of negative health outcomes in white and Latino, lesbian, gay and bisexual young adults. *Pediatrics*, 123(1), 346–52.

Sacchetti, M. 2009. Maine voters overturn state's new same-sex marriage law. *The Boston Globe*, 4 November.

SAGE. 2005. *Post-Event Summary Report Prepared for the White House Conference on Aging* [Online]. Available at: http://www.whcoa.gov/about/des_events_reports/PER_NY_09_28_05.pdf [accessed: 30 March 2010].

SAGE. *SAGE Harlem NORC Fact Sheet* [Online]. Available at: http://www.sageusa.org/uploads/Microsoft%20Word%20-%20SAGE%20Harlem%20Neighborhood%20NORC%20Fact%20Sheet%20-%20Jan%202008.pdf [accessed: 28 March 2010].

SAGE. 2009. *SAGE Harlem NORC Fact Sheet* [Online: Service and Advocacy for Gay, Lesbian, Bisexual and Transgender Elders]. Available at: http://www.sageusa.org/uploads/Microsoft%20Word%20-%20SAGE%20Harlem%20Neighborhood%20NORC%20Fact%20Sheet%20-%20Jan%202008.pdf [accessed: 30 March 2010].

San Francisco Human Rights Commission. 2003. Aging in the Lesbian, Gay, Bisexual, and Transgender Communities [Online]. Available at: http://www.sfgov.org/site/; uploadedfiles/sfhumanrights/docs/finalreport.pdf. [accessed: 17 August 2010].

Schmitz-Bechteler, S. 2006. Those of a queer age: Insight into aging in the gay and lesbian community. *University of Chicago Advocates Forum*, 26.

Sedgwick, E.K. 2008. *Epistemology of the Closet*. 2nd edition. California: University of California Press.

Servicemembers Legal Defense Network. 2010 [Online]. Available at: http://www.sldn.org/pages/about-dadt [accessed: 19 August 2010].

Severson, K. 2008. Saying 'I do,' making history, planning a party. *The New York Times*, 18 June, F1.

The sexes. 1975. *Time* magazine. 8 September.

Sexual Minority Assessment Research Team. 2009. *Best Practices for Asking Questions about Sexual Orientation on Surveys* [Online]. Available at http://www.law.ucla.edu/williamsinstitute/pdf/SMART_FINAL_Nov09.pdf [accessed: 28 March 2010].

Shah, D.K., Associate General Counsel, United States General Accounting Office. 2004. [Online: Letter to Senator Bill Frist, Majority Leader]. Available at: http://www.gao.gov/new.items/d04353r.pdf [accessed: 29 March 2010].

Shilts, R. 2007. *And the Band Played on: Politics, People and the AIDS Epidemic*. New York: St. Martin's Press.

Shippy, R.A. et al. 2004. Social networks of aging gay men. *The Journal of Men's Studies*, 13(1), 107–120.

Sidor, G. 2005. *Social Security: Brief Facts and Statistics*. [Online: Congressional Research Service]. Available at http://usa.usembassy.de/etexts/soc/crs_socsecurity2005.pdf [accessed: 30 March 2010].

Skolnik, S. 2001. Same-sex estate rights backed; state high court says gays may be entitled to partners' property in absence of a will. *Seattle Post-Intelligencer*, 2 November, B1.

Socarides, C.W. *How America Went Gay* [Online]. Available at: http://www.leaderu.com/jhs/socarides.html [accessed: 30 March 2010].

Sperry, L. and Prosen, H. 1996. *Aging in the Twenty-First Century: A Developmental Perspective*. New York: Routledge.

Sprigg, P. 2009. Homosexual activist Kevin Jennings not fit for Department of Education. *Insight* [Online]. Available at: http://downloads.frc.org/EF/EF09F64.pdf [accessed: 30 March 2010].

Starkey, J. 2008. Out of isolation: advocacy group assists Long Island gays and lesbians who grew up in less accepting times. *Newsday*, 1 February, B06.

Steakley, J.D. 1975. *The Homosexual Emancipation Movement in Germany*. New York: Arno Press.

Stein, E. 2001. *The Mismeasure of Desire*. New York: Oxford University Press.

Stein, M. 2004. *The City of Sisterly and Brotherly Love*. Chicago: University of Chicago Press.

Stevenson, D. 2002. Should addicts get welfare? Addiction & SSI/SSDI. *Brooklyn Law Review*, 68, 185.

Strauss, W. and Howe, N. 1991. *Generations: The History of America's Future 1584 to 2069*. New York: William Morrow and Co.

Sutherland, T. 2004. Senior vote growing much faster than that of younger voters. *SeniorJournal.com* [Online: 29 October]. Available at: http://seniorjournal.com/NEWS/Politics/2004/4-10-29SeniorVoteGrowth.htm [accessed: 29 March 2010].

Sutton, T.B. 2008. Births, marriages, divorces, and deaths: Provisional data for 2007. *National Vital Statistics Report* [Online: Centers for Disease Control and Prevention], 56(21), 1–6. Available at: http://www.cdc.gov/nchs/data/nvsr/nvsr56/nvsr56_21.htm [accessed: 28 March 2010].

Tam, B. 2008. Letter: What: If We Lose? in *Petitioners Trial Brief, Perry v. Schwarzenaggar* [Online]. Availiable at: http://www.lgbtpov.com/pdf/brief.pdf [accessed: 30 March 2010].

Tatara, T. and Kuzmeskas, L.M. 1996. *Reporting of Elder Abuse in Domestic Settings*. [Online: National Center on Elder Abuse]. Available at: http://www.ncea.aoa.gov/ncearoot/main_site/pdf/basics/fact3.pdf [accessed: 30 March 2010].

Terry, J. 1999. *An American Obsession: Science, Medicine, and Homosexuality in Modern Society*. Chicago: Chicago University Press.

The Killing of Sister George (dir. Robert Aldrich, 1968).

The Offences against the Person Act of 1861, in *Nineteenth-Century Writings on Homosexuality: A Sourcebook*, edited by C. White. New York: Routledge.

Toy, V.S. 2002. Not a place to leave a relative. *The New York Times*, 17 November, 14LI1.

Transcript of Oral Arguments. 2000. *Boy Scouts of America. v. Dale*, 530 U.S. 640.

Tripp, C.A. 2005. *The Intimate World of Abraham Lincoln*. New York: Free Press.

Turnipseed, T. 2010. Scalia's ship of revulsion has sailed: Will Lawrence protect adults who adopt lovers to help ensure their inheritance from incest prosecution? *Hamline Law Review*, 32, 95.

U.S. Bureau of the Census. 2004. Table MS-2. Estimated Median Age at: First Marriage, by Sex: 1890 to Present [Online]. Available at: http://www.census.gov/population/socdemo/hh-fam/tabMS-2.pdf [accessed: 29 March 2010].

Video. *Everything To Do with Schools* [Online]. Available at: http://www.youtube.com/watch?v=FijVUbUlV3s [accessed: 30 March 2010].

Vick, K. 2009. Maine set to vote on gay marriage. *Washington Post*, 2 November.

Von Kraft-Ebing, R. 1886. *Psychopathia Sexualis: A Medico-Legal Study*, translated by C.J. Chaddock. 1920. 7th edition. Philadelphia: F.A. Davis Co.

Walker, J. and Herbitter, C. 2005. *Aging in the Shadows: Social Isolation among Seniors in New York City* [Online: United Neighborhood Houses]. Available at: www.unhny.org/advocacy/pdf/Aging%20in%20the%20Shadows.pdf [accessed: 30 March 2010].

Waszkiewicz, E. 2002. Aging in transgender people: an annotated bibliography. *Trans-Health.Com* [Online]. Available at: http://www.trans-health.com/displayarticle.php?aid=74 [accessed: 29 March 2010].

Waysdorf, S.L. 2002. The aging of the AIDS epidemic: Emerging legal and public health issues for elderly persons living with HIV/AIDS. *Elder Law Journal*, 10, 47.

Weed, E. 1997. Introduction, in *Feminism Meets Queer Theory*, edited by E. Weed and N. Schor. Indiana: Indiana University Press.

Weistock, J.S. 2003. Lesbian friendships at and beyond midlife: Patterns and possibilities for the 21st century, in *Gay and Lesbian Aging: Research and Future Directions*, edited by G. Herdt and B. De Vries. New York: Springer: 177–210.

Weston, K. 1997. *Families We Choose: Lesbians, Gays, and Kinship*. New York: Columbia University Press.

Willis, G. 2009. Daredevil. *The Atlantic*, July/August.

Wilson, M. 2006. Lieutenant who won pension rights for her domestic partner dies at 49. *The New York Times* [Online: 20 February]. Available at: http://www.nytimes.com/2006/02/20/obituaries/20partner.html [accessed: 30 March 2010].

White House conference leaves out gay seniors, activists charge. *The Advocate* [Online, 15 December 2005]. Available at: http://www.advocate.com/news_detail_ektid23410.asp [accessed: 30 March 2010].

Woodell, D. 1997. Gay partner battles for rights even at the grave. *Austin American-Statesman*, 31 May, C8.

Woolf, M. 2009. Name, age … are you gay? Census may get personal. *Times Online* [Online, 15 November]. Available at: http://www.timesonline.co.uk/tol/news/politics/article6917400.ece [accessed: 28 March 2010].

Zeman, L.H. 1998. Estate planning: Ethical considerations of using Medicaid to plan for long-term medical care for the elderly. *Quinnipiac Probate Law Journal*, 13, 188.

Zernike, K. 2006. The bell tolls for the future merry widow. *The New York Times*, 30 April, 1.

Cases

Baehr v. Lewin [Haw. 1993] 852 P.2d 44.

Baker v. Nelson [Minn. 1971] 191 N.W.2d 185.

Boutilier v. Immigration and Naturalization Service [1967] 387 U.S. 118.

Bowers v. Hardwick [1986].478 U.S. 186.

Boy Scouts of America v. Dale [2000] 530 U.S. 640.

Bush v. Gore [2000] 531 U.S. 98.

Collamore v. Learned [Mass. 1898] 171 Mass 96.

Dale v. Boy Scouts of America [N.J. Super. Ct. App. Div. 1998] 706 A2d 270.

Dale v. Boy Scouts of America [N.J. 1999]. 160 N.J. 562.

Ex parte H.H [Ala. 2002] 830 So. 2d 21.

East High Gay/Straight Alilance v. Board of Education of Salt Lake City School District [C.D. Ut. 1999] 1999 U.S. Dist. LEXIS 20254.

Gill v. OPM [D.C. Mass. 2010].

Gillman v. School Board for Holmes County, Florida [N.D. Fla. 2008] 567 F.Supp 2d 1159.

Goodridge v. Department of Public Health [Mass. 2003] 798 N.E. 2d 941.

Hernandez v. Robles [N.Y. 2006] 855 N.E. 2d 1.

High Tech Gays v. Def. Indus. Sec. Clearance Office [N.D.Cal. 1987] 668 F. Supp. 1361.

In the Matter of the Adoption of Robert Paul P. [N.Y. Ct. of App. 1984] 63 N.Y. 2d 233.

In re Adoption of M.C.D. [Okla. Civ. App. 2001] 42 P.3d 873.

In re Guardianship of Kowalski [Minn. Ct. App. 1991] 478 N.W.2d 790.

In re Guardianship of Kowalski [Minn. App. 1986] 382 N.W.2d 861.

In re Marriage Cases [Cal. 2008] 183 P.3d 384.

Jones v. Hallahan [Ky. 1973] 501 S.W.2d 588.

Lawrence v. Texas [2003] 539 U.S. 558.

Langbehn v. Memorial Hospital [S.D. Fla. 2009] 661 F. Supp 2d 1326.

Lewis v. Harris [N.J. 2006] 908 A.2d 196.

Lofton v. Secretary of the Florida Department of Children and Families [S.D. Fla. 2000] 93 F. Supp. 2d 1343.

Martinez v. Monroe County [N.Y. App. Div. 2008] 2008 N.Y. App. Div. LEXIS 854.

Massachusetts v. HHS [D.C. Mass. 2010].

Nabozny v. Podlesny [7th Cir. 1996] 93 F.3d 466.

New State Ice Co. v. Liebmann [1932] 285 U.S. 262.

Perry v. Schwarzenegger. 2010. [2010 U.S. Dist. LEXIS 78816].

National Pride at Work v. Cox, [Mich. 2008] 481 Mich. 56.

Reed v. ANM Health Care [Wash. Ct. App. 2008] 148 Wn. App. 264.

Romer v. Evans [1996] 517 U.S. 620.

Singer v. Hara [Wash. App. 1974]. 522 P.2d 1187.

Strauss v. Horton [Cal. 2009] LEXIS 5416.

Vasquez v. Hawthorne [Wash. 2001] 33 P.3d 735.

Statutes and Regulatory Material

Alabama Code 2008. §16-40A-2(c)(8).

Arizona Statute 2008. §15-716(c)(1–2).

Arkansas Code 1987. §9-27-341(b)(3)(B)(i).

Colorado Statute 2009. §15-22-101.

Constitution of the State of Oklahoma 2007. Article II, §35B.

Department of Defense Directive Number 1332.14(8)(a)(1) (28 August 2008).

Hawaii Statute. Rev. Stat. Ann. §572C-1 to -7.

Florida Statute 2008a. §1006.147.

Florida Statute 2008b. §1006.147(3)(a)(1)–(10).

Internal Revenue Code 2004. 26 U.S.C.A. §402(c)(11).

Internal Revenue Code 1986. IRC §152(d)(2)(H).

Internal Revenue Code 2006. IRC §2(b)(3)(B)(i)).

Mississippi Code 2008. §93-17-3.

New Jersey Statute. N.J. Stat. Ann. §37:1–28.

South Carolina Code of Laws 2008. §59-32-30(A)(5).

Texas Health and Safety Code 2008. §163.002(8).

Virginia Code Annotated §20–45.3 (2005).

Uniform Probate Code 1990. §2–103.

United States Code 2005. 10 U.S.C. §654(b)(2).

United States Code. (Civil Rights Act.) 1964, Title II, 42 U.S.C. §2000(a).

United States Code. 2000. 38 U.S.C. §1722A.

United States Code 2000. 42 U.S.C. §414(a).

United States Code 2000. 42 U.S.C. §403(a).

United States Code. (Fair Housing Act.) 42 U.S.C. §3601.

United States Code 2004. 510 42 U.S.C §1396p(b)(2)–(2)(A)

United States Code 2003. 42 U.S.C.A. §3796(a)(4).

United States Code 2000. 38 U.S.C. §1710A.

Utah Code 2008. §78(B)-6-101(4).

Index